THE PRISM OF PIETY

Catholick Congregational Clergy at the Beginning of the Enlightenment

JOHN CORRIGAN

New York Oxford
OXFORD UNIVERSITY PRESS
1991

Oxford University Press

Oxford New York Toronto
Delhi Bombay Calcutta Madras Karachi
Petaling Jaya Singapore Hong Kong Tokyo
Nairobi Dar es Salaam Cape Town
Melbourne Auckland

and associated companies in
Berlin Ibadan

Published by Oxford University Press, Inc.
200 Madison Avenue, New York, New York 10016

Library of Congress Cataloging-in-Publication Data
Corrigan, John, 1952–
The prism of piety : Catholick Congregational clergy at the beginning of the Enlightenment / John Corrigan.
p. cm.—(Religion in America series)
Includes bibliographical references and index.
ISBN 0-19-506758-4
1. Puritans—Massachusetts—Boston—History—18th century.
2. Enlightenment—Massachusetts—Boston.
3. Liberalism (Religion)—Massachusetts—Boston—History of doctrines—18th century.
4. Liberalism (Religion)—Congregationalist churches. 5. Congregationalist churches—Doctrines—History—18th century. 6. Reformed Church—Doctrines—History—18th century. 7. Boston (Mass.)—Church history.
I. Title. II. Title: Catholick Congregational clergy at the beginning of the Enlightenment.
III. Series: Religion in America series (Oxford University Press)
BX7149.B7C67 1991
285′.9′09744—dc20 90-21105

1 3 5 7 9 8 6 4 2

Printed in the United States of America
on acid-free paper

For Ranger and Celia

Preface

In 1700 two slaves belonging to Mr. James Liblond named Grace and Derham were married at the newly formed Brattle Street Church in Boston. Another marriage, one of ideas, was also just under way in 1700 at the Brattle Street Church. It consisted in the bringing together, in the theology of the founders of the church, arguments about order and reason in a "beautiful" cosmos—such as those advanced by the popular English writer William Derham, among others—with the notion of the necessity for regeneration through supernatural grace. There is no further mention in the church records of the religious life of Grace and Derham. This book is about the other grace and Derham.[1]

I have endeavored in this study to describe the program of theological innovation at Brattle Street and several neighboring churches as a part of a process of intellectual and religious change that took place in Boston in approximately the first forty years of the eighteenth century. I have focused my investigation on a group of Congregationalist ministers who were at the center of this process of change. These ministers were essentially transitional figures, thinkers whose ideas represented a movement in New England from anxiety and pessimism about the predicament of human life in a corrupt world, toward a confidence in the rational order of the universe, and human capability to detect that order.

Following Henry F. May, Norman Fiering, and Theodore Hornberger, I have viewed the emergence of these new emphases in the theology of Boston Congregationalist ministers as a key part of the beginnings of an American Enlightenment. For May, a primary component of the "moderate Enlightenment" in America was the emergence of "Boston liberalism." A species of New England religion that combined aspects of Reformed theology with English latitudinarian emphases on reason and morality, Boston liberalism took shape in the first half of the eighteenth century in the writings of the Congregationalist ministers with whom we are concerned in this study. Fiering likewise has argued that "the First American Enlightenment" began in the early eighteenth century under the influence of philosophical Anglicanism, especially at Harvard and among the founders of the Brattle Street Church. Hornberger, writing about Benjamin Colman—who was the first minister at the Brattle Street Church—argued that Colman "exemplifies, as well perhaps as any colonial American, the early influence on this side of the Atlantic of the great ideas of the Age of the Enlightenment." Hornberger, like May and Fiering, saw "Anglican rationalism" as a major "Enlightenment" influence on Colman's thinking.[2]

The American Enlightenment was not a static, monomorphic phenomenon. In fact, Henry May has argued that it consisted in four distinct but sometimes overlapping movements between 1688 and 1815. As it evolved in various contexts in America throughout the eighteenth century, the Enlightenment developed emphases that sometimes were peculiar to context. I have not aimed in this study to unearth the entire root structure of the American Enlightenment, much less to catalogue the range of forms under which it appeared. Rather, I have sought to describe, first of all, how one key aspect of the Enlightenment in America, namely, the perception of unity, reason, and purpose in nature (including human nature), became a part of the thinking of a group of Boston ministers. Second, I have attempted to explain the ways in which these ministers reconciled—or were unable to reconcile—certain implications arising from such notions with their New England religious background. Accordingly, I have pictured them as having one leg in the Enlightenment and the other in a world of religious ideas drawn essentially from Reformed theology. Third, I have endeavored to show how in the first part of the eighteenth century, Congregationalism in Boston emerged from its first encounter with Enlightenment notions of reason and nature as a more emotional style of religion.

I have given particular attention to this last point. Previous scholarship for the most part has focused on the American Enlightenment as the "age of reason," while neglecting to comment on the ways in which passion, in religion as well as in other areas of eighteenth-century life, was accepted as part of the "natural man" alongside reason.[3] Twenty years ago, Peter Gay stressed that the "Age of Reason" was also, paradoxically, a "revolt against rationalism." For Gay, this revolt came about largely in connection with the liberation of sensuality and the passions from Christian doctrines and attitudes that had declared them to be worthless. According to Gay, "the Enlightenment's rehabilitation of the passions was essential to its rehabilitation of man as a natural creature." Taking my lead from Gay, I have sought to explain how certain Congregationalist ministers took a step toward accepting both the natural creature and passion.[4]

Over the course of the past thirty or so years, the catholick clergy (whom I shall identify shortly) have received regular attention from scholars. Such attention has been limited, however, almost entirely to passing references, or to limited treatments intended to serve as components of larger arguments. Moreover, in those cases wherein historians have taken notice of catholicks, they have in almost every case cast them as leading figures in a process of secularization believed to have taken place in New England in the early eighteenth century.[5] Such scholarship follows, for the most part, the view of Perry Miller, who, in *The New England Mind: From Colony to Province* (1953), offered an analysis of the catholick clergy that remains today the closest thing to a sustained discussion of their ideas. Miller viewed Colman and his catholick colleagues in Boston as a clerical "party," arguing that they wholeheartedly embraced latitudinarian claims for the capability of human reason and, in so doing, drifted from the covenant theology characteristic of New England Congregationalism.[6] I agree with some of what Miller has proposed, but I reject his thesis that catholick ministers lost interest in the covenant. The catholick clergy incorporated into their theology English ideas about cosmic order and human reason, but they did not sacrifice traditional ideas about sin and grace to that influence.

Readers who are familiar with Philip Greven's perceptive study of the "Protestant temperament" will recognize that my view of the catholick clergy corresponds in some important ways to his description of a "moderate" Protestant.[7] Greven does not make reference to the catholick ministers with whom I have been concerned in this book, however, so I am unable to comment in any substantive way on the similarities and dissimilarities of our approaches. Nevertheless, I have remarked at several points, as appropriate below, on how the catholick clergy were inclined toward the "moderate" approval of reason, passion, the human body, and religious diversity.

I have intended this book to serve, then, as a means by which some measure of clarity and depth might be added to future discussions involving Congregationalism in Boston, and as a study of a process of intellectual and religious change, in which new ideas were embraced, but old ideas were not abandoned.

I am grateful to the staffs of the Alderman Library, University of Virginia, to the Congregational Library, Boston, and to the Houghton Library, Harvard, for their help in locating books and manuscripts. I am likewise grateful to Virginia Smith of the Massachusetts Historical Society, Susan Moran of the First Congregational Church (Cambridge) Archives, Harley Holden of the Harvard University Archives, and Joyce Cannon of Winchester FDB. My research at these locations and elsewhere was made possible in part through the support of the National Endowment for the Humanities and by grants from the University of Virginia.

This book is better than it might have been because of the criticisms and suggestions offered by colleagues and friends who read the manuscript in its various incarnations. Among those I thank for their efforts in this regard are Jerald Brauer, James Childress, Jamie Ferreira, Gerald Fogarty, Winthrop Hudson, John Kloos, Benjamin Ray, and Jane Ulrich. Rodger Payne and David White subjected a late draft to detailed and painstaking criticism. Robert Cross, Conrad Cherry, Brooks Holifield, Charles Lippy, and Peter Williams also read the manuscript and offered encouragement that helped to propel me through the last stages of its preparation. Above all, I am grateful to my colleague Carlos Eire who read early and late drafts, sometimes on short notice, and suggested a multitude of improvements and clarifications. Finally, Cynthia Read of Oxford University Press, through her criticisms and support, proved the truth of the adage that the editor is the author's best friend.

Many times Sheila was somehow able to see behind my prose to what I meant to say, and to find the means for me to say it. Just as important, she obliged me by pretending to understand my disappearance into my work, and never failed in knowing when to rescue me from it.

Worcester, Massachusetts
May 1991

J. C.

Contents

The Prism of Piety

Introduction

According to most historians, New England, by the late seventeenth century, was an English colony that was beginning to reap the consequences—beneficial as well as disadvantageous—of profound social change. The growth of the population and new configurations of its geographical concentrations, the commercial development of the area's resources and the consequent expansion of the Atlantic trade, and the formal restructuring of political relations with England in the 1680s, among other changes, affected the everyday lives of New Englanders and challenged them in their thinking about the nature of society. At some times, and in some places, such changes bred severe anxiety, often with dramatic consequences, such as at Salem in the early 1690s. More commonly, New Englanders adapted to change, learning to live with it or even to exploit it and to strike a bargain between traditional ways of life and the forces that turned New England in new directions.

Among those persons who negotiated a tentative settlement between old ways and new were a small group of Harvard College graduates who lived in and around Boston. In speech and in print, these men frequently announced to the public their views about the changing world of New England and about the necessity for adaptation. They did not express themselves, however, in theories about land prices and bank solvency, or about tax rates and shipping tonnage, or about bridge construction and swamp drainage. Rather, as Congregationalist ministers, they drew on the theological and quasi-theological writings of their predecessors in New England, and to the lessons taken from these they added gleanings from their survey of English writers, in order to construct a response to change that was founded in an explicitly religious view of the world. These ministers interpreted the changing circumstances of New England life essentially as a signal calling for a rearticulation of personal and corporate religious self-understanding. Accordingly, they undertook to frame a definition of religion that comprehended the problems associated with the shifting foci of social life in early eighteenth-century Boston but that also conserved aspects of the theological orientation of previous New England generations.

This study focuses on the religious thought of the Congregationalist ministers who contributed to this project of theological innovation. Most important among these men were Benjamin Colman (H.C. 1692, S.T.D. Glasgow, 1731, Brattle Street Church), Benjamin Wadsworth (H.C. 1690, First Church), Thomas Foxcroft (H.C. 1714, First Church), Ebenezer Pemberton (H.C. 1691, Old South Church), and Nathaniel Appleton (H.C. 1712, S.T.D. Harvard, 1771, First Church, Cambridge). William Brattle (H.C. 1680, First Church, Cambridge) and Edward Holyoke (H.C. 1705, Second Church, Marblehead) were also associated with this group, Brattle being present at the beginning, and Holyoke representing a drift of the movement into new emphases after thirty years of its development. The group as a whole developed its characteristic emphases of thought under the ongoing influence and tutelage of John Leverett (H.C. 1680). Leverett, Wadsworth, and Holyoke served as presidents of Harvard, and Colman was offered the post but declined it. Pemberton and Brattle were tutors of the college (the latter serving as treasurer as well), and Appleton was a fellow of the college for over sixty years. All of these men, including Foxcroft, were well acquainted with the scientific theories and theological writings of English writers and became known for their exposition of those writings to New England audiences.

One hundred and fifty years ago, Josiah Quincy, who was then the president of Harvard, described the emergence in Boston, in the early eighteenth century, of a group of clergymen who "were eminently liberal in their religious views." He identified "Brattle, Colman, Pemberton, Wadsworth, and Appleton" as a "class of divines, which first appeared, when the civil power the clergy had wielded under the old charter, was beginning to be dissolved." Indeed, following on the loss of the original Massachusetts charter of 1629, the new provincial charter of 1691, with its provisions for a royal governor and for religious toleration and its discontinuing of church membership as a requirement for the franchise, pulled the colony into much closer orbit around England. The "liberal" clergy identified by Quincy responded to the restructuring of relations with England as part of a larger program of addressing social change in New England. And the chief plank of this program was their promoting among their congregations a "catholick spirit" in matters of religion. This catholick position implied, essentially, a willingness to overlook differences of opinion about the "smaller things" in religion, and, in particular, to avoid invective and censoriousness in observing the religious life manifest in congregations other than one's own.[1]

Those Congregationalist ministers identified by Quincy (and others since) as "liberal" I have called "catholick." Colman, Foxcroft, Appleton, and their colleagues commonly employed the term, in the sense that I here have outlined, in referring to their own thinking or to the views of those whom they admired as religious leaders. Most important among those religious leaders were certain members of the Anglican clergy, such as John Tillotson, Edward Stillingfleet, and Joseph Glanvill. From the sermons and essays of these so-called men of latitude, catholick Congregationalists borrowed extensively in their thinking about not only the nature of the church but the role of the faculty of reason in religion as well. Latitudinarians, seeking to guide English Protestantism toward a policy of moderation after the disruptive enthusiasms and political and religious zeal of the Civil War, had undertaken after midcentury to foster in England a broad church unity. The spirit of this movement made its way to New England, where it found a home at Harvard in the late seventeenth century. Under tutor (and later, President) Leverett, the study of latitudinarian writers led to the emergence at Harvard of a "catholick spirit." In 1699, with the founding of the Brattle Street Church, this catholick spirit began to emerge as part of the design of Congregationalism among certain congregations in the Boston area.

Catholick Congregationalism in the early eighteenth century was not limited to the promotion of religious moderation and understanding, however. As a catholick spirit emerged among certain members of the Congregationalist clergy, it took shape as a theological perspective characterized by the intertwining of four additional strands of thought. Colman and his catholick colleagues did not express themselves on matters of doctrine in precisely the same way, but the following emphases are present to one degree or another in the thinking of Colman, Pemberton, Wadsworth, Foxcroft, and Appleton.[2]

First, the catholick clergy were inclined to view the world, and the human body, as less threatening, less dangerous, than had their predecessors and some of their contemporaries in New England. Influenced by the theories of the English scientists Robert Boyle, John Ray, William Derham, and others, the catholick clergy increasingly came to perceive order and purpose in nature. Indeed, catholicks often exulted over the beauty visible in the works of creation, and they delighted in their perceptions of the power and majesty of God, the "father of lights," who ruled over creation. As a part of their confidence in the divine plan of order in creation, catholicks became more trusting toward human nature and, in particular, toward the emotions, or, in the language of the eighteenth century, the "affections." Believing that persons were furnished by God with reason that enabled them to detect regularity, arrangement, and system in nature, catholicks concluded that the faculty of the affections, with which persons were also endowed, likewise played an important role in the capability of the individual to respond to the spectacle of creation, to God, and to others. Accordingly, catholick ministers supposed that piety not only consisted in the faithful embrace of doctrine but was fundamentally an emotional experience as well.

Second, these ministers believed that body and soul, matter and spirit, functioned together in such a way as to form the whole person and that the affections were a product of the cooperation between these two sides of a person's nature. Catholicks interpreted the ideas of Cambridge Platonists such as Henry More, and other writings by both Anglican and Puritan writers, in such a way as to lead them to accept the body as a partner to the soul, and the affections as a partner to reason. Catholicks therefore expected that the affections, which were of great use in religion, could be and should be stirred by preaching, prayer, singing, and especially participation in the Lord's Supper. Moreover, for these ministers, even just the sound of music, or the sight of the moon, could elicit a response in which reason and the affections operated together so as to bring about both a deeper understanding of the majesty of God and the emotional experience of "delight" in the occasion. Catholick acquaintance with the new science and philosophy, then, influenced them not toward a rejection of emotion in religion, but, rather, toward its promotion.

Third, catholicks, for all of their emphasis on reason and order in the universe, believed that a vast gulf had opened between God and humanity as a result of original sin. They believed that the faculties had been vitiated by the fall and that it was only through regenerating grace that the faculties could be restored to health. Consequently, like their predecessors in the New England ministry, they explicitly preached the covenant of grace as the only means by which a person might be reconciled to God. They preached on the necessity for a conversion from sin to God, and they urged their congregations to make diligent use of the means of grace available to them in the church. Catholicks, however, were more inclined than their predecessors (and some of their ministerial colleagues) to depict the God to whom a person turned in conversion as a loving father, as a compassionate, adopting parent. Although they remained orthodox in their condemning "inordinate" affection to the world and in their forecasting of punishment for those persons who abandoned religion for worldly pleasure taking, they envisioned conversion more as a process of a person's being drawn to God in love than chased to him in fear. Moreover, their emphasis on love extended to their understanding of the aftermath of conversion, which they characterized not as a relentless, solitary combat against the flesh, but, rather, as the delightful association with other Christians, in a community governed by love. For catholicks, such community was founded on, and nourished by, the public expession of an emotional rather than a legal piety.

Fourth, catholicks understood that in actively seeking to raise the affections of their congregations, they ran the risk of creating a predicament in which elevated emotion might be distracted, or misdirected, into channels where it did not belong. The consequences of such error could be disastrous, both to the spiritual lives of individual persons and to the ordered love of the community. Accordingly, the catholick clergy preached the necessity for certain controls in the political and economic life of New Englanders. In so doing, however, they did not abandon their insistence on piety as a guide to social life. Underlying their pronouncements on good government, commercial ventures, and the moral life was their firm belief in the religious obligation to act in the world in such a way as to glorify God. And they continued to express confidence in the affectionate consociation of the regenerate as a legitimate basis for social order.

The "catholick spirit" among Boston-area Congregationalist clergy, then, consisted in several interrelated perspectives on the nature of church, the faculties, cosmic order, regeneration, and the moral life. In general, catholick thought was characterized by an optimism about the possibility for unity, understood not only as the unity among persons of differing religious backgrounds (Congregationalist, Presbyterian, Baptist, Anglican) but as the intertwining of body and soul in the person, and as the affectionate bonding of the individual to God and to others in the world.

Optimism of this sort was not shared by most other members of the Congregationalist clergy in the area. Among the previous generation, Increase Mather (H.C. 1656, Second Church), Samuel Willard (H.C. 1659, Old South Church), John Higginson (First Church, Salem), and Nicholas Noyes (H.C. 1667, First Church, Salem) had difficulty coming to terms with change in the seventeenth century, and, for the most part, they remained suspicious of nature, the flesh, and the affections. Moreover, they were inclined to a depiction of God as an angry judge, not as a loving parent. Among those ministers who were contemporaneous with catholicks, Joshua Gee (H.C. 1717, Second Church), Mather Byles (H.C. 1725, Hollis Street Church), Samuel Checkley (H.C. 1715, New South Church), and John Webb (H.C. 1708, New North Church) aligned themselves with the theology of Increase Mather et al.[3] Another group of third-generation ministers, namely Ebenezer Gay (H.C. 1714, First Church, Hingham), his South Shore colleague John Hancock the younger (H.C. 1719, First Church, Braintree), and John Barnard (H.C. 1700, First Church, Marblehead), emphasized, as did the catholick clergy, moderation, church unity, and reason, but they did not promote affective religion. Accordingly, I see these men as a wing of liberalism that might best be described as "rationalist" rather than catholick.[4] Finally, Cotton Mather, a man of enormous learning and accomplishment, was also a man of numerous contradictions. I have noted some of the ways in which his thinking was similar to that of catholicks, but I have treated him, finally, as closer to the thinking of his father Increase than to the catholick view of religion.

As I have already noted, catholick ministers ought to be located in history as a part of the first stage of an American Enlightenment. I add here that as catholicks appropriated and interpreted English scientific theories and theological arguments, they discovered that some of the ideas contained therein, which had come into being in part as an antidote to Puritan-related commotions in England, in fact were compatible with their own distant (but still determinative) Puritan background. The majority of latitudinarian thought consisted in a sober, moderate moralism, thoroughly informed by reason. One irony of catholick thought in Boston is that in spite of its indebtedness to English latitudinarian ideas, it was characterized by, among other things, its promotion of the affective dimension in religious life.

1

Catholick Moderation

Some of the ideas of catholick Congregationalists in New England were first articulated by Anglican clergymen and laymen writing after the English Civil War. The political and military battles of the 1640s and 1650s had crippled the authority of the English ecclesiastical establishment and so had set the stage for the emergence, during the Interregnum, of a host of radical religious sects known for their "enthusiasm" and "zeal." Englishmen such as Herbert of Cherbury (*De Veritate,* 1624) had for over a century sought to articulate a common religious ground for English Protestants. But the war and its aftermath provoked grave concern, and even despair, in the hearts of many about the prospect for unity among English Protestants. Consequently, there appeared, in ever-increasing numbers, sermons and books that stressed the necessity for moderation and comprehension, and the futility of narrow and rigid principles in religious matters. This irenical movement, which appeared in an early form in the Great Tew Circle that began to meet near Oxford in the 1630s, developed after the Restoration into the moderate Anglicanism of the seventeenth century that is commonly known as latitudinarianism.[1]

As Barbara Shapiro has written, latitudinarians combined in their thinking "the mutually reinforcing elements of latitude, moderation and rationality."[2] In their efforts to bring a measure of calm rationality to discussions about the future of Protestantism in England, in their urgent assertions about the dangers of sectarian enthusiasm and zeal, some latitudinarians came to question the usefulness to religion of passion of any sort. Eventually, certain of them cast a suspicious eye on emotion in general, whether that meant enthusiasm, zeal, passion, lust, or "affection". During the Augustan Age

(1690–1740), emotion in religion was in short supply. Horton Davies described the latitudinarian sermon of the period as typically a rational and unsentimental moral essay containing "cold good sense." Latitudinarian worship in general lacked "any element of holy excitement, of passionate pleading, of heroic challenge, of winged imagination." Other scholars have offered the same opinion. Hoxie Fairchild commented on how this "dull, broad, unenthusiastic protestantism" failed to satisfy the emotions. Norman Sykes, writing about "the reaction against 'enthusiasm' and the 'spiritual' preaching of many divines during the Interregnum," characterized latitudinarian preaching as "rationalistic" and a "descent into bathos." H. R. McAdoo described their religion as shallow, vague, and dispassionate "moralising," which edged "into coldness and indifference." The Anglican bishop Jeremy Taylor (d. 1667), who died just as latitudinarianism was emerging in England, reflected the mood of many persons connected with the movement when he rejected "ecstasies in prayer" in favor of "a life of justice and temperance, of chastity and piety, of charity and devotion." This mood extended to the Anglican church in New England as well, according to the Reverend Phillips Brooks of Boston's Trinity Church (originally Anglican). Surveying the two hundred years of history of Trinity Church, Brooks observed, "The character of the preaching they heard in those days in that ancient Trinity . . . is not hard to guess. . . . From the time of the restoration, enthusiasm had been in disesteem," and so Anglican preaching in Boston, like Anglican preaching in England, was "cold as marble."[3]

Latitudinarianism ought to be understood, however, not only in reference to its stance on the emotions in worship but in connection with the rise of science and the search for ways in which to carry out a program of free and unbiased intellectual inquiry in England. Accordingly, the ideals of the Royal Society, which was founded in 1660, were similar to those of the "latitude-men." Thomas Sprat, in his *History of the Royal-Society of London* (1667), pointed out that when the initial meetings of the group took place in the lodgings of John Wilkins, in Oxford, "their first purpose was no more, than onely the satisfaction of breathing a freer air, and of conversing in quiet with one another, without being ingag'd in the passions, and madness of that dismal age," the aftermath of the Civil War. In that "candid, and unpassionate company," in "such a gloomy season," Wilkins, Sir William Petty, and Samuel Hartlib, together with a circle of assorted scientists, set the terms for a program of investigation, analysis, and sober, moderate dissent that, they hoped, would enable their countrymen to be "invincibly arm'd against all the enchantments of enthusiasm." Wilkins himself eventually became the bishop of Chester, an influential position in London, and a man of latitude. His friend John Tillotson rose to the position of archbishop of Canterbury and became the most popular voice for latitudinarianism and a member of the Royal Society. Edward Stillingfleet, Joseph Glanvill, and Simon Patrick also belonged to this circle of devotees of the new experimental philosophy and brought their ideas about "scientific" sobriety and moderation in religion to pulpits or lecture halls throughout England. The generally moderate temperament of the latitude-men and their confidence in the future of broad church religion are well represented in the writings of Wilkins, Tillotson, Stillingfleet, Glanvill, and Patrick.[4]

Wilkins, Tillotson, Stillingfleet, and other Anglican church leaders agreed on many points as far as religion was concerned, though certainly they did not agree on everything. Consequently it is best to view latitudinarianism as a spectrum of religious ideas generally related but showing shades of differences as well. Most important among those differences was the attitude of these men toward emotion in religion. Stillingfleet and Glanvill are very good examples of the kind of dispassionate religion to which historians often refer in connection with the latitudinarian movement. Patrick and Wilkins, on the other hand, allowed and even tentatively encouraged a place for the emotions in their view of religion. Tillotson fell somewhere between these two positions but was probably closer to the former than to the latter.

Edward Stillingfleet (1635–1699), chaplain to Charles II in 1667 and later bishop of Worcester, published his *Irenicum* in 1659 on the eve of the Restoration. His purpose was to persuade his countrymen away from "party religion" and to "allay the heat and abate the fury . . . of contention" that had arisen during Cromwell's regime. Stillingfleet argued that the "distempered heat of men's spirits" had so seriously damaged religion that posterity likely would recall the time as one "when men talked of religion most and lived it least." The culprit in this turmoil was zeal, and the censoriousness and narrow view of religion associated with it. Stillingfleet was concerned less with piety than with a determination of the duties of religion, including the observance of religious rites and customs. He pointed out the great diversity of religious forms in the "primitive church" and argued that instances of censuring, "by inconsiderate zeal," were "resented by other Christians" in earliest Christianity. He claimed as well that in matters of religion, those duties or ceremonies that were instituted by the lawful authority of the church (in cases where divine law and natural law were indeterminate) were not to be understood as permanent and unchangeable fixtures of Christian worship. Such things were not "unalterable, but may be revoked, limited, and changed, according to the different ages, tempers, inclinations of men, by the same power which did determine them."

Stillingfleet developed this argument in numerous other books and sermons. In *A Rational Account of the Grounds of Protestant Religion,* he took up the matter—as did most of his colleagues at one time or another—of the meaning of "catholick church," endeavoring to define it against the claims of authority made by the church of Rome. Sprinkling his argument with numerous references to Cyprian and other Fathers, Stillingfleet argued that the word *catholick,* as it was used in the early church, was not a specific reference to the church of Rome, and that some of the Fathers in fact had viewed the church of Rome as a "member" of the catholick church. Accordingly, "the formal reason of any particular churches having the denomination of catholick, must come not from any communion with the church of Rome; but from the owning of the catholick and apostolick faith, and joyning in communion with those churches which did own and acknowledge it."[5]

Joseph Glanvill (1636–1680), also onetime chaplain to Charles II and rector at Abbey Church in Bath, was, like Stillingfleet, very concerned about the danger of zeal. Richard Westfall has observed that Glanvill "hated and feared enthusiasm," and his "antipathy for sectarians, or enthusiasts" emerged as "a hearty repugnance which crept into everything he wrote." In *Catholick Charity* (1669), Glanvill wrote that "there is nothing hath done the world more mischief, than indiscreet, unseasonable zeal for truths" when persons do not distinguish between what is necessary to know, and what is not. Madness, frenzies, and "unmortified affections" lead to careless quarrels, so that "when the passion is raised, the judgement is gone." Glanvill affirmed that the "intent" of religion essentially was "to direct us to govern our passions, and subdue our appetites," not "to teach us systems of opinions."

Glanvill had stated this view of passion and religion previously, just after the Restoration, in *The Vanity of Dogmatizing* (1661). Arguing that "enthusiastic effects" are a "deceit of our imaginations" and claiming that "religion bribes the judgement to the most notorious inequality," Glanvill suggested that most of the disagreements between persons about religious truth came about "when the affections wear the breeches, and the female rules." Years later, Glanvill reaffirmed that "enthusiasm is a false conceit of inspiration," and declared that "the real philosophy, and knowledge of God's work, serves religion against *enthusiasm,*" a "dreadful enemy." Scorning reason and moderation, the enthusiast teaches his followers "to lay stress upon all raptures, heats, and mysterious notions, while they neglect" or even reject "plain Christianity."[6]

The first more or less systematic statement of the beliefs of the latitudinarians appeared in 1662, under the title *A Brief Account of the New Sect of Latitude-Men.* Its author, S. P., was Simon Patrick (1626–1707), who was later the bishop of Ely. Patrick explained his tongue-in-cheek reference to the latitude-men as a "sect" by stressing that this was not a movement whose aim was the destruction of the religious and social fabric of England. Instead, latitude-men sought a "vertuous mediocrity" between the rites and ceremonies of the Roman Catholic church and the principles of the fanatic conventicles. Latitude-men were trinitarian and orthodox and embraced the liturgy of the Church of England, but they did not condemn other forms of worship. Typically, Patrick reinforced his announcement of the thinking of latitude-men by claiming that the movement was guided by the voices of the Fathers of the church.

Preaching at St. Paul's many years later, Patrick detailed his view of the importance of toleration and the dangers to religion posed by human judgment biased by passion. In *Two Sermons One against Murmuring, The Other against Censuring,* Patrick observed that a person might judge of others "inwardly" or "outwardly," as, in the latter case, through "words and speeches." He suggested that between the two, "there is no small difference, and this is the distinction which ought to be carefully observed; because it may be lawful to pass a judgement upon men's actions in our own thoughts, when we ought not to signifie it to others by our words." Moreover, noting that passions cause "noise" and "tumult" within a person, he warned that a person's seeking to discover faults in others might indeed be an enterprise undertaken "meerly to please some bad affections." A natural infirmity of mankind, "the strength of the passions," made life unstable and unpredictable, and a person did well to keep at a distance from passion, lest it fester into censorious zeal. Such was, in effect, the advice he gave his hearers when he preached at the funeral of John Smith, the Cambridge Platonist. Of the deceased, Patrick declared, "Least of all would he endure than any passion should lodge in him, till it was become a cankered malice and black hatred."[7]

Patrick did not entirely condemn emotion in religion, however. It seems that he moved gradually toward the notion that there was a role for the affections in religion. More important, he came to view public worship as a particularly valuable activity because it encouraged the union of persons in affection. Patrick, whose religion was described by John Tulloch as a "practical mysticism," wrote late in life that "the greater signs of ardency of desire, and warmth of affection, there appears in those with whom we are assembled, the more feeling we shall naturally have of it ourselves." Explaining the relation of personal piety to public worship, Patrick succinctly stated the importance of the affections as follows: "The sum of this argument is, that no man is so warm alone, as in a crowd; so our spiritual fervor is more quickned [*sic*] in an assembly of pious worshippers, than it is apt to be, when we are retired by ourselves."[8]

John Wilkins, like Patrick, mixed advocacy of moderation with a limited encouragement of emotion in religion. Wilkins (1614–1672), master of Trinity College, Oxford, was one of the founders of the Royal Society and eventually became the bishop of Chester (1668). He was the author of several scientific works, one of which, *The Discovery of a World in the Moone* (1638), a discourse on lunar inhabitants, eventually earned him the ridicule of the Royal Society antagonist Robert South, who referred to him as the "Archbishop of Cuckoo," and another wit, who could not resist a reference to a clerical "man in the moon." And this was in spite of the fact that Wilkins's theory put him in the company of the respected scientists John Ray and Christian Huygens.

A collection of sermons published in 1682 (prefaced by Tillotson) included a meditation by Wilkins on Phil. 4:5, "Let your moderation be known unto all men, the Lord is at hand." In explaining the Christian duty of moderation, Wilkins asserted that " 'tis a virtue inclining us to such a kind of benign and equitable temper in our conversing with one another, whereby we may endeavour to preserve concord and amity in our treating concerning those things about which we differ." Wilkins noted that although the actual word *moderation* appeared only rarely in Scripture, its "meaning" was in fact often commanded by God. After all, God himself was moderate and merciful. Moderation, he stated, was good for the individual, as well as for "humane society in the general."

In his influential *Of the Principles and Duties of Natural Religion* (1675), Wilkins, remembering "the pernicious doctrines of the antinomians, and of all other libertine-enthusiasts whatsoever," stated his concern for the control of passion in no uncertain terms: "I am from the nature of things morally certain, and cannot make any doubt of it, but that a mind free from passion and prejudice is more fit to pass a true judgement, than such a one as is byassed by affections and interests."

Wilkins, however, did not entirely rule out a place for the affections in religion. Barbara Shapiro, in her intellectual biography of Wilkins, suggests that he was either a moderate Anglican or a moderate Puritan, her point being that Wilkins, because he evidenced a modified Calvinism in some of his views, might be seen in his connections with Puritanism as well as with Anglicanism. If this is true, we ought not to overlook in Wilkin's writings possible sympathy to the emotional emphases present in English Puritanism at midcentury. Indeed, Wilkins occasionally preached on the importance of a vital piety in religion, and this included qualified recommendation of "warmed affections" in worship. So, in a discourse on prayer, Wilkins warned against the "two extreams" that posed a problem to prayer. In one case, "men depend altogether on sudden suggestions" to enliven their spirits, while others "confine themselves to the help of books and particular set forms." But Wilkins suggested that, especially for the "beginner," the use of "set forms" in worship could be useful in stirring the affections. Wilkins in no way supported an enthusiastic or ecstatic form of worship. Rather, he sought to channel the emotional aspects of "personal" religion into acceptably social manifestations, while avoiding the overimposition of structures that might deaden prayer. At the same time, he believed that some carefully controlled stimulation of the affections was important to worship, and to that end he proposed the use of "premeditated formes, as may be the most effectual to this end, namely to excite the affections." Wilkins's sense of the power of language itself (as opposed to language understood merely as a vehicle for the communication of doctrine) is evident in his recommendation of the use of "set formes" as a means to "engage the affections."[9]

Tillotson (1630–1694), the most popular preacher of his time in England, "abhorred the anarchy of private religious inspiration," according to John Marshall. He sought to frame a program for peace and comprehension among English Protestants, to heal the religious wounds that came with the war. "The manners of men," he wrote, "have been almost universally corrupted by a civil warr [*sic*]. We should therefore all jointly endeavour, to retrieve the ancient virtue of the nation." Tillotson sought to reinstate a religion that was free of "the extremes both of superstition and enthusiasm," which "flourished in the age of our immediate forefathers." In a sermon entitled "The Danger of Zeal without Knowledge," he explained that the word *zeal* was generally used in Scripture in a "bad sense, for a malicious and furious rage." Since zeal was "one of the most ungovernable passions of human nature," great knowledge and judgment were necessary to manage it. As an example of zeal without knowledge, Tillotson pointed especially to those persons who would argue "blind with rage" over religion, and particularly the externals of religion. Zeal without knowledge was "a greater and fiercer zeal for the externals of religion; than for the vital and essential parts of it." And only a "gross ignorance of the true nature of religion" would lead a person to "a loud and zealous outcry against rites and ceremonies, and the imposition of indifferent things in religion." In place of zeal, Tillotson recommended catholick charity, and the catholick patience of Benjamin Whichcote, a moderate Anglican whom he upheld in a funeral sermon in 1683 with words of high praise: "he was of all men I ever knew the most patient to hear others differ from him."

Tillotson's ideas about passion, although not identical to those of Stillingfleet or Glanvill, were nevertheless closer to the thinking of those men than to the views of Patrick and Wilkins. Tillotson warned against the "tyrannical power of the lusts and passions," which "blind and bias" judgment. Religion for him consisted in sober morality, not emotional piety. In fact, the purpose of religion was to bridle the passions, not to excite them. According to Tillotson, "the lusts and passions" of men "darken their minds even by a natural influence," and so, "now religion doth purifie our minds, and refine our spirits, by quenching the fire of lust, and suppressing the fumes and vapours of it; and by scattering the clouds and mists of passions." But in spite of this, Tillotson occasionally was given to pronouncements such as the claim that knowledge of God "will ravish our affections." And, even though his sermons may have been largely sober expositions of a rationalistic morality, at least some of them were of such a quality as to move one American reader to tears.[10]

Latitudinarians, while differing in some ways with regard to their understanding of the place of emotion, all advocated "catholick" charity in religion. Drawing a lesson from the Civil War and its aftermath, they believed that the future of English Protestantism lay along a path marked by comprehension, not separation. They condemned religious zeal as misguided enthusiasm for pure religion, and they stressed instead morality and unity and, as we shall see, the role of reason in religion, as well.

The movement of ideas and customs across the Atlantic from England to America has been described in various ways in recent scholarship. David Grayson Allen has pointed to the influence of English custom in the structuring of land and agricultural systems in New England. Richard Bushman has suggested points of similarity and differences in style between Old and New England. Other scholars have analyzed English influence on the development of social theory, material culture, and family life in New England and in other British colonies in America in the seventeenth and eighteenth centuries. It is important to keep in mind, however, that New Englanders nevertheless to some degree experienced a sense of estrangement from dominant English patterns of culture during most of the 1600s, and that it was only at the end of the century that Americans took steps toward a rapprochement with English ideas and customs. Once begun, this process of Anglicization steadily gained force and clarity, so that, as T. H. Breen remarked after surveying the development of political thought in colonial New England, "The movement toward a cultural Anglicization was well rooted by 1700." Catholick Congregationalism emerged in New England as a part of this process of Anglicization. So third-generation ministers in New England, Harry S. Stout points out, were "thrust into a larger Anglo-American world where they discovered . . . that they could enjoy the benefits of England's culture" without departing from the covenantal theology that since the early days of New England had constituted for them a self-referential framework. These "congregational 'liberals,' " according to Stout, could thus "enjoy the best of both worlds."[11]

In religion, the growing influence of Anglicanism on New England was most startlingly evidenced in the defection at the 1722 Yale commencement exercise of Samuel Johnson, Timothy Cutler, Daniel Brown, Jared Eliot, John Hart, James Wetmore, and Samuel Whittlesey. These Yale tutors (Cutler and Brown) and ministers, partly through the influence of the Society for the Propagation of the Gospel minister George Pigot, came to doubt the validity of their Congregational ordinations and determined to seek Anglican orders at the hands of a bishop in England. Johnson, who admitted late in life that he "never liked enthusiasm," was driven by a particularly thoroughgoing concern for church purity. He not only sought reordination but, confessing grave doubts about his Presbyterian baptism, decided for rebaptism as well. Johnson's fears were by no means peripheral to the concerns of New England's Presbyterians and Congregationalists. Discussion about church purity (and clerical authority) was common, as was curiosity, even practical interest, in Anglican ceremony. William T. Youngs, Jr., has suggested that, in fact, Congregational ordination ceremonies moved closer to the Anglican pattern in the years following the Yale defection.[12]

"The noise of Yale College," wrote Judge Samuel Sewall, a member of the Old South Church in Boston, "came to me gradually; at first we heard some uncertain rumblings; at last the plain and loud thunderclaps astonished us." The Yale incident was the exception, rather than the rule, however, when it came to New England's reception of Anglican religious ideas. For thirty years, students at Harvard, by virtue of the efforts of the tutor and eventual president John Leverett, had been exposed to latitudinarian ideas about moderation and the role of reason in religion. The "infiltrating ideas that heralded the century of Enlightenment" in America had been trickling into Harvard—according to Samuel Eliot Morison—since the initial appointment of John Leverett (H.C. 1680) as tutor (later, president) in 1685. The Leverett curriculum, refined over the course of four decades, was organized in such a way as to include the reading of latitudinarian writers together with Reformed, and, especially, English Puritan theology and the Cartesian-flavored theology of Dutch writers. Harvard ministry students were more likely to seek common threads between Anglican writers and their own Congregationalist backgrounds than to abandon New England for Old. Adaptation, rather than transilience, was the likely product of a Harvard education.[13]

John M. Murrin has suggested that Harvard was "hopelessly catholic" by 1730. Well before the 1730s, however, Harvard had taken on a "catholick spirit." Benjamin Colman, in a letter to Bishop White Kennett of Peterborough dated 1725, reflected on his education at Harvard over thirty years earlier, "I was proud of my own humble education here in our Cambridge, because of the catholick air I had there breathed in." In fact, Colman also believed that it was "the free and catholick spirit of the seminary" that "took [the] generous heart" of Thomas Hollis, the English benefactor of the college. Colman himself recommended a "free and candid spirit" in church government and discipline to some Irish friends in 1736. All of this openness, this moderate temperament, Colman attributed to "the generous principles of a enlarged catholick spirit cherished in me by cially Tillotson. Foxcroft cited Tillotson on a remarkably broad rang of topics, including those titled regeneration, beatific vision, restitution, God, divinity of Christ, Christ as a mediator, truth of the Christian religion, excellence of the Christian religion, conscience, natural religion, how Satan works, and justifications of religion. Stillingfleet and Wilkins also were cited under this last heading, as well as elsewhere in the notebook.

Foxcroft sometimes made such specific references to latitudinarian writings that it is possible to identify precisely sources of (or, at
least, influences on) some of his ideas.[20] In three such cases involving
vritings by latitudinarians, the arguments made by the authors are
nost instructive for understanding the kinds of ideas that Congrega-
onalist ministers like Foxcroft found useful in the thinking of their
ngland brethren. The first two cases involve references to Still-
gfleet and to Wilkins, under the heading "justifications of religion."
e reference to Wilkins is clearly to his sermon on Phil. 4.5, which I
e noted. In this sermon Wilkins stressed the importance of mod-
ion, giving the doctrine as "1. A duty enjoined, moderation," and
e specifically he pointed out the necessity for "concord and amity
r treating concerning those things about which we differ." The
hat this sermon is cited under the category of justifications of
n suggests that Foxcroft supposed that at least one reason that
n ought to be embraced was that, in fact, it taught the duty of
ation. It would be difficult to find a more "catholick" point of

croft's citation of Stillingfleet is clearly to a sermon preached
hall, taking as a text Lk. 7:35 ("But wisdom is justified of all
lren"). Stillingfleet summarized the argument as follows:
cepts of our religion are plain and easie to be known, very
the nature of mankind, and highly tending to the advan-
se who practice them, both in this and a better life." As in
s sermon, the theme of cooperation among persons in
important to the argument. Stillingfleet, in describing the
" of religion in this life, emphasized morality and stressed
the "doctrine delivered by Jesus" tended to preserve and
cooperation among men and women that was necessary
th functioning of society, the "civil interests of the

case involves Foxcroft's reference, under the heading
Christ," to a sermon by Tillotson that was focused
ecessity for Christian love among the faithful. Outlin-

my tutor, Mr. Leverett." By way of confirming this, Colman's son-in-law, Ebenezer Turell, who wrote a biography of Colman in 1749, reported that Colman over the course of a lifetime wrote a great many letters to persons in New York and New Jersey, as well as in New England, for the purpose of "healing divisions, and quenching fires kindling and flaming among parties, pastors, and brethren."[14]

Colman's claim that he was "nurtured on the reading of liberal episcopalian authors" was one that any student who studied at Harvard under the tutors Leverett and William Brattle (H.C. 1680) might make. According to Henry Newman (H.C. 1687), Leverett and Brattle recommended "the reading of episcopal authors as the best books to form our minds in religious matters, and preserve us from those narrow principles that kept us at a distance from the church of England." (Moreover, this was at a time when Increase Mather, the embattled absentee president of the college from 1685 to 1701, "thundered out anathemas upon all that went to the Church of England as apostates from the primitive faith.") Newman added that William Brattle personally was "much in love with the beauty and order of the Church of England and the learned men at the head of it." But William, like his brother Thomas Brattle (H.C. 1676), the treasurer of the college, did not leave Congregationalism for the Church of England. As the *Boston Post News-Letter* reported of Thomas Brattle, there was among his noteworthy qualities "his catholick charity to all of the reformed religion, but more especially his great veneration for the Church of England, although his general and more constant communion was with the nonconformists." It is not surprising to find Henry Newman concluding that there were twenty times more friends to the Church of England in America "since these gentlemen governed the College."[15]

Leverett himself, in the course of his tenure at Harvard, came to emphasize God's benevolence rather than his power and justice. Arthur D. Kaledin, Leverett's biographer, has stressed that the tutor "felt that the 'true catholick Church' was, during his time, travelling a dark passage" and that he sought in Scripture the answers to the problems posed by religious parties in New England. But, according to Kaledin, Leverett's "intense Scriptural fundamentalism . . . served as a liberalizing force. Whatever was not warranted or forbidden by explicit divine prescription" was left to human judgment. Leverett thus was attracted to theories stressing the cultivation of reason, and the more or less scientific discovery of moral laws, in order to help him in articulating religious duty. (Leverett and William Brattle were elected to the

Royal Society in 1714.) Consequently, "in response to the challenges of the Enlightenment, [Leverett] magnified precisely those strains of seventeenth-century Puritanism—its naturalism and rationalism" that were to become so important for reasonable religion in the middle and late eighteenth century, and he set these in a context that affirmed God's love for humanity.[16]

But it was Leverett's role in organizing the curriculum and the library of the college during his years of service there as a tutor and as the president (1707–1724) that contributed the most in the long run to the emergence of a moderate, catholic temperament in his students. As Michael G. Hall has recently written, the latitudinarian movement "was more a movement of temperament than an attack on doctrine," and its temperament was "cool, complacent, agreeable." Some of Leverett's students seem to have grown into this temperament, in part through the habits of reading—the authors and the topics—that they formed while in residence at the college. Such habits naturally also determined much of the direction of their later intellectual development as ministers or as laypersons.[17]

The curriculum that Leverett bequeathed to Benjamin Wadsworth, on the latter's election to the presidency of the college in 1725, had shaped those habits by emphasizing the traditional as well as the new. Accordingly, freshmen were required "to dispute on Ramus's definitions, Monday and Tuesdays in the forenoon"; to study grammar; to read the Greek testament; and to learn Hebrew, among other things. Upperclassmen recited William Ames's Puritan *Marrow of Theology,* the works of the Dutch Cartesians Franco Burgersdyck and Adrian Heereboord, an assortment of writings by Johannes Alsted, and the physics of Charles Morton, who arrived in Charlestown from England in 1686. Students also studied the natural philosophy of John Ray, William Derham, and Robert Boyle and learned St. Thomas Aquinas and the church Fathers as well.[18]

And, of course, students read latitudinarians, especially Tillotson. Norman Fiering, surveying Tillotson's popularity in the colonies, in fact has argued that Tillotson was a key figure in the beginnings of the Enlightenment in America. Tillotson's books turn up on library lists and catalogues throughout the colonies. Ebenezer Pemberton (H.C. 1691), who was employed as the Harvard library keeper while he was working on his second degree, managed to accumulate later during his years as the pastor of the Old South Church an impressive library of his own. When it was sold after his early death in 1717, the catalogue announcing the sale listed Tillotson's *Works* and *Sermons,*

together with numerous volumes by Stillingfleet, including the *Ir*
cum and *Sermons;* Patrick's *Discourses* and other writings; and
kins's *Sermons* and *Of the Principles and Duties of Natural Rel*
The Harvard Library catalogue of a few years later (1723)
works by Stillingfleet and Wilkins and other moderate Anglic
ers. At the same time that this catalogue appeared, a com
investigators drawn from the Harvard Board of Overseers
discover "What are the books in Divinity, which are most
particularly recommended to the students?" They even
able to report that "by some information given, the wo
son, Sherlock, Scott, and Lucas, are generally most
Hancock, Jr. (H.C. 1719), the father of Governor Joh
immediate predecessor to the rational-minded Lemu
1739) at the First Church in Braintree, was the colle
ing this time (1723–1726). In his college common
corded, among other moderate wisdoms, Tillots
belief in God was valid because it was reason
"Johnny" Barnard (H.C. 1700), who was hired t
ling public collection of books in Boston and
congregation in Marblehead, developed a pa
the course of explaining the importance of
warning parents "never to correct in a passi
be looked upon but as the effect of passi
enduring influence of Tillotson, John Q
later, wryly observed in his diary that,
heard a sermon preached, he supposed
plagiarized] from Tillotson.[19]

One of the most telling, and mos
influence of latitudinarian writers in
book of sermon subjects kept by
Foxcroft was born in Boston and
Colonel Francis Foxcroft, a leadin
Thomas, however, became a Co
fifty-two years as pastor at Bos
mon for clergy in America and
sermons or simply for medita
range of headings various ref
to Scripture. Foxcroft's note
God," listed dozens of sub
as many as fifteen or twe
some of the most freque

ing the importance of the example of Christ in this endeavor, Tillotson emphasized "the great example which is here propounded to our imitation: as I have loved you" so also should you love one another.[21]

Gleanings such as these, entered by Foxcroft into his subject notebook, indicate that the influence of latitudinarian writers was, in his case, extensive. This supports the Harvard Overseers committee report that Tillotson's writings were among the most used volumes at the college and shows that Foxcroft knew of and approved the ideas of other latitudinarian writers. Moreover, Foxcroft's notes suggest something further about the transmission of ideas from England to colonial America. Foxcroft, like his colleagues Colman, Wadsworth, Pemberton, and Appleton, followed custom by seldom footnoting his writings. That is, he was not in the habit of identifying for his audience the source of a particular argument or idea. (His citation of Tillotson in *A Discourse Preparatory to the Choice of a Minister* is itself a rare exception in this regard.) Consequently, it is not easy to determine his or his fellow ministers' intellectual indebtedness by searching for revealing footnotes. One insight that comes from analysis of his subject book is that scholarly study of seventeenth- and eighteenth-century library lists, of references to books in correspondences and records, and of a particular writer's educational background and ideas is more likely to uncover that writer's intellectual indebtedness than will the search for revealing footnotes.[22]

It is manifestly clear that the literary tastes of Foxcroft, Leverett, the Brattles, Colman, Pemberton, Wadsworth, Appleton, and others among the Harvard "new curriculum" circle were not identical to the tastes of some of the area's other ministers and leading laymen. Indeed, eventually there was outright conflict over the direction in which Leverett had piloted the college. Increase Mather, who accepted the office of president of the college in 1685, was at least partly responsible for the appointment of Leverett and Brattle that same year. But whatever promise for the support of orthodoxy that Mather had detected in the new tutors at that time apparently did not come to fruition over the sixteen-year term of Leverett's presidency. According to Morison, there were "signs of a growing coolness" between the two in 1697, when Increase Mather, speaking at William Brattle's First Church in Cambridge, suggested that the tutors look back to Jonathan Mitchell (H.C. 1647, d. 1668), a former tutor and defender of orthodoxy, as a model for their own work as educators: "A Few words let me speak further to you, who belong to that nursery, for religion and learning, which has for a long time been the glory, not of

Cambridge only, but of New England. If the fountains be corrupted, how should the streams be pure?" Mather then advised at least two of the men presumably in attendance that day: "Say each of you, Mitchell (once a tutor in Harvard College) shall be the example, whom I will imitate!"[23]

From Mather's account in his *Autobiography* of his expedition to England (1687–1692) to secure a charter for Massachusetts, it would seem that he was eager enough to receive the assistance of Tillotson in that endeavor, but this cordiality apparently did not extend to the ideas of Tillotson. After 1697, relations between Increase Mather and Leverett deteriorated, and other persons, such as Pemberton, who was appointed a tutor that year, were drawn into the fray. Eventually, a Mather party, which had taken shape not only in connection with the problems at Harvard but as a result of other factors of change as well, took up the fight against a Leverett party. Cotton Mather, whose broad interests and extensive reading distinguished him above most of his colleagues, was provoked into declaring that the divinity books that the students were reading had "rank poison in them." Edward Holyoke (H.C. 1705), who emerged from the Leverett party in the 1730s to become the president of Harvard, years later was still replying to the same sort of criticism as that which Cotton Mather had made. Defending the college against the accusations made by the itinerant George Whitefield, Holyoke stated that "the aspersions upon us, as to the principles there prevalent, & the books there read, were unjust."

Party lines eventually took clearer shape, as differences of opinion became incidents of party interest. Judge Sewall, a formidable ally of the Mathers though he was a member of Pemberton's church, censured Holyoke's almanac for having an Anglican bias. Johnny Barnard, who claimed to have clinched for Holyoke the president's office by remarking to Governor Belcher that Holyoke was of a very "catholic temper," was originally under the care of the Mathers, having assisted in the preparation of a pamphlet defending them from a literary assault made against them from another quarter, by the merchant Robert Calef. Barnard's mistake was to become friendly with Colman, and this mistake cost him a position at North Church, where Cotton Mather persuaded the voting members to overlook Barnard's candidacy. (Barnard seems eventually to have detached himself from both parties, however.) Cotton Mather also seems to have started a "whispering campaign" against Foxcroft, when some remarks he made were taken to mean that Foxcroft was a Church of England man. Joshua Gee (H.C. 1717) began a whispering campaign of his own, when, in the interests of demonstrating support for and solidarity with the Mather party, he declared that Cotton Mather in fact hated the writings of Tillotson. Pemberton, who was known for his short fuse, needed no whispering campaign to announce his feelings of frustration in his dealings with the other side. Suspecting the Mathers of complicity with Judge Sewall in a cause against him, the minister, according to Sewall's diary entry, exploded: "Mr. Pemberton with extraordinary vehemency said, (capering with his feet) If the Mathers ordered it I [Sewall] would shoot him through." Benjamin Wadsworth (H.C. 1690), who was Foxcroft's colleague at First Church, was for a while claimed by both parties. He ended up in the Leverett camp and eventually had to fight the efforts of the Mather-Sewall party to expel him—along with Colman and Nathaniel Appleton—from his position as a fellow of the Harvard Corporation. He was successful in defending himself, and, in fact, he was offered, after the death of Leverett, the office of president, which he accepted (1725–1736). Even Governor Bellomont was aware of party differences in 1699, when, in a communication to Sewall, he contrasted "Mr. Mather's selfishnesse and pedantick pride" to the "vertue, learning and merit of Mr. Brattle and Mr. Pemberton."[24]

Leverett and Brattle for the most part ran the college, with Increase Mather often distracted by pastoral obligations in Boston and by the disputes and adventures in other areas into which he and his son Cotton seemed inevitably to fall. Increase left the president's office in 1701, however, when the General Court determined to make the position full-time. Rather than give up his responsibilities at North Church, Mather resigned and was replaced by Samuel Willard (H.C. 1659), then the vice president, who was installed as "acting President," and served the college for six years. Willard, who labored over the course of many years to articulate covenant theology to his audiences at Old South Church, was, with Increase Mather, a leader among the second generation in New England, at least as far as religion was concerned. Although he remained to the end a conservative, he could on occasion be somewhat broad-minded, as evidenced, perhaps, by his choice of Ebenezer Pemberton as his assistant at Old South. Pemberton was probably never perceived by anyone as a raving reformer, who might subvert the authority and order of the churches. However, at the time of his installation at Old South in 1700, his catholick views were already well known. Indeed, Willard wanted him as an assistant at Old South "but felt obliged to move slowly, because he was already identified as a liberal and a friend of John Leverett and William Brattle."[25]

Willard's selection of Pemberton as an assistant, Judge Sewall's toleration of him as his minister, the frequent cooperative enterprises between the various churches (for example, on fast days), the sharing of pulpits, and other such seeming anomalies suggest that party politics at Harvard did not lead to an entirely disputatious relationship between the Mathers and the Leverett corner. Accordingly, the disagreements that emerged in connection with the running of the college should not be taken as indicative of utterly clear party lines that were defended to the end. It should be remembered that Increase, and especailly Cotton Mather, were by no means ignorant of the arguments of science or natural theology, or even the catholick views of latitudinarians. Together with Judge Sewall, John Webb (H.C. 1708), and Samuel Checkley (H.C. 1715) of the New North Church, Joshua Gee, and some of the older ministers in Massachusetts, such as John Higginson, Nathaniel Noyes, and James Allen, the Mathers sought to preserve orthodoxy but endeavored as well to avoid causing disunity among the churches. Clearly, religious differences became more visibly outlined in the process of the party disputes at Harvard. And some of these differences were sharp enough to make compromise unlikely. But such differences nonetheless should not be understood as indicative of an all-encompassing theological opposition of new ideas to old ways. Catholicks did not abandon orthodoxy for the glitter of English ideas, and noncatholicks did not uniformly reject all of the ideas of English writers after 1660.[26]

By way of bringing the party dispute into relief it might be reiterated that those who read and approved of the latitudinarian books did not flee Boston meetinghouses for membership in the Anglican congregations of King's Chapel, or, later, Christ Church. There was already some degree of cooperation with the Anglican clergy before the 1690s, and relations gradually improved over the course of the next fifty years (though rumors of an Anglican bishopric in later decades obviously damaged the Anglican image). Benjamin Wadsworth, in the course of his trip to Albany in 1690 to meet in treaty with representatives of the Five Nations of the Iroquois, found himself listening to a chaplain who read aloud the "Common Prayer before each of the English sermons" (including his own) that were preached to the mixed group that made up the expedition. He gave no indication that he found this disturbing. John Murrin has written that the rise of the "catholick spirit" contributed to the relaxation of harassment of Anglicans in Massachusetts Bay after 1740. But tensions did not disappear entirely. The Harvard Corporation, for example, decided to continue to deny seating as college overseers to Church of England ministers in 1727, explicitly reaffirming a ruling that had been initially stated in August 1699. Nathaniel Appleton, the nephew of President Leverett and brother-in-law to President-to-be Holyoke, followed William Brattle into the Cambridge pulpit on the latter's death in 1717, thereby receiving something like de facto certification as a catholick. Appleton, nevertheless, worried in his later years that "the Church of England should thrust itself in among us."[27]

Carl Bridenbaugh, in his study of Anglican "ecclesiastical imperialism" in the colonies at the end of the seventeenth and during the eighteenth century, asserted that Benjamin Colman desired some rapprochement between Anglicans and non-Anglicans in Massachusetts but that Colman did not wish to adopt Anglican forms of worship. Although it is true that Colman did not wish to adopt Anglican liturgy, he nevertheless came to believe that some changes in the order and discipline of the Congregational churches were necessary. Colman graduated from Harvard in 1692, and after taking his M.A. degree in 1695, he sailed for England. After a series of misadventures, including his capture by pirates and a brief imprisonment in France, he found his way to London, where his connections landed him duty as a supply preacher, which provided him temporary assignments, such as a short term with a congregation in Cambridge. He eventually settled in Bath, where he became close with the poet Elizabeth Rowe (née Singer), and it was there that he received a letter from some New England friends calling him back to Boston.[28]

In Colman's absence, a group of Boston merchants, led by the Harvard treasurer Thomas Brattle and John Mico, had begun to lay plans for the founding of a new church in Boston. With the support of Leverett, William Brattle, Pemberton, and the Reverend Simon Bradstreet (H.C. 1693) of Charlestown, they contacted Colman, offering him the position of minister to the church. Colman received the invitation at Bath in June 1699. The undertakers of the church took pains to assure Colman that their design did not arise from uncatholick motives of separation or party interest, writing him that "this affair is neither begun nor carried on by strife or faction." As we shall see, the inclusion of this line reflected the difficult circumstances of the New England churches in the late seventeenth century. As T. H. Breen has written, a "factious spirit which had divided congregations throughout New England" had emerged on the heels of the Halfway-Covenant, and various other theological disagreements, in the 1660s. Theological factionalism and controversies over the related issues of ministerial authority and church purity, such as the one that led in 1669 to the forming of the Third Church by persons dissatisfied with the policies of the First Church, seemed to threaten the very order of the religious establishment. In fact, the religious predicament of New Englanders was in some ways similar to the problem of "zeal" that occupied latitudinarians in England. The letter to Colman did not detail these problems, however. It offered as one reason for the formation of a new congregation the information that there was a shortage of good pews in other meetinghouses. Colman was persuaded by the undertakers' letters to receive a Presbyterian ordination in England and to return to Boston, which he did in November 1699.[29]

In December, Colman was installed as minister, and the congregation met in the church for the first time. More important, however, the undertakers published in December a short *Manifesto* outlining their principles. Among the innovations it proposed were the following three articles: (1) the right of all members, communicants and noncommunicants alike, to an equal voice and vote in the choosing of a minister; (2) the removal of the requirement of a public relation (or confession) for admission to the church; and (3) the reading of Scripture without explication, or, as it was sometimes called, "dumb reading."[30]

The church building that was constructed for the Brattle Street congregation, with its tower and spire, followed more closely a style of architecture of London churches than that of New England Congregational meetinghouses. But the popular name for the church was not drawn from its architecture or its location (as were the names Old Brick, New Brick [also known as the "Revenge Church"], Old South, New South, West, Hollis Street, and so on). Rather, it was christened by its detractors "the Manifesto Church" for its departure from tradition, as suggested by the December statement. Predictably, the Mathers were furious with Colman and the founders. Cotton Mather wrote in his diary in January 1700: "I see Satan beginning a terrible shake unto the churches of New England; and the innovators, that have set up a new church in Boston, (a new one indeed!) have made a day of temptation among us. The men are ignorant, arrogant, obstinate, and full of malice and slander, and they fill the land with lyes, in the misrepresentation whereof, I am a very singular sufferer." Those persons who had published "under the title of a Manifesto" the articles of the new church had not only "assaulted all the churches of New England" but had threatened by their action to "utterly subvert our churches."[31]

Nicholas Noyes and John Higginson, the latter called by Judge Sewall the "hammer of heretics," wrote to Colman on the last day of 1699, with the warning: "We advise you that the word manifesto in the frontispiece is offensive." Among the assorted heresies that the church might be guilty of was the provision to extend the voting franchise to all who belonged to the church. But the members of the Brattle Street Church could not themselves agree on what the proposal meant until 1704. Moreover, the issue was not forced until July 4, 1715, when the congregation met for the first time to vote on the hiring of a new minister to assist Colman. Nevertheless, the very notion of an equality of members posed a challenge to the sense of many in New England that the church was guided essentially by the minister and the visible saints, or those who had been accepted into full communion (and who were, as a result, guided by God). Samuel Willard, who was not as active as the Mathers in condemning the Manifesto Church (he seems to have spent more time in his study refining his system of divinity) but like them was a defender of orthodoxy, surely must have seen the danger in this article of the Manifesto. Willard, in the 1690s, on several occasions, had stressed to his congregation at Old South Church that, in the deliberations leading to a choice of a minister, "he had a negative [veto], and was not only a moderator." Indeed, this exercise of authority was perceived as necessary so as to prevent the church's becoming a "democracy," at a time when forceful, authoritative leadership of the churches was most urgently needed. And Increase Mather had made precisely this point twenty-five years before the founding of the Manifesto Church, arguing that concessions to democracy in church order would lead to anarchy.[32]

Higginson and Noyes, in their letter of rebuke to the Manifesto Church, had identified as a particular problem the proposal that there be no "publick and personal profession of your repentance toward God" as a condition for admission to communion. The proposed omission of a public relation of one's experience of humiliation before God for sin was viewed by many as a major departure from tradition, and it was on this point especially that the defenders of orthodoxy sensed a potential subverting of the New England churches. Since the early years of the Bay Colony, the test of a relation had been required for persons seeking admittance to the Lord's Supper. One purpose of the relation, or "confession" of the course of one's conversion from sin, as it was known to Thomas Shepard of Cambridge sixty years earlier, was to afford the faithful, the "visible saints," an opportunity to make an informed judgment as to the likelihood that a person was regenerate (the judgment in almost every case was positive). But resistance to the practice had surfaced as early as the 1670s, when Solomon Stoddard of Northhampton, seeking to discover ways in which to invigorate the piety of his congregation, had argued that "the practice was taken up at first but as a useful thing, yet many now make it an ordinance. There is as much weight laid on it as if it were a divine institution."[33]

Stoddard's reasoning on the matter was precisely the approach taken by Colman and his colleagues in 1699. They suspected that some persons were so frightened by the prospect of having to confess the story of their conversion that they kept themselves away from the Lord's Supper rather than face the congregation. Thinking like the Stillingfleet of *Irenicum,* the Brattle Street founders decided, apparently as had Stoddard, that the personal spiritual benefits that might arise from a person's participation in communion outweighed the potential danger of allowing an impostor to slip into the fellowship of the church. The test of a relation, being a human invention rather than a divine direction, was deemed expendable. The First Church in Cambridge (Brattle, Appleton), the Old South Church (Pemberton), and the First Church in Boston (Wadsworth, Foxcroft) all either substantially modified or dispensed with the requirement for a public relation during their years under catholick pastors.[34]

The Brattle Street decision to read Scripture without exposition and to recite publicly the Lord's Prayer and other "set forms" of prayer possibly was the most threatening of the innovations that were proposed. "Dumb reading" was based on the notion that the language of Scripture, and especially of the Psalms, was itself a powerfully affecting instrument of devotion. Increase Mather, in his public response to the *Manifesto,* a work entitled *The Order of the Gospel* (1700), decried these practices, identifying the adoption of "set forms" of prayer as "syllabicall idolatry." What disturbed Mather probably was not simply the fact that the new church, by approving these practices, had symbolically drawn itself closer to the Church of England. So much was obvious from viewing the church building. Rather, as Teresa Toulouse has argued, Mather suspected that set forms and dumb reading "encouraged a misguided sensuous delight." Colman's friends Mrs. Rowe and Isaac Watts (the latter the author of a translation of the Psalms that became popular in America), together with some other literary-minded Dissenters in England, had in the latter part of the seventeenth century become interested in the capability of ornate language, in poetry and prayer, to raise and stir the affections. Mather, who was suspicious of the affections, in part because of their connection with the physical body, consequently discountenanced the apparent Manifesto plan to reach the affections with "sensuous" language. Mather believed that the better course was to instruct his listeners through the exposition of sound doctrine. As we shall see, Colman and his catholick colleagues perceived no inherent contradiction between doctrinal instruction and language that stirred the affections.[35]

Latitudinarians, writing after the English Civil War, were extremely wary of religious "zeal." Extolling the virtues of a moderate, catholick religious temperament, they sought ways in which to prevent any further the fragmentation of Christianity in England into "enthusiastic" parties, each of which might claim for itself a monopoly on religious truth. In America, one result of the appointments to Harvard of the tutors Leverett and Brattle was that a rising generation of Congregational ministers in Massachusetts were exposed to such latitudinarian thinking. Some of those ministers—men such as Colman, Foxcroft, Pemberton, Wadsworth, and Appleton—were influenced by latitudinarian thought to the extent that they become "catholick Congregationalists." These ministers rejected zeal to the extent that they believed, as Wadsworth wrote in 1701, "Christians may differ from one another in some smaller things" of religion and it was crucially important that they "keep the unity of the spirit in the bond of peace."[36] They did not abandon discipline, however. They encouraged criticism of sin as it was lodged not only in institutions but in individuals as well. However, they made it clear that such criticism was not to be made in anger, but in love: "When we go to reprove or rebuke others, this should not proceeed from revenge, ill will, or any such principle, but it should proceed from love to God and to our neighbour." Catholicks, drawing ideas from across the spectrum of latitudinarian thought, came to emphasize the importance of the affections in a kind of zealous love to God and neighbor, as opposed to a zealous anger at and hatred of any departure from Congregational orthodoxy in New England.[37]

2

A Beautiful Order in Nature

Historians often have pointed out the magnitude of social change that took place in Massachusetts in the last three decades of the seventeenth century. The growth of the population of New England, the development of the Atlantic trade and the diversification of the economy, and problems arising from the shortage of land in eastern Massachusetts all contributed to change, and so also to the fears of some persons that religion was in decline. As the world became more complex and as patterns of social life adjusted to increasing complexity, older notions of social order, status, and authority—which had been received from the immigrant generation to the Bay Colony—came under review. New Englanders after the mid-1660s reaped the "fruits of diversity," or dissension, disunion, and factionalism in civil and ecclesiastical politics, and the worry and confusion that went with them. This process was accelerated in 1684, when the English overseers of Massachusetts revoked the Massachusetts Bay charter and created the Dominion of New England. The loss of the charter meant that self-government was replaced by a political system controlled by a royal governor. The "city on a hill" that was the Bay Colony was drawn into the larger world of New England religious and political life, and into observance of English legal statutes, which included religious toleration (according to the Act of Toleration [1689]). Some ministers, such as Increase Mather, interpreted the departure from the way of life of the founders as an ominous sign. Even before the loss of the charter, Increase had warned, "There is a great decay as to the power of godliness amongst us. Professors are many of them of a loose, carnal, ungirt conversation. . . . Professors of religion fashion themselves according to the world." The lessons of history, of biblical history, accordingly ought to be taken to heart: "Thus if we look back into the old world, they were minding little besides their sensual pleasures, until the very day when the flood came."[1]

Ministers called their congregations to account for their departure from godliness, and they stressed the necessity of reformation from the world, in jeremiads, a sermonic form featuring, in addition to accusations of personal and collective deviancy, an emphasis on the terror of God's judgment. However clearly their congregations heard them, it is obvious from the rhetoric that ministers sensed a contamination of society and that they understood this to be a result of persons' having too much "affection to the world," as the Reforming Synod of 1679 stated the problem. Church purity demanded a separation of the individual, and the congregation, from the world.[2]

As the Atlantic Ocean narrowed in width in the late seventeenth century and New Englanders increasingly were drawn into closer contact with English ways and ideas, ministers warned against the temptations of pride and other vices that followed wealth and power. But at the same time, ministers seem to have conceived New England as distanced from Europe, perhaps more than ever before, by "the great Atlantick flood." In fact, while worrying about the worsening predicament of New England as it was pulled ever closer to England, ministers, paradoxically, forcefully expressed the view that Massachusetts was a fragile and endangered outpost of civilization tenuously perched on the brink of a "howling wilderness." Clerical reflection on the nature of the North American wilderness was rarely systematic, but as it was expressed in sermons and other writings, it nevertheless displayed in simple form a kind of logic that was manifest as well in certain other aspects of religious thought in early New England, including theories about the affections. Accordingly, a brief consideration of the leading features of ministers' thinking about wilderness in the latter part of the seventeenth century is offered here as an introduction to discussion of theories about the affections.

The unpredictability of the wilderness, the possibility that the chaos of the wilderness might at any time spill over the hedgerows into the protected garden of the settlers, posed for New Englanders an urgent problem. A sense of the danger inherent in such unpredictability and potential chaos was expressed in various ways by colonists who believed that in this world, the agents of Satan worked constantly against the faithful. William Bradford, of Plymouth colony, early on connected the "howling wilderness" with Indians who were "cruel, barbarous, and most treacherous." William Wigglesworth, in

God's Controversy with New-England (1662), made the point more precisely: "Beyond the great Atlantick flood / There is a region vast, / A country where no English foot / In former ages past: / A waste and howling wilderness? Where none inhabited / but hellish fiends, and brutish men / That devils worshipped." To colonists, the Indian often represented evil, and the danger of descent into chaos. As Richard Slotkin has observed: "Through the darkness the Indian flitted, like the secret enemy of Christ, or like the evil thoughts that plague the mind on the edge of consciousness. Like the Devil, Indians struck where the defenses of good were the weakest and, having done their deed, retreated to hiding."[3]

The fear of being engulfed in chaos, expressed through references to the wilderness and sometimes more specifically to the Indian, was expressed in other ways as well. Black dogs, wild animals in the forests, natural catastrophes such as floods or earthquakes, and other such New World phenomena constantly reminded New Englanders that "the world is satanic and dark." Jonathan Mitchel, whom Increase Mather had recommended to his Harvard opponents as the model of a tutor, had used the phrase "errand into the wilderness" to describe the settlement of New England. Other ministers adopted the phrase in their own sermons or otherwise explored the symbolism of wilderness to reinforce their warnings about the threats facing New England after 1670. Samuel Danforth (*Errand into the Wilderness* [1671]) argued that the unbridled lusts and passions and sensuousness of New Englanders were provoking God to give up the people entirely to the wilderness, through the chaos of a flood or an earthquake. Samuel Willard, Urian Oakes (a former president of the college), and Cotton Mather made essentially the same arguments in the 1680s. Nicholas Noyes and John Higginson referred constantly in their sermons to the wilderness of New England, the latter pointing out in 1663 that persons did not originally come to New England for the purpose of accumulating wealth or cultivating a life of sensuality, "nor had we any rationall grounds to expect such a thing in such a wilderness as this." Increase Mather still was making this point sixty years later, by asking: "What did our fathers come into this wilderness for? Not to gain estates, as men do now, but for religion. . . . But, Ah, degenerate New-England, what art thou come to at this day?"[4]

The terrors of chaos, as symbolized by the wilderness, were everpresent. Indeed, it should be understood that New Englanders' fear of chaos was an integral and necessary part of their religious worldview. They could not allow their consciousness of the threat posed to them by chaos, represented in one way by wilderness, to slip away from them any more than they could give up their reflection on religious expressions of order, stability, and continuity. Reflection on the chaos of the wilderness was as much a part of their awareness of the "sacred" as was the experience of order and discipline in the fellowship of the saints. The reason for this is that for many New Englanders, the wilderness of the New World—although indeed it sometimes seemed the manifestation of chaos—also represented a powerful, dynamic, revivifying influence on religious life. Of course, New Englanders were by no means the only persons to hold such a religious worldview. In fact, the expression of a sense of blending of destructive and creative forces in the symbol of the wilderness (or forest or desert) had been an occasional feature of Christian thought for over a thousand years (and perhaps since the early church). But certain aspects of colonists' experience in New England contributed to the intensification of this kind of thinking after 1670 or so. In some cases that experience amounted to perception of a wave of nearly insurmountable problems that followed in the wake of closer economic and political ties to England. But churchgoers also were to an increasing extent reminded by their preachers that the founders of New England had left England because of the too-highly elaborated system of ecclesiatical organization and rules of religious conduct that they had experienced there as repressive. Accordingly, the settlement of the New World was presented—as the historian of religions Mircea Eliade might say—as a reinforcing (or even a recreating) of pure religion through a descent into chaos. As Charles Hambricke-Stowe has pointed out, extant narratives of the captivity of New Englanders by Indians demonstrate the presence of this understanding of the recreative properties of wilderness on a personal level. Hambricke-Stowe writes, "When New Englanders were forcibly taken into the wilderness by those perceived as Satan's minions," the journey, as it proceeded "farther and farther into the chaos of the wilderness" became a "transforming spiritual ordeal in which the drama of death and resurrection was once again played out in the soul." Wilderness, then, conceived as the representation of chaos, was often—to borrow a phrase from Jonathan Z. Smith—"sacred in the wrong way," or the "bad sacred," and so threatened to overturn the social and religious order. But, like the ancient Israelite's perception of the desert, it was also a "life-giving power . . . insuring vitality and fecundity."[5]

The wilderness was often conceived as chaotic and dangerous, but sometimes as recreative as well. The affections were viewed similarly, as powerful and useful to the spiritual life but also as unpredictable and potentially dangerous. It is important to understand this in order to appreciate that New Englanders such as Willard, the Mathers, Noyes and Higginson, Webb, Checkley, and some other ministers, in spite of their often obvious suspicion of emotion, were not entirely unemotional men, nor did they preach sermons that unqualifiedly condemned all emotion. It is because they understood well the power of the affections that they feared them. Rodney Fulcher has argued that these men "belonged to a generation that had found no place for the man of feeling within their midst," and David Leverenz has written that in Willard's theology, "feelings are deliberately slighted." Robert Middlekauff has characterized Samuel Sewall's religion as one of "emotional detachment." But these assessments are not entirely accurate. More instructive is the insight of Middlekauff that Increase Mather's distrust of the affections emerged from a concern that the affections "often arose" from "carnal ends" and in "the service of lusts." It was the connection of the affections with the sensuous, the carnal, that made them dangerous. It should not be overlooked, however, that the affections, some of which could be aimed against sin, were also understood to be a potentially useful weapon in the battle against evil, lodged as it was in the world, and so could not be wasted. Accordingly, even those ministers who greatly feared the disruptive potential of the affections sought ways in which to employ them in religion. Most often, these ministers ultimately emphasized fear of God and hatred of sin, rather than God's loving adoption of the faithful as children or the bonding of the saints in affection in this world. To borrow terms from Rudolf Otto, it might be said that there was more of the *tremendum* than of the *fascinans* in their view of the Holy.[6]

Congregationalist ministers in the seventeenth and early eighteenth centuries were influenced by a view of the affections that had descended from Aristotle and St. Thomas Aquinas, through English Puritans, to New England. From Aristotle's *De Anima* Thomas drew lessons about the soul that contributed to his framing an outline of the soul's capabilities in *Summa Theologica* and *De Veritate*. According to Thomas, the physical world was related to the soul as its matter and its instrument. The soul, as known by the objects of its activity, was divided into three grades: (1) the vegetative soul, which, as the lowest grade of the soul's powers, acted solely on the body, as the force underlying nutrition, growth, and generation; (2) the sensitive soul, which was more extensive in scope than the vegetative power, having as its object anything related to the senses; and (3) the rational soul, whose object was not only the sense world but universal (incorporeal) being. Such a division of the soul into three parts, founded on a perception of the way in which specific activities of the soul transcended by degrees inanimate bodies, in essence "fractured" the soul into various faculties. And, as Rodney Fulcher has argued, this fracturing, which "worked against an organic conception of the soul," was passed along to Puritans.

Against this background of a fractured soul, Thomas developed his understanding of the passions. Arguing that "what intelligence grasps is of a different class from what sense grasps," he posited an intellective appetite as distinct from a sensitive appetite "which contains the soul's passions." The passions—love, desire, hate, fear, and so on—came about through a relation of body and soul, form and matter. Proposing that "all passions seem to be in connection with the body," Thomas explained passion as a process involving the excitation of an appetite on the heels of an apprehension of good or evil, and consequent bodily changes. Though the body itself did not "cause" the passion, its participation in the process was fundamental to the constitution of a passion. Ideally, reason directed the sensitive appetite in its operations, so that "emotional desirousness" did "respond to the higher part of the soul, the part of understanding or reason and of will." But Thomas expressed misgivings about the capability of the rational soul to direct and control the passions properly, in a lengthy discussion entitled "The sense appetite as a cause of sin." Stressing the physical aspects of the operations of the sense appetite, he argued that "an emotion of the sense appetite" could move or control the will "indirectly" and that this could happen in two ways. On the one hand, he argued that when one faculty was heavily concentrated on a certain activity, "other faculties have little or no energy at their disposal." Accordingly, by the "law of distribution" (or, "distraction"), "when the sense appetite is fired by emotion, the will, which is the rational appetite, has little or no force for its own activity." On the other hand, the emotions of the sense appetite could simply become so powerful as to overwhelm reason, not in such a way as to control the will directly, but to distort rational judgment, and thereby indirectly to influence the act of will following from judgment.[7]

To this scheme were added over time other ideas drawn from Plato, Augustine, Albertus Magnus, and a host of other theologians and classical writers, so that, when English Puritans began to articulate their understanding of the passions, they did so with reference to an admixture of theories about the soul and human faculties that was not always logically consistent. One description of the general problem of the faculties in Puritan theology was offered by Perry Miller, who wrote that, on the one hand, Puritans drew from scholasticism the notion of reason as "a principle of action, a power or faculty by which truth was discovered in sensibles." From Plato, Augustine, and Reformed theology, on the other hand, "came the conception of reason as itself the source of truth, the container and giver of ideas through inward intuition or recollection." Writers such as the moderate Anglican Edward Reynolds (*Treatise of the Passions* [1640]) sought to alleviate some of the tension in this system by articulating in detail the troublesome relation of reason to the will and its manner of operation in the faculty of the "understanding" as a guide to the will. But the thorny problem of the relationship of the soul to the body—and, in particular, the capability of the passions, which were closely engaged to the body, to distort judgment and lead the will astray—remained to plague Puritan writers. If the world was, as John Winthrop believed, a "dung heap," and the body, as the Cambridge (Massachusetts) pastor Thomas Shepard believed, a "menstrous cloth," then the rational soul, which was charged with apprehending, judging, and embracing the Word, stood in jeopardy through its association with the body. The capability of the passions to influence (at least indirectly) the will toward sin became more menacing to morality and personal discipline in the context of a worldview that did not look kindly on the physical body, or material existence in general.[8]

But like the wilderness, which was dangerous yet sometimes useful, the passions, or the affections, could not be ignored. The affections, in fact, could prove beneficial to the spiritual life when they were carefully managed so as to invigorate and reinforce the process of repentance in a person. Specifically, ministers in New England throughout much of the seventeenth century adopted a strategy, with regard to the use of the affections, that was focused on the engendering of fear of God and hatred of sin and separation from the flesh. This approach to the exciting of the affections in fact offered a built-in precaution against the danger that the affections might overpower reason and cause irreparable damage to the soul. By encouraging affections that reinforced the separation of a person from the temptations of the flesh, ministers were, in a sense, aiming the passions against themselves. If separation from the temptations of the flesh was understood to promote spiritual purity, and if the affections were themselves located in that part of the human constitution that included sensory perception, then by employing the affections in the service of distancing oneself from the world, a person was at the same time distancing himself from the affections themselves. Accordingly, the excitation of affections that reinforced separation from the world also, paradoxically, functioned in such a way as to prevent the affections as a whole from gathering such power as to allow them to usurp reason or seduce the will. The tendency among Puritans in the early seventeenth century to destroy their connections to the world while availing themselves of what it might offer in the way of spiritual inspiration has been described in other literature, and we will return to it in this study. But the point to be made here is that for much of the seventeenth century ministers in New England were keenly aware of the dangers of a "fleshly" life, and, accordingly, they were suspicious of the affections. However, by employing the affections in such a way as to facilitate separation from the world, they were able to harness the powers of the affections to the yoke of repentance and, in the bargain, not worry about overexciting the affections, and thereby endangering reason and the will.[9]

Ministers who were most vocal in their concern that New England was in danger of being swallowed up by the wilderness tended to worry most about corrupted flesh, the evil world, and the untrustworthiness of the affections. Samuel Willard, the Mathers, and those ministers who labored more or less to preserve the ways of the founders generally viewed the social changes of the seventeeth century as threatening to godly order in the churches. Surveying the dramatic rise of egoistic economic activity, the accumulation of fortune, and the adoption of prideful, ostentatious English custom (such as the wearing of wigs, one of Judge Sewall's favorite whipping boys), some ministers concluded that "carnality" was the culprit in the perceived decay of religion. In preaching against carnality, they stressed the necessity for "separation" from the world and from sin. Their theology, accordingly, was tipped toward fear of God and terror of hell, and to obedience and duty, and tipped away from a vision of God that was characterized by divine love, tenderness, and compassion.

Samuel Willard, who has been called a "preacher of orthodoxy in an era of change," stressed throughout his ministerial career the necessity for constant repentance. He did not conceive the relation between God and the individual as a warmly affectionate one. As Leverenz has correctly observed, God as a father is depicted in Willard's sermons "with a striking absence of love and tenderness." Willard "assumes patriarchal distance, not loving or anxious bonds." For Willard, as for many of the second generation, shame, guilt, and a vision of God as a judge were to the forefront of religion, "with tender mothering buried in the future rewards after the body dies." The body, argues Leverenz, was understood by Willard, Mather, and their orthodox colleagues as an impediment to the experience of loving bonding. Leverenz, writing from a psychoanalytic perspective, interprets Willard's *The High Esteem Which God Hath of the Death of His Saints* (1683) as follows: "His fantasy is of death from the body's 'Case' so that the soul can become a sweet-smelling invisibility." Indeed, among the second generation, "quite unabashedly, sermons were meant to be repressive, at least of carnal feelings," and so, there is a prominence in sermons of the time of the "negative oral imagery of 'devouring' hell," and other such terrifying imaginings.[10]

In explaining the nature and purpose of repentance, Willard emphasized the importance of what he called the "separating affections." In the last year of his life (1707), in a sermon that was later included in his enormous *The Compleat Body of Divinity* (1726), Willard explained that "repentance ever supposeth evil, in the thing repented of. In repentance there is a separation from the thing" that "must needs employ the separating affections in the exertion of it." The "separating affections" were of key importance in religion. The most important of this class of affections was hatred, and from this the other separating affections followed. Willard wrote, "Now Hatred is the primitive separating affection," and among those affections that were "derivative of hatred" was the "insatiable desire" to be rid of sin. Willard explained that desire might be understood as "a craving after the enjoyment of an absent good," or as an affection aimed at the connection of a person with a pleasurable object. However, Willard made clear that by using the term *desire,* he did not intend to suggest an attraction to what was perceived as good, but, rather, "the contrary to which is under present consideration: tho' improperly it may be called a desire, tho' not after the thing, but of getting away from it." The separating affections derived from hatred, but a thoroughgoing hatred of sin, in oneself as well as in others, amounted to zeal. In his election sermon of 1682, Willard had encouraged the magistrates to "check and restrain" the "many sins, some very crying," that plagued the land, warning his audience that "great industry and zeal is needful here when sin is grown impudent." When Willard recommended zeal, he meant an intensity, specifically, of the separating affections, zeal primarily "from a thing" as opposed to "to a thing."[11]

Increase Mather spent much of his life resisting attachment to the world. Sometimes this took the form of an expectation of the end of the world. After the appearance of blazing stars in the heavens, he confided to his audience in 1681, "I am perswaded that the floods of great water are coming." At other times, he simply expressed himself in warnings such as "Beware of an heart glued unto the world." Observing that pride and lusts corrupted the soul, Mather argued that even "the holiest heart in this world has a great deal of impurity in it: there is sin in it and all sin is impurity." The affections, whether they were tickled by "syllabicall idolatry," or even by strong preaching, were not to be trusted. Pointing out, "Men may well be affected towards faithful ministers of God, and yet not go to heaven," Increase drew the following lesson from Scripture: "The Jews were mightily affected with a sermon which they had heard Christ preach concerning the bread of life, so as that with much affection they said, Lord, Evermore give us this bread Joh. 6.34. Notwithstanding this pang of good desires, these men after a while went back from Christ, and walked no more with him." Conversion, as Mather described it in the revealing title *Awakening's Truth Tending to Conversion* (1710), was a matter essentially of separation, and he seems to have accepted the usefulness of the "separating" affections to that enterprise. Answering the question of what is "implyed in conversion," he responded, "a being turned from sin, satan, the world & self." It was useful, then, for a person to become angry at these evils, because, in fact, "zeal implies anger," that is, "an affection of anger that is lawful." Fear, guilt, and shame also were useful. No doubt Mather intended to stir all three of these emotions with his warning that parents who failed to guide their children into good Christian habits would have to endure for eternity the knowledge of their children's terror and suffering in hell.[12]

Following generally in this pattern of thinking about the world and the affections were other second-generation ministers, some of whom stressed certain points more than others. Urian Oakes recommended zeal, arguing, "Zeal is an intense degree of sincere affection to God and to his service." But Oakes emphasized primarily that "there is so much rooting in the earth, that there is little growing upward, heavenward." Accordingly, it was necessary for persons to "renounce all confidence in creatures," to "mourn for, hate and loath those wayes that will be bitterness in the end." Jonathan Higginson worried that "godliness, is exceedingly decaying and expiring in the countrey." He stressed, "A real willingness to part with sin is the immediate affect of those afflicting affections of fear, shame, grief and hatred which are found in humiliation," and he proposed prayer to loosen the will and the affections from "special sins." Nicolas Noyes, Higginson's colleague at the First Church in Salem, versified (in a manner reminiscent of Wigglesworth) about "an holy soul with flaming zeal," observing, "The more the flesh is hack'd, and hew'd / The more corruption is subdu'd."[13]

Those among the younger generation who concurred with their elders in this view of the flesh and the affections included John Webb, Joshua Gee, Mather Byles, and Samuel Checkley. Webb (H.C. 1708), who seems to have come by his position as the first minister of the New North Church through the intercession of Cotton Mather in 1714, preached against irreligion and sinful lusts and singled out Harvard College for special reprimand in this regard. For Webb, "Satan and this evil world are as inveterate enemies to us as sin and self." Webb worried that only earthquakes, thunder, and lightning, or, possibly, the sight of a public execution (as in the case of Matthew Cushing, who was condemned to death for burglary, bad language, and, it would seem, unruly passions), would wake sinners out of their sleep. Cushing, said Webb, "was once or twice sadly overcome with strong drink" and he "once and again fell into violent transports of passion . . . and under a kind of Satanic impression." Cushing, at the age of twenty-two years, should have been an example of restraint, since the "affections" were, in youth, "more easily addressed to their proper objects." Webb urged zeal on rulers, so that they might "make head against the growing iniquities of the time," and he affirmed that persons must at all times "fear the Lord with a religious fear."[14]

Joshua Gee, Cotton Mather's young colleague at Second Church, was "bitter against every one who had liberal views of Christianity" and was referred to by Charles Chauncy (who was himself outspoken against some aspects of the revival in the 1740s) as having "principles rigid to the highest degree, and his charity as cold as death." Urging the "narrow way," and especially the "solitariness of that way," on his congregation, Gee preached regularly on the topics "the constant warfare between the flesh and spirit" and "the evil appetites and inclinations of men." Preaching at the funeral of Cotton Mather, Gee proposed that the death of God's servants "gives us reason to fear approaching judgements," and in that vein he instructed the faithful to discourage "interferring lusts and passions" and to seek to enter at the strait gate.[15]

Mather Byles (H.C. 1725), the nephew of Cotton Mather and the first minister of the Hollis Street Church, believed that "in a little time the dark minutes will all be over and endless light will dawn" as the dead are revived: "O how different this magnificent glory, from the doom of the present world!" Byles made quite clear his views on the body—in its earthly form—in *A Discourse on the Present Vileness of the Body* (1732), wherein he argued the extreme position that "our body was vile, even in the purity of its first creation." The body, for Byles, was like Willard's body a "case" for the soul: "All its appetites are vitiated and disorder'd, and it leads the soul about like a malefactor in chains." The body itself was sick, continually racked by fevers and infected by airborne distempers. Indeed, according to Byles, "our daily eating and drinking, proclaim a feeble body, that would faint and die if these were omitted." Accordingly, the movement of the affections to embrace anything about the world was a terrible error, so that if "our desires tend to this world, let us immediately check the inordinate affection, and say 'No, I have renounced these long ago.' " Byles, who at various times affirmed that religious "enthusiasm" was a mistake, also advised against "ambitious garb" in which the vile body might be dressed, no doubt a reference to English dress, with its "pomp glitter and empty show," and "fopperies."[16]

Samuel Checkley (H.C. 1715) became the first minister at the New South Church in 1719. He was the son of Colonel Samuel Checkley, who had worn a periwig to make his relation to the Old South Church in 1685, but Samuel the younger does not seem to have inherited his father's ease with English fashion. For Checkley, the "world we now live in is full of trouble, our days in it few and evil." Like Webb, he found himself in a position to preach to a man under the sentence of death, in this case for the crime of murder. Checkley, stressing "the sensual and depraved appetite" of persons, urged his auditors to consider how Solomon spoke "ironically" of this: "Go young man, take thy fill of sensual delights . . . these carnal pleasures . . . whatsoever . . . will gratify thy sensual appetite." For Checkley, "lusts and passions" led to "confusions and uproars in society," and, indeed, the terrible crime of murder was committed by persons "who in the heat of their passion" took on an "angry, passionate, quarrelsome, revengeful spirit, and temper."[17]

Cotton Mather usually joined forces with these ministers in the preaching of imminent doom, the depravity of the body, the volatility of the affections, and the necessity for zeal and personal and corporate purity. But Cotton Mather, as those who have studied him have allowed, was a man of numerous contradictions and inconsistencies. It therefore is not a simple matter to explain his thinking in relation to either catholick congregationalists or the more traditionally minded ministers. He did not fit well into either camp. At times, he agreed wholeheartedly with the views of his father and of others who worried over the decline of religion in New England. At other times he seemed to uphold vigorously some of the same ideas as did the catholicks.[18]

There certainly is no lack in cotton Mather's writings of evidence for his opposition to the flesh, the world, and the devil, those "three idols, to which all ungodly men devote themselves." Philip Greven, in fact, has made Mather a model of the "evangelical" temperament (as opposed to "moderate"), which included as a fundamental component of its outlook "a sustained hostility toward the body and all its manifestations and demands." This hostility is apparent in the following entry that Mather made in his diary in 1711:

> I renounce the FLESH. I make no further Allowance to, and Provision for, the *Flesh,* than God allows me. I durst not please the *flesh,* with anything that is displeasing to God. I rebuke, I restrain, I deny the *Flesh* in its irregular inclinations. I don't place my chief good in having my *Flesh* accomodated. I renounce the WORLD. I do no wicked thing to gain the *World;* would not sin for the *Gain of the whole World. . . .* The *sinful Customes* of this *World* do not carry me down the Stream thereof. I renounce the DIVEL. I do not hearken to my grand Adversary. I am afraid of his *Devices.* My Life is a continual *Warfare* against his *Temptations.*

In *Conversion Exemplified,* Mather made essentially the same point, again stressing together the evil of the world and the flesh, this time in rhyme: "vile flesh, thy raging lust, and sordid ease / my winged soul now shall not serve and please. / False world, thy laws shall be no longer mine."[19]

Analyzing Mather's view of the world, Robert Middlekauff has written, "All his life Cotton Mather accused himself of sin that rendered him indescribably filthy." Accordingly, Mather was inclined to rhetoric about the suffering of the spirit in a fleshly world, as in his lament: "O soul, grievously vexed with devils, which throw thee into the fore of passion." And some of Mather's sermons were liberally sprinkled with encouragements for the cultivation of "separating" affections. What is striking, however, is the lack of references in his writings to a role played by "connecting" affections in religion. Mather sometimes referred to the importance of love of neighbor, or the importance of having "the love of thy saviour flaming in" the heart. But in sermons wherein one might expect to find doctrine about the power of the affections to bond a person to Christ, there often is none, or only a passing reference to love of God. And this is true even when the sermon was about conversion, as in *Conversion Exemplified* (1703), *The Greatest Concern in the World* (1718), *The Converted Sinner* (1724), *The Resort of Piety* (1716), and *The Tryed Professor* (1719), which proposed ways to "make sure of sincerity in the profession of religion."[20]

According to David D. Hall, "The Mathers insisted upon separation of church and world." More specifically, "purity of membership (a purity tested at the Lord's Table)," and "a life-style of asceticism: this was the 'primitive' system to which the Mathers were faithful. Their fidelity extended to the fundamental myth of the Puritans, the idea that saints and worldly men were at war with each other." But it would be unfair to conclude that the Mathers, for all of their concern about church purity, were opposed to church unity of any sort. Neither Cotton nor Increase had the stomach for a long battle with the Manifesto Church. After a period of about a year following the church's founding, during which time Increase Mather published *The Order of the Gospel,* Colman answered with *The Gospel Order Revived.* Cotton Mather rebutted Colman with another short pamphlet, the air began to clear, and a fragile peace, and cooperation that came with mutual respect, settled once again over the Boston churches. Increase Mather may even have taken a step toward the toleration of other religious views over the next twenty years, participating as he did in the ordination of a Baptist minister in 1718.[21]

Cotton supported, with Increase, the *Heads of Agreement* that had brought together Congregationalists and Prebyterians, in 1691, as the United Brethren. Moreover, shortly before his death, he published a book of advice to the new generation of ministers, advising them to take on a "catholick spirit." And he even seems to have accepted eventually the argument that a "public" relation was not a necessary requirement for church admission (at a church other than his, at least). Unfortunately, shortly after the United Brethren campaign, Cotton took up arms against "high-flying" Anglicans, and he also found himself repeatedly on the defensive against the ideas of other Congregationalist ministers, including Colman, Pemberton, and Simon Bradstreet (H.C. 1693) of Charlestown. Moreover, in spite of any hints he may have dropped about relaxing his standards, he remained vitally concerned with church purity. Silverman is likely correct in his judgment that Mather's ecumenism caved in to more pressing requirements for doctrinal purity, especially after 1720. In any event, Cotton Mather was not a liberalizing force in New England when it came to polity and church discipline. Certainly, it was not because of any innovations launched by Cotton Mather that Daniel Neal, an English nonconformist, saw fit to write in 1720: "It must be allowed, that the churches of New-England were formerly very narrow in their principles, and uncharitable to those who differed from them; they had no notions of liberty of conscience; but were for forcing men to their public assemblies by fines and imprisonment, but I must . . . [now] inform the world, that they are men of truly moderate principles."[22]

Catholicks, like more traditionally minded Congregationalist ministers, of course also experienced the social changes of the late seventeenth and eighteenth centuries. Both groups also were exposed, in some measure, to the theological ideas of moderate Anglicans and to the theories of English scientists. Exactly why some Congregationalist ministers gravitated toward a catholick point of view cannot be definitively stated, however. Several possibilities suggest themselves.

Colman, Pemberton, Foxcroft, Wadsworth, and Appleton did not belong to the generation of Willard Oakes, Higginson, Noyes, and Increase Mather. The story of the motivations and struggles of the founders of New England, of the "errand" of the first generation to covenant together as pure churches of the visible saints, was for the third generation not as richly detailed a memory as it was for their elders. This does not mean that the myth of New England's founding was for Colman any less compelling than it had been for Increase Mather. Rather, it suggests that the grandchildren of the founders were at a sufficient distance from the earliest years of the colony to be able to "idealize" their history. That is, following the sociological sense of the term, they could overlook some contradictions and anomalies in their history in order to construct categories of analysis that strengthened the case for the importance of certain key aspects of that history.[23]

The Leverett curriculum at Harvard, as noted, also was an important factor in the development of catholick Congregationalism. But ministers such as Gee, Checkley, Webb, and Byles were also educated at Harvard, and they did not become catholick. It appears that catholicks simply found the arguments of Latitudinarians (and other, "scientific" writers) more persuasive than did their classmates. And Leverett's personal influence must certainly be suspected in the case of Appleton, who was the president's nephew. Perhaps Edward Holyoke, who was brother-in-law to Appleton and who shared some catholick views, was also drawn into a more serious consideration of catholick ideas through family connections. Foxcroft, because he was raised in an Anglican household, may have been more sympathetic to Tillotson and other Anglican writers (and English ways) because of that. Colman's time spent in England, after he received his Harvard degrees, and, particularly, his friendship with Mrs. Rowe while there, probably contributed to his support of innovation in religion in Boston. Personality probably was not a factor in Pemberton's catholicity: Pemberton's bad temper was well known, especially to Judge Sewall. However, Wadsworth and Colman evidenced in their demeanor qualities that led Perry Miller repeatedly to characterize them as "peacemakers." According to Miller, both men were by nature conciliatory, irenical, agreeable. Such a disposition certainly would not have hindered their adoption of a tolerant, open attitude as far as religion was concerned.[24]

Some historians have proposed that the articles of the Brattle Street Manifesto were designed to close some of the distance between Congregational and Anglican forms of Christianity because the men who organized the new church were themselves wealthy merchants who wanted their religion to follow the rest of their lives in becoming more "English." Larzer Ziff has written that the merchant founders desired a "church order" that was "cleansed of the crudities of primitive Puritanism," that would "reflect the dignity of their stations and the politeness of their times." Although the Brattle Street Church came to be known as a congregation that included many wealthy persons, it is unlikely that Anglican "church order" provided status, since, as Bruce Steiner has shown, Anglican congregations in New England were hardly "assemblies of aristocrats." In any event, a mere longing for things English does not explain the emergence of the theology preached in catholick meetinghouses.[25]

All of these factors certainly contributed to the emergence of catholick Congregationalism. However, it was the fact of the loss of the charter of 1629 that is most important in understanding the movement toward "openness" in religion in and around Boston. The necessity for ministers to come to terms after 1691 with the new charter—

and its apparent obstacles to self-government, and therefore, to the "errand"—was, if not entirely the mother of invention as far as catholick Congregationalism was concerned, at least a key catalyst for change. Specifically, by providing an incentive for reconceiving the relationship with England, it set the stage in Boston for the favorable reception, at least among some persons, of the latitudinarian emphasis on moderation and tolerance in religion.

The new charter forced New Englanders to "reinvent" themselves. This process took place over many years leading up to the American Revolution, but catholicks were among the first to articulate a new interpretation of the meaning and mission of New England. Bruce Tucker has identified Colman, Foxcroft, Wadsworth, Appleton, and Holyoke as key figures in the reinvention of the meaning of New England, and its history, after 1691. According to Tucker, the second generation "had become convinced that God had chosen New England as the model for reformed Christendom, and that generation had attempted to preserve its New World haven from English corruptions, particularly toleration." The third generation, and succeeding ones, however, understood "their new dependence on the mother country," and so became "convinced that the Anglo-American world was to be the nerve center of the final reformation." Colman and his colleagues came to view the inauguration of closer political ties with England not as subversive of the errand but as beneficial to New England, because it would extend to New Englanders more clearly the civil and religious rights and liberties of Englishmen. In this way, it would serve to protect the errand, particularly from the sort of harassment that New Englanders had experienced at the hands of Governor Andros, who, as the ruler of the Dominion of New England from 1686 to 1689, had seriously disrupted the civil and religious lives of Bostonians, going so far as to demand the use of the Old South meetinghouse for Anglican services. The events of 1684–1691 caused some New Englanders to think about their history and about their relationship to England. The product of such thought, among catholick Congregationalists, was a revised corporate identity, and this included a history that idealized and conserved some of colony's past, but it included as well an enlarged sense of a common project of religious reformation with the mother country.[26]

Fundamental to the articulation of a new corporate identity was the adjustment made by catholicks in Congregational thinking about how individuals were related to each other in such a way as to form the whole society. Catholicks softened the rhetoric of the second generation about the dangers of the affections, and, although not abandoning the view that the affections *could* be dangerous (just as they did not abandon the covenant), catholicks expressed an understanding of the affections as useful in religion, in a public context as well as in a private context, by virtue of their capability to facilitate a closer relationship with God and, in fact, to nurture a sort of religious solidarity with others.

Arthur Kaledin described the founding of the Brattle Street Church as a response to "the waning of Puritan emotional intensity" in the latter part of the seventeenth century: "A man for whom the emotional rather than the intellectual meaning of Christianity was more important would have felt more at home at Brattle Square than at Boston's other Congregational churches." The Brattle Street Church was not as short on doctrine as Kaledin suspected, but Colman, as Perry Miller, Larzer Ziff, Teresa Toulouse, and others have pointed out, certainly was a promoter of emotion in religion. Indeed, as Harry S. Stout has observed, many ministers of the third generation were more inclined than their predecessors to preach the importance of an "exhilarating," "experimental religion." Colman probably had been influenced toward emotional religion by Leverett, who, in the late seventeenth century, had begun "to tip the balance in favor of God's more benevolent characteristics," in Congregationalist theology. Leverett, who used little in the way of shorthand in his notes, regularly substituted the symbol ♡ for "heart," which suggests that he often thought or wrote about the emotional side of religion, as in his assertion "It is the piety of the heart which is the soul that animates all the religion of our lips and lives." Certainly, other ministers spoke of the piety of the "heart." But for Colman (and probably for Leverett as well), the meaning of "heart" religion included a recognition of the role played by the affections in drawing a person, and bonding a person, to God and to neighbor.[27]

A preliminary sense of catholick recognition of the importance of the affections, especially those that "connected" rather than "separated," can be had here with reference to a few catholick writings, beginning with some by Thomas Foxcroft. Foxcroft affirmed in 1726 that ministers should shepherd their flocks with "the lively passions of tender fathers." By 1729, he had further developed the idea of tender fatherhood, so as to be able to explain the relation between God and the faithful in these same terms. His sermon on this theme, in which he took as his text Matt. 13:43 ("Then shall the righteous shine forth as the sun in the Kingdom of the Father. Who hath ears to hear let him hear." [KJV]), was one of his most popular. He delivered it over a dozen times between 1729 and 1760, in various Boston meetinghouses and in others along the coast as far south as Newport. Foxcroft told his audiences that God was their father and that they were his adopted children. Through that adoption, persons would come to know "the unspeakable joy and consolation they shall have in a sense of and love of God . . . & the most intimate communion with him." Foxcroft went to great length to describe the qualities of God, under such headings as "holy," "compassionate," "powerful and wealthy," "faithful," and others that stressed only the positive, constructive emotional aspects of the individual's relationship to God.[28]

The experience of such emotion was by no means limited, for Foxcroft, to the privacy of the closet. Those ministers who had preached declension in the previous century had on rare occasions granted to the "connecting" affections a place in the religious life. But because, for them, such affections were so dangerous—they posed a particular threat to the social cohesiveness of the community—they were usually confined to the "closet." For Foxcroft (like Simon Patrick), the affections that turned persons wholeheartedly toward God were appropriately intensified in a public setting. He stated this in a sermon preached in the early 1720s, in language similar to Isaac Newton's description of his experiments with prisms. In the treatise *Opticks* (1704), Newton had discussed the resolution of light into the colors of the spectrum and the recombination of colors back into light. In describing this latter phenomenon, Newton wrote, "There was no red, no yellow, no green, nor purple to be seen any longer, but from a confusion of them all there arose one uniform white color." Foxcroft, stressing the importance of group worship, wrote: "The union of many devout souls in a joint presence, mutually raises and enlivens their affections. As a collection of many dispersed *rays* into a narrow compass, gives them a greater light and heat . . . even so the concurrence of a multitude in the solemnities of God's house, tends to kindle and diffuse a common ardour in the worshipping assembly."[29]

Other catholicks, in addition to their constant references to "religion of the heart," also stressed God's love and mercy, and his tender parenting of the faithful. Wadsworth told his audiences that it was important to honor God with the affections; "We should keep our hearts and affections intensely engaged" in the seeking after spiritual rewards. Wadsworth pointed out, "God's law extends to the heart, to the powers, affections, motions & actions" of the soul, and he ob-

ason, More's theology was influential at Harvard. The library con
ned, by 1723, many of his published works, including volumes of
lected philosophical and theological works and *An Explanation of*
Grand Mystery of Godliness (1660). Pemberton's 1717 list also
uded the latter work, and his *Mystery of Iniquity,* as well. Cud-
th's *Intellectual System* was in the Harvard Library, and his *Dis-*
se of the Lord's Supper was on Pemberton's list. It also is possible
some of the ideas of the Cambridge Platonists might have come
ew England through personal connections, as Cudworth's
er James settled in Scituate, Massachusetts, where he became
s with Henry Dunster, the first president of the college.
cote had connections to New England as well. Moreover, sev-
ew Englanders, or three-fourths of those who immigrated to
ngland as clergy between 1636 and 1647, were educated at
dge, and of these, twenty were connected with Emmanuel
which was a center of Puritanism, and later of Platonism
rth preached and published throughout the 1640s). John Cot-
n Harvard, and Thomas Hooker were among those who
d from Emmanuel.[35]

bridge Platonists, like latitudinarians, disapproved of the
thusiastic religion that had troubled England during and
ivil War. But the Cambridge Platonists, unlike the latitudi-
ere willing to accept emotion, even "enthusiasm," into a
e in religion. Cudworth, preaching before the House of
n 1647, questioned the capability of "cold theorems and
ry and jejune disputes, lean syllogisticall reasonings" to
living notions of heavenly truth." Warning his audience
id not come to earth "to kindle a fire of wrangling and
dispute among us," Cudworth recommended instead a
onious affection" between persons "in these jarring
ffections were part of "the strong magick of nature,"
verything to that place which is suitable to it, and to
belong." And those persons drawn to God, who
he secret mysteries of the divine," would not languish
rowing language from the Bible, Cudworth averred
move his "fatherly bowels" of compassion and by
y" answer those who implored his help. Elsewhere,
ned that the "mystical notion which is contained" in
rriage" between a man and a woman was applicable
een Christ and the church. In the course of explain-
h was not new to Protestantism and certainly not to

served several corollaries of this rule governing the connection between God and humanity, including the fact that Christ had adopted the faithful as his own children and that Christians were obliged to observe the "twin duties" that "go together, & and can't be separated," loving God and loving one's neighbor. Pemberton, in a series of sermons in early 1697, emphasized in different ways that "God is infinite in his mercy & therefore he is inclined thus to keep & conduct his people." Ten years later, in a series of sermons on the Incarnation, the two natures of Christ, and Christ's redeeming sacrifice, Pemberton stressed that God's love for humanity was "incomprehensibly great." Preaching in 1709 at a public fast, the sort of occasion on which a sermon was often organized around the theme of God's judgment, Pemberton made no reference to judgment at all, preaching instead on the mercy and love of God, and his protection of the faithful from danger.

Appleton, like Colman, often referred to God's "benevolence," as in his assertion that God guides and protects humanity "with a love of benevolence." Appleton also spoke at length about the important role of the affections in the cultivation of piety. In his most ambitious theological treatise, *The Wisdom of God in the Redemption of Fallen Man,* Appleton argued, "When the affections are once stirred up and engaged, they serve very powerfully to enlighten the mind, perswade the will, to remove discouragements."[30]

Colman observed that among the faculties of the soul were the "affections and passions to excite and quicken, move and urge us." Colman was for the most part an optimist in matters of religion, and so he emphasized God's love and benevolence and the constructive, positive side of the affections, rather than their separating capabilities. In *The Hope of the Righteous* (1721), for example, he explained the ways in which "human hope is a cheering and exhilarating passion." After a visit to Boston by Whitefield, Colman informed his audience that he would be unhappy to "see your affections cool and go off!" Even in his sermon preached to a society of young men in Boston, he stressed the goodness of creation and emotion. The society every few years invited the local ministers to instruct them, in a series of sermons over the course of six months or a year, and they were used to hearing sermons about the depravity of the body and the danger of falling into sins of passion and lust. Colman surpised them, and probably some of his colleagues, with a sermon stressing the divine workmanship reflected in the human body, and he encouraged his audience: "Youth is thy beautiful, thy lovely and acceptable time.

This is thy prime and bloom, the flower, vigour and strength of thy life." And he encouraged them actively to seek wives, in order to be able to "place your affections, give away your hearts," to another.[31]

Colman's favorable view of the human body in his sermon to the young men was shared by other catholicks (to varying degrees). Moreover, catholicks' willingness to recommend the affections in a way that their immediate predecessors (and, some of their contemporaries) did not was closely related to their acceptance of the body, their attitude toward nature as a whole, and, particularly, their belief in order and reason in creation.

Catholicks became acquainted with theories about the orderliness of creation and about human capability to detect that order through their exposure to the writings of latitudinarians, English scientists, and the Cambridge Platonists. But these ideas were not entirely foreign to Puritan writers in the sixteenth and seventeenth centuries. In fact, as Lee W. Gibbs has argued, the "technometry" of William Ames and other English Puritans had already included arguments for the importance to religion of the systematic investigation of order and reason in nature. Against this background, catholicks studied new theories about the physical world and the faculty of reason, and from this "new learning" and science of the seventeenth century, they drew lessons that helped them to articulate in their theology a view of the world that was less hostile to the flesh, and more accepting of the affections, than was that of the Mathers and their circle.[32]

The Cambridge Platonists included Benjamin Whichcote, provost of King's College; Ralph Cudworth, master of Christ's College; Henry More, also of Christ's College; and John Smith, a pupil of Whichcote who later was associated with Queen's College. Like the latitudinarians, they tended toward moderation in matters of religion, but their mood was best summed up by Whichcote, when he wrote that there was "a secret genius to humanity; a bias that inclines him to a regard of all of his own kind." Belief in the possibility of union with God and with others, and union of faith and knowledge in the individual soul, was central to the thinking of the Cambridge Platonists. According to H. R. McAdoo, "The Cambridge Platonists, the scientists, and the latitudinarians, spanning by their works the latter part of the century, were moving in the same direction," namely, toward the conclusion that reason and faith cooperated in religion.

The Cambridge men came to embrace the Platonic philosophy through the influence of the Platonic Academy of Florence, of which Marsilio Ficino (d. 1499) was the head, together with his protégé Pico

della Mirandola (d. 1494). By way of Erasmus, John
and Thomas More (d. 1535), this late Renaissance
its way to England, where it eventually found a hom
the turmoil of the midseventeenth century. The
drawing on Plotinus, had fashioned a philosop
which was a notion of "beauty" as the investmen
Not form itself, but the vision of the form in the
ful. Cambridge Platonists, building on this n
stand the material as an extension of the spi
emanation of form. Resisting Cartesian du
recognized a strong bond between nature an
and reason. Ernst Cassirer described their
that experience was always a mixture of th
and the "spiritual and intellectual," and
"reconciliation between God and the wor
bridge Platonists argued "the fusion of
reality," and, according to Sykes, they
nence with Christian mysticism. Gerald
sized their belief in "the essential unit

For the Cambridge Platonists,
faith to form the whole person, and
in the trademark saying of Which
candle of the Lord." Cudworth, w
explained similarly, "As all the
their candles at the suns flame,"
enliven a person's heart. The
Platonists and the latitudinaria
tained a vaguely Calvinistic en
predestination), sometimes o
latter tended toward morali
who followed them, the Pl
ceived as excesses of enthu
less, because of their confi
door for some measure of

Norman Fiering has
the 1680s of More's ethi
philosophical liberalism
ments in support of pie
ogy of the Cambridg
affectional religion, e
ous with existing ter

Puritanism, Cudworth made clear, however, his Platonist point of view. Citing the "masters of the cabala," he suggested that they had "a kind of secret and mystical divinity remaining in part yet amongst them," which was, he approvingly noted: "i.e. that everything that is below hath some ROOT above."[36]

Henry More addressed more specifically than Cudworth the matter of the affections. In *An Explanation of the Grand Mystery of Godliness,* More admitted that "inordinate affections" were a danger to religion, but he proposed as well, "There is indeed some use and advantage in all the animal affections." In fact, More claimed that the purpose of preaching was "to raise the affections of the auditors to the love and pursuit of such things as are commanded us by the precepts of the Gospel." One significant aspect of More's understanding of the affections was his belief that the "animal affections" were influenced by the humors of the body and that, in spite of this profound linking of the affections and the physical world, they nevertheless were valuable to religion.

More, guided in his thinking by a notion of union, as opposed to separation, of body and spirit, wrote at length on the beauty and usefulness of the human body and of nature in general. Indeed, as Cassirer has argued, beauty and a "principle of creative love" as a uniting force were at the center of More's thinking. More related with delight wonder stories about serpent charming, astral travel, and strong winds that threw down the gallows at a hanging of witches. Elsewhere, in *Enthusiasmus Triumphatus* (1662), More specifically explained how enthusiasm was affected by, among other things, the eating of meat, and infection of the body by disease. In this short book, More "wanted to preserve the emotional energy of enthusiasm for the cause of religion and virtue without the taint of antinomian madness." He did this by arguing for a natural connection between the body and religious emotion, between the corporeal world and spirit.[37]

The Cambridge Platonists were not the only Englishmen who marveled at the created world: at the body, plants, and animals, and physical forces such as magnetism. Interest in natural science, supported by the Royal Society, blossomed in England in the seventeenth century and quickly spread to New England. Of particular interest to New England ministers were the vaguely theological writings of English scientists. Among works of this sort available to Boston-area ministers were William Whiston's *A New Theory of the Earth,* William Derham's *Physico-Theology* and *Astro-Theology,* and

John Ray's *The Wisdom of God in Creation.* The importance of writings such as these, which stressed reason and design in creation, was that they offered arguments in support of a religious view of the world as orderly, rather than as unpredictable, unreliable, and spiritually dangerous. Basil Willey, in evaluating the effect of natural science on religious thinking in the early eighteenth century, observed, "The physical world, in spite of its divine origin, was traditionally held to have shared in the fatal consequences of the fall of man, and to have become the chosen abode of the apostate spirits." According to Willey, "Nature was full of pagan divinities turned devils, and to meddle with it was to risk damnation." But the new science contributed to a "changed attitude toward nature," which "meant that nature was rescued from Satan and restored to God."[38]

The scientists' understanding of the cosmos was different from the vision of the Cambridge Platonists, however, in that scientists such as Robert Boyle were not guided in their thinking by a sense of union between God and the world. Barbara Shapiro has gone so far as to argue that, for Boyle, "matter was devoid of spirituality." This does not mean that Boyle was not religious, however, but that his thinking about God and nature was characterized by an emphasis on the acquisition of rarified knowledge of cosmic order, and it included recognition of the distance bewteen God and the created world.

In *The Christian Virtuoso* (1690), Boyle explained his science precisely in these terms. The title referred to the activities of "a virtuoso, who, by manifold and curious experiments, searches deep into the nature of things." According to Boyle, God had so manifested himself in creation "that a moderate degree of understanding, and attention, may suffice to make men acknowledge his being." The virtuoso, by virtue of his diligent and careful scrutiny of the works of God, reaped the reward of belief in God that was superior to that of the casual observer. Boyle nevertheless emphasized "the immense distance between the creator and his creatures," arguing that the distance "is so vast, that all divine attributes, or perfections, by immeasurable intervals transcend those faint resemblances of them, that he has been pleased to impress, either upon other creatures, or upon men." The virtuoso, then, did not discover the union of the human spirit with the divine, as did the Platonists, but, rather, sought for "abstract truths; by which term I mean here such truths, as do not at all, or very little, gratify men's ambition, sensuality, or other inferior passions or appetites." For Boyle, and for the virtuosos generally, religion tended toward a kind of intellectual delight in the discovery of order and design in the universe, rather than an assent to God that was a product of appetites or passions, or, ironically, "sensuality."[39]

Cambridge Platonists wrote about union with God and the connection between spirit and matter. The virtuosos delighted in abstract truths about the order of the cosmos. Latitudinarians, as we have seen, urged openness in matters of religion. Latitudinarian writers did not contribute as much as did the virtuosos to a change in attitude about nature in the seventeenth century, but they were able to explain in their theology the role of reason in religion. And since a more trusting attitude toward the affections developed in New England alongside a heightened sense of the importance and usefulness of reason, it is likely that latitudinarian writings were of some influence in New England on this count. Catholick Congregationalists borrowed from them some arguments about the reasonableness of religion and added those to what they had borrowed from the Cambridge Platonists (the unity of creation, including the union between spirit and matter) and from the scientists (appreciation for cosmic order).

New Englanders learned arguments for the importance of reason in religion from essays such as Joseph Glanvill's "The Agreement of Reason and Religion" (1676) and Edward Stillingfleet's *Rational Account of the Grounds of the Christian Faith* (1662). From the latter, New Englanders learned that "the true notion of God is most agreeable to the faculties of men's souls, and most consonant to reason and the light of nature: i.e. that the idea of God, (or that which we conceive in our minds when we think of God) is so far from being any wayes repugnant to any principle of reason within us, that it is hard to pitch on any other notion which has fewer entanglements in it." John Wilkins, in *Of the Principles and Duties of Natural Religion* (1675), likewise argued that "the nature of man . . . doth consist in that faculty of reason, whereby he is made capable of religion, or apprehending a deity, and of expecting a future state of rewards and punishments." Moreover, for Wilkins, there was a "primary and natural obligation to piety and virtue, which we commonly call the law of nature . . . and consequently, nothing contained in the word of God, . . . can be interpreted to dissolve the obligation of moral duties plainly required by the law of nature." Wilkins, in his own sermon subject notebook, which was published in 1693, cited under "natural religion" a host of authors ranging from Aquinas to Baxter to Lord Herbert of Cherbury (*De Veritate*). From such authors he drew lessons about religion and "that faculty whereby we apprehend, compare and judge of moral things, called reason." For Wilkins, "things themselves, which appearing by the light of nature, to be necessary unto our well-being, is called natural law, or law of nature. . . . Obligation resulting from the observance of such things. Duty."[40]

Tillotson also stressed the role of reason in religion, writing that "religion is called the knowledge of the holy." Even more than other latitudinarians, Tillotson undertook in his preaching to provide to his audiences "arguments" about the nature and purpose of religion, and much of his effort in this regard was aimed at proving why religion was the best "knowledge." For Tillotson, then, "all supernatural revelation supposeth the truth of the principles of natural religion," and, accordingly, "reason is the faculty whereby revelations are to be discerned." Recognition of the truth of revelation came not through a stirring of the affections, but, rather, by way of the faculty of reason, because knowledge of religion—like knowledge of anything else—had to be "learned." Tillotson argued: "Whatever doctrines God reveals to men are propounded to their understandings, and by this faculty we are to examine all doctrines which pretend to be from God, and upon examination to judge whether there be reason to receive them as divine, or to reject them as impostures." For latitudinarians, the moral teachings contained in Scripture were the best evidence of the reasonableness of religion. Such "natural laws" as charity, justice, and equity coincided with the instruction given by divine revelation, so that "Christian religion propounds the most powerful arguments to perswade men to the obedience of these laws." Duty was known by revelation and by "the light of nature," which cooperated in impressing arguments on the rational mind.[41]

Latitudinarians, as we have seen, preached catholick tolerance, but, with some exceptions, they remained suspicious, to one degree or another, of the affections. Catholick Congregationalists were influenced by latitudinarian writers toward religious "openness" and acceptance of religious differences among persons. But catholicks were more favorably inclined to the affections than were such latitudinarians as Stillingfleet or Tillotson. Catholicks in New England encouraged an emotional religion, and they came to this position, in part, through the influence of some English writers but also through their reflection on the Puritan theology that formed much of their immediate religious background. Specifically, they were influenced in the following ways:[42] (1) the influence of Cambridge Platonism was present as a foundation in the catholick belief that reason and faith, spirit and matter were not incompatible; (2) from the scientists catholicks learned that God was detectable in his works, and, especially, that nature, ordered by laws, was predictable and consistent in its workings; and (3) from latitudinarian writers catholicks drew not only a lesson in religious toleration but the equally important lesson that reason itself was a trustworthy guide to religious truth. There was, of course, some overlapping of influences (for example, Cambridge Platonists, as well as latitudinarians, stressed the capability of reason). But in our seeking to understand the attitudes of catholick Congregationalists toward the affections, it is most useful to see the influences of these three groups according to this scheme.

The ideas of writers such as Tillotson, Boyle, and More became important to New Englanders after the Massachusetts charter was revoked. In the wake of the inauguration of the new charter, Congregationalist ministers who were seeking ways in which to understand their new relationship with England decided that New England no longer was an isolated fortress of religious purity in a surrounding wasteland of cultural decadence and personal lusts run rampant. "Wilderness," a symbol for chaos that threatened the community of the faithful, accordingly was no longer an appropriate symbol, at least for some ministers, of the world that was geographically or conceptually "outside" New England. The tendency among some ministers to conceive New England as something other than a garden surrounded by wilderness was reinforced by English ideas about order in nature. Basil Willey's claim that the new science rescued nature from Satan may be particularly appropriate in the case of New England. The new science provided to ministers ideas about order and predictability in nature that served to reinforce their departure from the theme of wilderness in their sermons. Moreover, as Harry S. Stout has observed, "along with scientific discoveries and the ennoblement of reason came a more approachable, manlike God" who supervised the operation of creation "according to flawless designs of structure that proceeded from self-perpetuating laws and principles."[43]

Nature was less threatening because its order could be "seen" by the light of reason. Darkness in the physical world, first of all, was dangerous: this was a fact of history for Wadsworth, who observed that "darkness and horror often go together. We read, Ge. 15.12. That Abraham had an horror of great darkness." Darkness understood as a predicament caused by sin was also lamentable, as in Appleton's worry about "the darkness & blindness" of a soul in sin. But against this darkness, ministers came armed in the eighteenth century with vocabulary that described the luminescence of God, nature, and reason.[43] Wadsworth was just one of many ministers who began to refer to God as "the father of lights." Appleton, in a long discussion of religious light, appropriated a more traditional, Biblical phrase, arguing that just as the sun gave natural light, so was Christ the light of the world. Colman wrote that "God is light. So he presents himself to us," and he asked his congregation, "Who can behold the sun when it shines, or the moon walking in brightness, and not own the God that is above?"[45]

The brightness of God extended to his works, and to reason itself, as in the terms "the light of nature" and "the light of reason." Colman, reflecting on the "works of God," asked his audience to "but observe and consider that light which God has made for us to see by." Colman believed that "the invisible things of him from the creation of the world, are clearly seen, being understood from the things that are made," and this ought to lead the faithful to "the meditation of his glories as they shine forth in the works of creation." Foxcroft preached that "the glory of God is very conspicuously display'd in the things which his hand hath formed; so his creatures and works, with the greatest justice, challenge a room in our thoughts, and demand our deliberate attention to them." Wadsworth was more specific in his claim that there were "many things . . . that may be known by the light of nature," and these things included seven truths about God: He is eternal, unchangeable, "immense, boundless in his being," omnipresent, omnipotent, holy and righteous, and "a spiritual being."[46]

God was visible by the "light of nature," that is, through a process of rational reflection on impressions brought by the senses to the soul. Knowledge of the world acquired through the senses was important for religion. Wadsworth told one congregation that the soul was "a rational agent . . . hence knowledge is necessary to the welfare of the soul." Wadsworth explained, " 'Tis the divine power, that upholds or preserves the natural powers . . . that upholds in men, the animal faculties of seeing, hearing, smeling, &c. and that does concur with these faculties in such sensations," leading to the acquisition of knowledge. Appleton explained further to his fellow ministers that "light is that by which we are able to see things, and come to the knowledge of them. It is that which enables the eye to view objects, their magnitude, their distance, their form, their color, their beauties, and their deformities." Accordingly, "by means of the light we behold the works of God . . . all of which declare his glory." And regarding the attributes of God himself, Appleton argued (just as had Wadsworth), "So that by the things which are seen by means of light, the invisible things of God are also discoverable, even his eternal power and Godhead." Colman's claims for reason, "the law and light of nature," were stated most clearly in his influential *God Deals with Us as Rational Creatures* (1723). Therein he argued, "We ought to use the reason God has given, yea, and to reverence it: It is the rule and law of the eternal and perfect intimate mind inscribed on us and for us." Therefore, Colman declared, when it came to living according to God's laws, "Our souls move upon these motives if either reason or sense be hearkened to."[47]

Reason was not merely a tool by which a person might be provided with knowledge about the attributes of God, however. As important as knowledge about God was a correct understanding about the relation of the individual to God. Colman, using a phrase that became more common as the eighteenth century wore on, explained this relationship as follows: "The light of nature teaches us that there is a God and that he ought to be worshipped by us." Foxcroft was more precise, emphasizing that the collective obligation of persons to God was also to be discovered by the light of nature: "The worshipping of God publickly, is to be refer'd to the head of *natural* religion. . . . Public worship, in the general, is a dictate of *nature.* Natural light tells us that, as we are God's creatures, . . . we do (by consequence) owe worship to him." Scripture, of course, taught the same lesson, but for Foxcroft, and for other catholicks, the light of nature did not contradict Scripture. Rather, it provided support for what was known by faith. Most importantly, it provided such support by proposing that the five senses of the human body could be relied on to furnish a person with impressions that indicated the existence of God, suggested at least some of his attributes, and demonstrated the necessity for the public worship of him.[48]

Catholicks believed that the senses could be trusted to play a role in providing to a person knowledge of God and that the human body was not necessarily an impediment to spiritual advancement. In fact, among catholicks, there emerged a view of the body that stressed its positive aspects, and, indeed, its holiness. In this sense, catholicks were similar to the "moderate" Protestant temperament described by Philip Greven.[49] So, for Foxcroft, the human body reflected in miniature all of the excellencies of creation. Foxcroft wrote: "Man is a building of God, a house built by the King of Glory. The Lord is the Creator of the world, both the greater and lesser world. Man, for his various excellencies, is called a *microcosm,* a little world." One argument for the excellence of the body was the fact that Christ had been human, so that, in fact, "It was Christ who built this fair and beautiful fabric. He was the first framer of this house, as well as the first possessor of it." Appleton, making the same point, pointed out that Elijah and Enoch "did pass immediately soul and body into heaven." Wadsworth and Colman also stressed the bodily assumption of Elijah and Enoch, Colman explaining, at the funeral of Cotton Mather, that there had been three cases of bodily assumption into heaven: "Enoch before the law, Elijah under it, and Jesus Christ under the gospel oeconomy."[50]

Wadsworth was not thoughtlessly uttering a cliché when he encouraged his audience to love their neighbors and to "wish them the best in body and soul." The body was the earthly home of the soul. According to Colman, the body would be exquisitely glorious after the resurrection, "yet as the body now is, it is wonderfully made, set up and kept up. Call it a tabernacle: it is a finer and noble one in itself; like that of Moses, a work of great design, and whereon much art and cost and care was bestowed." This tabernacle was sometimes described as "curious," signifying wonder, as in Appleton's referring to "our bodies (designed for the temples of the Holy Ghost, and that God has curiously wrought in the lower parts of the earth, and made in such a fearful and wonderful manner as we now behold them)." Moreover, the body was not simply a passive "tabernacle," an inert casing for the soul. Rather, as Colman pointed out, the body was created to use and enjoy creation. Colman exhorted his audience to "look thro' the visible creation, and see the provision made thro'out it all for the entertainment of man, his soul and body. . . . What beauties for our gazing eyes? What pleasing sounds for our ears? What delicacy of foods for our palates?" Colman urged his audience to "but look in one another's faces, and observe their beauty and comely proportion." And he declared, "How beautious, healthy and athletic then is the body?"[51]

In an orderly, interconnected universe, the body was useful, even beautiful, and the testimony of the senses was not only to be trusted but embraced. The world, now ordered, was seen as less threatening; the body itself was less dangerous, less corrupt; and the affections seemed more trustworthy. For catholicks, the sight of the moon or the sounds made by a songbird could stir the affections, which were, after all, of the body. Just as information conveyed to the rational soul through the senses could serve as a basis for knowledge of God, so also might sensory experience raise the affections, which were of considerable use to religion.

Catholicks believed that the affections could be influenced through stimulation of the senses, and I will suggest in the next chapter more specifically how catholicks understood the practice of this theory. There is one point that should be added here, and that is that there was occasionally a vaguely Cartesian flavor in catholick statements about the faculties. Reason was, after all, wrote Foxcroft, "that excellent power in man, by which he is nearly ally'd to the angelic world, and advanced above the level of sensitive beings here below. 'Tis one essential character of the divine image instamp'ed on man at his creation." The "light of reason" made possible the recognition of God's glory in the works of creation, but its operation was not always contingent on the testimony of the senses. Colman, who, as noted, often spoke about observation of the works of creation as a way of knowing God, nevertheless seems also to have promoted a kind of intuitive reason: "We think, we speak, we reason and discourse, and form idea's [*sic*] of things we never saw, and whereof bare matter and outward form can give us no intimation."

In the thinking of catholicks, there remained something "mysterious" about the faculties. Catholicks did not explicitly claim that the affections were acted on directly by God, as would Jonathan Edwards, who, in linking the will to the affections, argued that both were infused with grace in such a way as to be directly, physically transformed. However, catholick thinking was not structured in such a way as to exclude all possibility of such an understanding. The theoretical foundation for such a notion, drawn (most immediately) from English Puritanism, was reflected in Wadsworth's declaration "But how often has God spoken to us . . . by the secret motions of his Holy Spirit." Colman was aiming at the same point in explaining that "from within thy self thou knowest in a very great measure what God is." Appleton, likewise, seems to have acknowledged that religious truth was available to a person independently of sensory experience when he preached that what God required of men and women "apears [*sic*] from the very light of nature & whatever we experience in our selves." But neither Appleton nor other catholicks developed these suggestions in such a way as to integrate them into a larger scheme of theology. As ministers with a responsibility for the spiritual nurturing of their congregations, they were more inclined to think about how the affections might be stirred through preaching and other means.[52]

Some ministers remained disinclined to allow a place in religion for the "light of nature." Mather Byles, as late as the Great Awakening, was still referring to seventeenth-century "carnal reason." Joshua

Gee continued to prefer the "narrow way" and the "strait gate" to "the blindness of a carnal mind." Increase Mather's writing about the natural world, his biographer points out, remained "blurred and contradictory," and "in the end, he chose to believe in an inscrutable God over against a world knowable through science." John Webb and Samuel Checkley seem to have moved in the 1730s to some measure of acceptance of "the light and law of nature," but like Ebenezer Gay, John Hancock, and Lemuel Briant on the South Shore; John Barnard on the North Shore; and John Hancock the elder in Lexington, they remained suspicious of the affections. Webb and Checkley dutifully carried the heavy Calvinist baggage of human depravity and saw disruption in passion of almost any sort, fear of God excluded. Gay and Briant established reputations as preachers of "rational religion" and frowned on emotional preaching. Barnard quoted Tillotson and was a close friend of Colman, and he came closer to balancing head and heart then Checkley or Briant, but he nevertheless worried regularly about the dangers of excited affections, and he bragged about his role in rescuing the people of Marblehead from Whitefieldian "disorders and confusions." And Higginson and Noyes wrote to the founders of the Brattle Street Church rebuking them, "You might have found some other direction and obligation to relative duties between pastor & flock, and brother & brother, besides the dictates of the *law of nature*."[53]

All of these ministers at least occasionally referred to the "heart" in their sermons. Some expressed a desire not only for less party among churches but for ecumenical endeavor as well. Some of them became so rationalist in their theology as to approach Arminianism. But none of them attempted a theology, as did catholick Congregationalists, that brought together belief that knowledge of God could be acquired through scrutiny of an orderly universe with the idea that the affections could be trusted to provide some measure of direction to the person seeking God. Indeed, as I will suggest further along, catholicks, in fact, attempted more than this. First, however, I will explain how catholicks, in their sermons, did not not simply refer in passing to "the heart" but believed that it was important actually to rouse the heart, to "stir" the affections. And their ideas about how the affections could be stirred were related to their shifting of emphasis from the view, held by their immediate predecessors, that the affections tilted precariously on the edge of falling into evil cooperation with the flesh, toward a view of the affections as operating within a body united to a soul.

3

Raising the Affections

Catholicks believed that the soul and the body were united in the person, and, therefore, it seemed to them possible to influence the soul *through* the body. In reaching this conclusion and in reflecting generally on the functioning of the affections within a person, catholicks likely were influenced by Henry More, Charles Morton, and such English Puritan writers as William Fenner. Such influences, absorbed together with others that were closer to home, contributed to the emergence among catholicks of a view of worship that recognized the importance of preaching, prayer, and singing that would raise the affections.

Ebenezer Pemberton wrote in 1704 that each person was an "embodyed Spirit": "Man, in his composition stands related to both worlds: By his body to the visible world, which is made up of *gross* matter; by his soul to the invisible world of the spirits." But the relation of the individual to both worlds was not to be understood as disjunctive in its quality. Rather, Pemberton explained that "an organised body is at present an essential constituent part of man: In vital union between which and the soul man's moral life consists." Foxcroft proposed essentially the same view, arguing that although the soul was "invisible thinking substance, distinct from our material and animal part," nevertheless each person was a "compound of matter and spirit." Colman preached in typically upbeat tones about the matter: "Most wonderful is the strict union of soul and body . . . by a most tender sympathy [they] share in each others joys and sufferings." And Appleton suggested, "The happiness of the soul in its separate state is not the full and compleat happiness of the man; for the body is an essential part of the human constitution, and there is not a perfect man but where soul and body are united." Death, then, as Foxcroft wrote, was the destruction "of the vital union between soul and body."[1]

Not all ministers were inclined to see the relationship of body and soul as the union of flesh and spirit. Increase Mather stressed that the soul was influenced to "ignorance and error" while in the body, arguing that it could become sinless only on leaving the body. For Mather, "The soul is a spiritual substance and not of the same matter as the body." Moreover, "There is flesh and spirit in continual combat," and so, as far as the souls of the faithful were concerned: "This world is not their own: It is not their home. On earth they are strangers and pilgrims; not earth, but heaven is their home." Joshua Gee likewise informed his congregation, "The soul being so vastly superiour to the body, and the powers of understanding and reason so much above the bodily senses," there was little in common between "mere brutal creation" and the "high-born soul."[2]

For catholicks, however, with their view of the union between body and soul, the body could cooperate in the spiritual improvement of the individual. The "beautiful" body, connected to the soul, was useful to the soul, rather than detrimental to its health. And, most important, the affections, which were at least partly of the body, could be actively utilized in religion. In conceiving in this way the relation of the body, soul, and the affections, catholicks shared a great deal with Henry More. For More, the strong bond between soul and body was like "the attraction of the load-stone." According to More, the souls of both men and beasts existed before the bodies that they would inhabit were created. The soul found its way to a created body in the same way that an eagle or hawk or kite on high was drawn to the smell of food on the ground, so that the soul is lured to "that matter that is so fit a receptacle for her to exercise her efformative power upon." In this way "may a soul be conceived to quit her airy vehicle within a certain period of ages, as the Platonists hold she does."[3]

As we have seen, More believed that the "animal affections" could be influenced by the chemistry of the body, as, for example, through the eating of meat. But these animal affections, or passions, were not clearly distinguished by More from emotions that might arise in connection with religious life. More's "passions," all of which had some inherent connection to corporeal existence, shared something as well with emotions that a person might experience in heaven. Accordingly, as Norman Fiering has written, "More's passions" were "confused but fertile compounds of body and soul, will and intellect, appetite and sensation." Catholicks, drawn to the idea of the union between body and soul, also understood the affections to be partly a product of sense experience but nevertheless capable of connecting an individual, through the rational soul, to the divine.[4]

Charles Morton (1627–1698), who settled in Charlestown in 1686 and for a few years tutored students in his home, was the author of a system of "ethicks" and a treatise on the nature of spirits, both of which were used at Harvard, as was his "Synopsis of Naturall Philosophy." Together with his *The Spirit of Man* (1693), these works evidenced an assortment of ideas, drawn from far-ranging sources, and Morton is probably best described as eclectic rather than systematic in his thinking. With regard to the nature of the relationship between body and spirit, however, it is clear that Morton supposed the unity of the soul and the body and that he believed that some passions arose from a mixture of soul and body. Morton proposed a general "definition": "A passion is an intense or vehement act of the sensative appetite which by it inclines too or shuns a good or evil perceived by the senses, proposed by the fancy, & that with some non-naturall change in the body." Following this definition, then, Morton explained that certain passions were common to both man and beast, because they belonged wholly to the sensitive appetite and "are seated organically in the heart." Such passions would include love, hatred, and fear. However, certain passions arose partly from the "organicall" side of a person, and partly from the "inorganicall powers." Passions such as shame, emulation, and commiseration were "common passions but intimately conjoined with some rational act of the mind and the soul, they are of a mixt nature, & so subjected partly in the mind partly in the sensative appetite." And Morton proposed to students the following rhyme by which to remember the lesson: "Man's proper passion are of nature mixt / Partly in the mind, partly in the appetite are fixed." Morton also stressed that "the passions are not evil in their own nature but only as they are irregular. In their nature they are good, . . . & in man may be helpers and furtherers of virtue, as love of God, hatred of evill, & etc."[5]

The ideas of More and Morton about the cooperation of matter and spirit, mind and body, in the affective dimension of life were similar in several ways to those of William Fenner, the English Puritan author of *A Treatise of the Affections* (1642). As Charles Cohen has pointed out, among English Puritans, the term *heart,* like *spirit,* was not finally, and precisely, defined. Both terms, however, and especially *heart,* seem to have connoted a combined physical and spiritual entity, so that the heart might be understood in English Puritanism as "the exemplar of both material and spiritual life." In fact, some ministers, such as Richard Sibbes, connected the spiritual sense of the heart with the heart understood as a physical organ, so that at times the two "meanings melt together," and the "organ and inner man fuse." Fenner's treatise was important for one reason: it explained the affections in this context of the relation of soul and body. Fenner's intention seems to have been to rescue the affections from a position of inferiority among the faculties. Accordingly, he argued against the notion that the affections were merely aspects of physical appetites. He was careful to point out that he did not agree with Aristotle that the affections were to be located in "the unreasonable sensitive part" of a person. Instead, Fenner argued that they were to be seen as "the forcible and sensible motions of the heart, or the will" to or from good or evil.

Although arguing for a more elevated view of the affections, Fenner nevertheless did not insulate the affections from the body. Fenner believed that they were closely related to the body in at least two ways. On the one hand, the affections, seated as they were in the will or the "heart," "make humours" that cause a person to blush, tremble, cry, and so on. He stressed, moreover, that in cases in which there was a very strong apprehension of good or evil, "not only the soul is deeply affected, but the body is mightily compatible." On the other hand, although the affections might cause the body to tremble, the apprehension of good or evil might cause the affections to be stirred, as well. Drawing on the popular Old Testament passage Lam. 3.51, "Mine eye affecteth my Heart," Fenner explained that when the church "beheld the lamentable distresses of the daughters of Sion, this stirred up the affection of pitty in her heart."

For Fenner, the inclination of the will and the inclination of the affections were largely the same, and the affections ultimately required regenerating grace in order to be inclined constantly toward God. Fenner wrote that a person "cannot set his affections on Christ." "But," he added, "he may raise up his affections a good way towards Christ." Accordingly, "the minister that preaches must stir up affections," and Fenner offered a checklist of ways in which that might be accomplished, including certain uses of the voice, the stamping of feet, waving of the arms, and so forth.[6]

Fenner was cited by Wadsworth and Foxcroft and was known to other New Englanders. Some scholars have argued that his theories ought to be reckoned a significant influence on the development of ideas about the affections in New England. However, it should be noted that catholicks did not have to look exclusively to Fenner for an example—or a theory—of preaching to reach the affections. They could observe at home in New England the work of Solomon Stoddard (H.C. 1662), who served a large congregation at Northampton from 1669 to 1729 and experienced during that time several "seasons" of "refreshment," during which unusually large numbers of persons were converted. Stoddard objected to the reading of sermons and argued instead that "when sermons are delivered without notes, the looks and gesture of the minister, is a great means to command attention & stir up affection." Stoddard disdained "meer rational discourse" as "a dull way of preaching" and stressed the importance of preaching to rouse the affections. This much catholicks could understand. But Stoddard so differed from the emergent catholick viewpoint in other ways that his possible influence on the thinking of ministers like Colman or Foxcroft or Wadsworth (all of whom cited him extensively) could not have extended beyond such practical advice on preaching. Stoddard was ruthlessly Calvinistic, so much so that he believed that "natural reason," even though it might be "advantaged with external revelation," was hopelessly deranged. In place of instruction to the rational faculties, Stoddard offered as preparation for conversion the excitation of the "separating" affections, or, more specifically, the engendering in a person the terror of hell. Arguing, "When men don't preach about the danger of damnation, there is want of good preaching," Stoddard supposed that only the fear of hell would force persons to apply themselves diligently to personal reformation, to a fruitful utilization of grace, when it was bestowed.[7]

It should not be assumed that catholicks denied the importance traditionally placed on the faculty of the understanding in religion. Catholicks, unlike Stoddard or Fenner, did not tip religion away from a concern for rational appeal to the understanding, and overwhelmingly toward the affections. Rather, they raised the affections to a status that they had not enjoyed under the leading figures of the second generation (or even some of the third generation). They sought to position the affections alongside understanding as a channel by which grace might flow to the individual. Catholicks did not abandon doctrine. They continued in their sermons to insist on the necessity for the clear exposition of the Gospel. Moreover, catholicks remained visibly faithful to the covenant of grace, believing that regeneration was possible only through the mercy of God in supplying supernatural grace to a person. Catholicks instead moved perceptibly away from their predecessors and some of their contemporaries through their approval of a close relationship between the corporeal body and the affections. They believed that the affections could be roused through an appeal to the senses and that this process contributed directly to the spiritual development of a person.

Catholicks did not arrive all at the same time to this point of view, nor did they express in identical ways their understandings of these ideas. Colman was the first among them to propose the usefulness of the affections and bodily senses working together in religion in *The Government and Improvement of Mirth* (1707). Writing principally for the instruction of young people, Colman explained that any sort of "sensual excess" was folly and that it would contribute directly to the degeneration of holiness in a person. However, Colman also explained, "Mirth may be decent and good, since it is a shadow of heaven." Colman described in detail the ways in which mirth was useful in refreshing the body and the soul. Mirth, he wrote, "lifts up the hands that hang down in weariness, and strengthens the feeble knees" so that "we renew our labors again with vigour." Mirth, moreover, was eminently social in its nature, not something to be feared. Mirth, wrote Colman, ought to become "the habit of chearfulness," and he emphasized that it should "not accompany us just to the doors of the church, or of our closets, and there take leave of us."

Colman explained further that the responsible consumption of alcoholic beverages was also a help to body and soul. Mirth that was too loud or too long was immoderate, and therefore to be avoided, and drink that caused immoderate mirth was accordingly to be avoided as well. But for Colman, the connection of body and soul actually made possible the enlivening of the heart through alcohol, and, in fact, as long as imbibing remained a "refreshment" and did not become the basis for a "Drunken Club," it was acceptable. Colman reminded his audience, "Nature is the best physician," but, quoting Scripture, he proposed as well: " 'Your heart shall rejoice and your bones shall flourish as an herb': There is a natural influence and causality in the one unto the other. Cordials serve to cheer and keep up the spirits from sinking."

After explaining that mirth was a refreshment to both body and soul and that alcohol could be useful for essentially the same reason, Colman finally proceeded to discuss a more specifically "religious" activity within the context of the relationship of body and spirit. Noting the "pleasure and delight which mankind generally take" in the singing of Psalms, Colman argued, "Nor is this a sensitive pleasure meerly." He proposed that the singing of Psalms was an excellent worship and praise of God but that it was especially valuable because "it strikes so strongly on sense and imagination, and by them has the more forcible access to our affections." He also stated clearly that "our spirits being imbodied are naturally come at by impressions from our senses, and more particularly by the eye and ear." "Musical notes" may be addressed to the passions and so might introduce into the mind "ideas" that provoke either "laughter or seriousness." Colman then concluded, "He that throws away his senses and natural powers, must his reason and religion too."[8]

Nathaniel Appleton, like Colman, understood the union of body and soul in a person—the "whole man"—to mean that the affections could be influenced by the singing of Psalms. Appleton first of all described the cooperation of the senses and the spirit: "We must consider our selves compounded of body as well as spirit, and as having bodily and sensitive organs, as well as rational and intellectual faculties." Appleton explained that "these sensitive and rational powers are so blended together in our present constitution, that they very much affect each other, and depend upon each other." The union of body and soul, sensitive and rational aspects of human nature, was so close that those activities that were pleasing to the senses could be particularly beneficial to the spirit. Appleton concluded: "And now, as singing and making a melodious noise does greatly affect and please our senses, particularly our hearing, so it serves, as we find by experience to raise and exhilerate our spirits, and to put the whole man into a more lively and chearful frame."

Appleton, moreover, explicitly rejected the notion that it was merely the *words* of the Psalm, rather than the singing of the words, that affected a person. He stated that "if they have been holy songs that have been sung, they have stirred up holy and devout affections much beyond what the bare reading of them would have done." Such a phrasing of his support for Psalm singing was no doubt intended as a response to those who had placed the value of Psalm singing in the recitation of words and had overlooked the significance of pleasing and affecting music.

Those who labored to preserve theological orthodoxy most often emphasized the power of Scripture as "Word" (in this case, the Psalms) to instruct and persuade. Cotton Mather, in his published remarks on singing, entitled *The Accomplished Singer* (1721), stressed at the outset of his discussion of the topic that ministers be certain to take five minutes, before the congregation sings, to give "a short exposition, expressing the lessons of piety to be found in the verses now sung." For Mather, the singing of Psalms was important for the same reasons that Scripture of any sort was important. "As in the reading of sacred scriptures in general," wrote Mather, so also with singing: "that is, to fetch lessons out of every verse, and then turn them into prayers." Mather argued that "while we do by the action of singing put our minds into a due posture for it. We should first *hear* what the glorious God speaks unto us." As far as singing itself was concerned, Mather did not view the activity as a way in which the testimony of the senses (the sound of music) influenced spirit. He objected to the "confused noise of a wilderness" that plagued singing in church services, and he wished to remedy it with the introduction of a more orderly method of singing, the so-called new way, which would restore a measure of order to worship and would, as Laura L. Becker has argued, encourage discipline generally within the church.[9]

Catholicks preached about the affections in connection with other kinds of worship besides Psalm singing. Appleton commented on the enlivening of the affections through the recitation of the Lord's Prayer (and for this, he, like Colman, could have experienced the scolding of Increase Mather for those who advocated the use of "set formes"). Appleton wrote that the person who prays "will very much help to enlarge his heart in love unto him, he will find his affections stirred, and inflamed by the very petition." In a series of sermons preached in fall and winter 1721, Appleton moved line by line through the Lord's Prayer, explaining the meaning of the language, in statements such as the following, which addressed the first line: "It teaches us to come with the affections and dispositions of children to such a father."[10]

Such a lesson was wholly in accord with Appleton's views on preaching. As early as 1720, Appleton had already explained that because "ministers exhort as well as teach, then their sermons ought not to be taken up with the theoretick or speculative parts of divinity." Apparently, his hearing George Whitefield confirmed this belief in him, judging by Harvard tutor Henry Flynt's observation that Appleton's preaching became more lively after Whitefield's visit. In a sermon preached in 1741 and "occasioned by the late powerful and awakening preaching of the Rev. Mr. Whitefield," Appleton reiterated this understanding, explaining that "sometimes the most labor'd, learned, rational, accurate sermons shall go without any success; when others more plain, less studied, less methodical and accurate, will be accompanied with mighty power." Appleton did not wish to abandon the rational exposition of doctrine, but he believed that it was the duty of ministers to rouse the passions of his auditors and to find a vocabulary appropriate to the task. "If the preacher be wise," preached Appleton, "he will seek to find out acceptable words, even such expressions as will move the passions, and work upon the affections of the people." At the same time, however, the minister must be engaged in "informing their judgements, and awakening their consciences by offering rational convictions to them; without which the former will come to nothing."[11]

Wadsworth, like Fenner, knew that the "eye affecteth the heart," that "when the eye or ear, brings external objects to the view of the mind" a person is "affected with hope, fear, joy, grief, and the like." Moreover, Wadsworth supposed that "affecting" was not merely the rational consideration of a "truth" or doctrine that was obvious in what the eye surveyed. Rather, the testimony of the eye and the ear caused the affections themselves to respond. The voice was, for Wadsworth, particularly important in this regard. During his expedition to Albany in 1694, Wadsworth, whose father had been slain by Indians when he was a child, observed with satisfaction that the Indians came to the treaty place, to meet with the king's representatives, "singing all the way songs of joy and peace." Preaching several years later, he affirmed that "the voice is to be used in prayer, because it may be a means to stir up our affections." "Our affections ought to be lively and fervent in prayer," Wadsworth argued. Explaining that as "the eye dos frequently affect the heart, so dos the ear," Wadsworth concluded that "the rise of the voice in prayer has a tendency to move and stir our affections." It was in this spirit that he suggested another advantage of the voice, pointing out that "people are apt to forget what they heard, and some need to have the same things repeated" to them, or they will be "apt to grow dull and dead" in their "affections for spiritual things."[12]

Thomas Foxcroft, as we have seen, believed that public worship itself served to enliven and intensify the affections. But for Foxcroft, preaching nevertheless was to be carefully styled so that it would not only inform the understanding but "inflame the affections" of auditors as well. Foxcroft explained that religious instruction given by ministers to their congregations was to be a mixture of appeals to the rational faculties and language that would kindle the affections. Explaining this point, Foxcroft wrote: "The Italians have a proverb . . . Duro con duro non sat bon muro, hard stones heap'd up will not make a good wall." A sermon consisting solely of the presentation of doctrines to the understanding served auditors poorly. Rather, the hard stones of doctrine were to be "soften'd" with language that would not "chase the passions." Ministers were to avoid relying on "academical terms and philosophical nicety of diction" and "scholastic accuracy, and metaphysical distinctions." Rather, Foxcroft wrote, "As to language," ministers were to preach "with the most lively colours."[13]

Foxcroft's preaching was itself filled with "lively colours" and other language that described the spiritual life in ways that would appeal to the senses. From the "father of lights," the "fountain of living waters," came the "river of his pleasures." The saints, as they grow in holiness, "are made to drink larger draughts of the river of his pleasures." Public worship caused the blossoming of "a *special* perfume" that came with the "confluence of pious breathings." Worship was also like a "consort of musick." The words of Christ were "sweeter also than honey," and the saints "taste the special goodness of God." Even in the course of warning against the exclusive attachment of the affections to the "delights of sense," Foxcroft described heaven as a place where the saints, drawn together through the "utmost heights of mutual affection," enjoyed "the most pure & perfect, sweet, solid and satisfying pleasures." These "inconceivable pleasures," Foxcroft predicted, would "ravish our happy souls."[14]

Ebenezer Pemberton believed that some sermons were to be aimed at the exposition of doctrine, whereas others should stir the affections. As Harry S. Stout recently has argued, the "regular sermons" that ministers preached often were directed toward exhortation, and the encouragement and support of piety. "Occasional sermons," or those preached on special days (such as election, fast, and thanksgiving days), more commonly addressed an issue involving the necessity for a clarification or application of a point of doctrine, particularly with regard to the collective life of New Englanders. Pemberton's discussion of the use of language in sermons seems to be in line with this distinguishing between two types of preaching. Pemberton, who often complained about the dangers of "lukewarmness in religion," stated that "An orthodox creed, & an enlarged knowledge of the doctrines of the Gospel, is not able of itself to save any." The will and the affections were to be actively involved in religion as well. Sometimes, then, a minister should seek to stir the affections, and this involved a certain kind of preaching: "An address to the affections will admit that language which may not be so proper when the understanding for its information is immediately apply'd to." Pemberton explained further that "there is a difference here also to be allowed between one auditory and another; between common discourses and such as are made on some special occasion."

Edward "Gutts" Holyoke, like Pemberton, believed that ministers were obliged sometimes to speak to their audiences "in that peculiar hortatory manner as shall best win their affections and passions." Holyoke accepted that "sudden flashes of light" might "break in upon the mind" and that "the saint may feel this very sensibly, and it is a joy unspeakable and full of glory."[15]

Catholick Congregationalists were not the first New Englanders to suppose that devotion could be enriched through the cultivation of an awareness of the physical world. Charles Hambricke-Stowe has shown that various kinds of private meditation were practiced by Puritans in England and New England in the first half of the seventeenth century. But this "meditation" should not be confused with the sort of activity that catholicks had in mind when they recommended that the affections be stirred through stimulation of the senses. The first generation of New Englanders, as E. Brooks Holifield has argued, took a "distrustful posture toward visible symbols of any kind" and so were largely opposed to "sensory piety." Their attitude toward the physical world and, in particular, their understanding of the relationship between the world and the affections were colored by a deep suspicion of worldly or material images.[16]

The early settlers of New England, in their devotional meditations, sometimes drew a lesson from the observation of nature or the activities of everyday life (such as milking a cow or stoking a fire). But, as Michael Clark has argued, "the Puritans were not led to a contemplation of God through the excitation of the affections by a corporeal image." According to Clark, Puritans such as William Ames, John Cotton, Thomas Hooker, and Thomas Shepard utilized in their reflection on images drawn from nature a hermeneutic that "was based on the destruction of the image from which it departed." For Clark, Puritans relied on a complicated scheme of interpretation, when it came to drawing some lesson or inspiration from a corporeal image. This scheme was designed to "rupture the connection between significant sign and the image," so that what was left was meditation on a passage of Scripture or a point of doctrine that presented itself, through allegory or similitude, to the mind. Those who practiced meditation observed that the exercise indeed ended with the discovery of enlivened affections. But the process itself was understood in a way that removed the significance of the image.

Spontaneity and directness were lost in the process, so that the religious meditations of Puritans tended toward what Robert Middlekauff has described as "routinized emotion," or the transmutation of "raw feeling into feeling sanctioned by their code" of morals. Baird Tipson has made essentially the same point in his analysis of the piety of Thomas Shepard, arguing that Shepard's meditations, which Tipson thinks were representative of seventeenth-century New England piety, were an expression of "intellectualized piety." According to Tipson, the "assumption, often supported by references to faculty psychology, that experience simply provided raw data upon which the Puritan intellect was discretely to reflect, has misled scholars of Puritanism. In Shepard's case, intellectual expectations virtually created experience." Because for Shepard, meditation was "tied to particular biblical verses," it "remained mediate." as Urian Oakes later asserted, one of the functions of intellect was to "frame, and shape, and mould" the emotions. In short, seventeenth-century New Englanders, in their meditations, were inclined to discount the value of an emotional response to sensory experience and, instead, through a hermeneutic of "destruction," aimed at transmuting sense experience into comprehension of doctrine.[17]

The attitudes of the first generation toward the world did not become the attitudes of all later New Englanders. According to Holifield, a strong interest in sacramental piety, or "sensory piety," emerged in New England in the early eighteenth century.[18] We should recognize that catholicks were at the forefront of that movement. Catholicks saw order in the world and beauty in the body. They believed that the affections, which were partly of the body, were valuable to religion when stirred by reading, preaching, prayer, singing, the sacraments, or simply the vision of creation. For catholicks, the feeling of "delight" in nature could contribute substantially to the reinforcement of spiritual well-being. Catholicks expected, as Wadsworth wrote, "to see God's glory with delight." "Heart" religion, for Colman, Foxcroft, Appleton, and the others, accordingly referred to a kind of piety that included a strong emphasis on the excitation of affections that would draw the individual toward God and neighbor.[19]

Catholick piety of the heart, moreover, was not "intellectualized" as was the piety of Shepard, for example, or even Cotton

Mather. In the first place, the intellectualizing "tradition" in New England meditation was focused on the elicitation of feelings of anxiety and unworthiness, and disgust with the fleshly sins, not with the experiencing of joy and delight that followed on the heels of a vision of "beauty" and "order" in creation. The "experimental knowledge of God and Christ" that Appleton recommended in 1728 surely included a sense of sin, but it also contained a strong dose of what Colman called "the bare apprehension" of "excellencies." When we hear Colman exclaim, "What surprising pleasures do the varieties of wondrous use and beauty give to our contemplative and devout minds!" we ought to take seriously his choice of the word *surprise.* Spontaneity is suggested as well in Colman's ejaculation "O what a joy does it give us?" to see the works of creation. Colman, discussing the "various beauteous" things that "surround us and present themselves to our sight," declared, "What must we think first of but the God that made all these things? . . . that is to say, the first thing that occurs to the rational mind, upon surveying his own body and the visible universe is the greatness and glory of its creator." The simple delight of the sound of music—recommended by catholicks as a way to stir the affections—or the joy of observing the moon was not a highly mediated, intellectualized emotion. And it was this sort of experience that set the tone for other kinds of emotion experienced in connection with religion.[20]

Catholick emphasis on the affections should not be taken to mean that intellect suffered in catholick theology. Robert Middlekauff's claim that piety and intellect were closely related in "puritanism" is as true for catholicks as it was for Cotton Mather or Thomas Shepard. In fact, as the last quotation from Colman suggests, the "aesthetic" response of catholicks to nature was actually a mixture of intellect and affection. But intellect did not overwhelm emotion. For Middlekauff's "puritans," a "highly articulated moral code displaced certain kinds of emotions." For catholicks, on the other hand, the affections were understood as actually guiding the intellect, at least some of the time (and, more broadly considered, as contributing actively to the organization of social life as well). As Appleton argued: "When the affections are once stirred up and engaged, they serve very powerfully to enlighten the mind, perswade the will, to remove discouragements." As body and soul, flesh and spirit, were connected, so also were the affections and the intellect.[21]

This is not to say that catholick expressions of joy and delight in nature's beauty were entirely unmediated by intellectual and cultural categories. It is unlikely that the expression of emotion, in any culture, is not shaped in some measure by ideas. And, of course, catholicks, like other clergy, were quick to adopt wording drawn from Scripture to assist them in their expressing emotion. Ebenezer Turell wrote that Colman "often made use of Scripture, not for proof and illustration only, but for the sake of the inspired language."[22] In short, there might have developed among catholicks some habitual, even ritual forms for expressing a response to the perception of beauty, but this in itself does not amount to routinization.

I do not wish to imply that noncatholick ministers wanted only the icy truth of doctrine and an emotional life of unrelieved anxiety. Nevertheless, we ought to pay attention to the differences between the emotional dimension of their religion and that of catholicks. Tipson points out that Shepard lived out his life on a "treadmill" of anxiety characterized by a "feeling of inadequacy and unworthiness." Cotton Mather had his private raptures and joys, and he experienced a wide range of emotions from despair to ecstasy. "But," writes Middlekauff, "few" of those emotions "brought peace and repose." Mather, and some of the ministers who looked to him for leadership, were genuinely concerned with religion of the "heart." But this religion of the heart was not identical to that conceived by catholicks. Fear of God and humiliation and shame for sin were the major components of Mather's religion of the heart. Mather's preaching, moreover, did not include—as did catholicks'—much in the way of provisions for the exciting of what might be called the "connecting" affections. Rather, it was directed toward the experience of satisfaction and confidence that accompanied the recognition of the truth of divine revelation. Mather's preaching may have suffered on this account: Captain Brown of Concord reported that after years of listening to Mather preach, he "supposed he was not converted by it." When Joshua Gee, Samuel Checkley, Mather Byles, or John Webb referred to religion of the heart, he had in mind essentially the same experience of guilt, shame, and humiliation, relieved by an occasional, conditional feeling of confidence that God had reinforced his repentance with the gift of grace.[23]

Catholicks, of course, were interested not only in the affections but in doctrine. Moreover, catholicks did not assume that excited affections were proof of the presence of saving grace. Edward Holyoke reflected the catholick position when he explained that a stirring of the affections, as much as it might *contribute* to spiritual improvement, was not, in the final analysis, a sign that one had "the Spirit of God." Moreover, the union of body and soul in a person in no way meant that all "feelings" were "religious." Accordingly, excited affections were no guarantee of regenerate status. In conjunction with knowledge of God acquired through a purified understanding, the affections were of great use, but neither the understanding through "right reason" nor the affections could substitute for the grace of God.

This much is clear from Holyoke's letter to George Whitefield, written in 1744, possibly in response to the criticisms of New England's ministers (and Harvard College in particular) that were contained in Whitefield's recently published *Journals*. Holyoke informed Whitefield, "Some [persons] have very gross ideas of the word *Feeling* as if it were to be taken with respect to matter." People did not feel the Spirit of God "in their hearts & breasts as they do their food & drink in their stomachs." It was generally acknowledged, wrote Holyoke (who likely knew well such things), that a "gross corporeal sensation" of pleasure could always be expected to follow the consumption of good food. The "feeling" of the "Spirit of God," however, did not come about in this way. As much as good preaching might be involved in a raising of the affections, it was only with the cooperation of grace that authentic experience of God was possible. Moreover, the raised affections were not a sure sign of grace. And it was certainly wrong to assume that any stirring of the affections—by preaching, music, and so on—would cause God to act to provide grace. God could not be forced to act.[24]

In catholick thinking, the affections did not operate within a person apart from the rational faculty. In the person made up of the union of body and soul, the affections sometimes played a key role in influencing him toward God. But emotional experiences in the meetinghouse, or in the closet, or on the street, whether they were experiences of joy or shame, were not be taken as a sure sign of election. Catholicks, for all of their declarations about reason and order in the universe, the availability of the light of nature, and the beauty of creation, still believed that without regenerating grace, a person was lost to sin, no matter how aroused were his or her affections.

4

Love Flowing from Grace

Catholicks believed that regeneration was necessary for salvation.[1] Faculties such as the understanding and the affections were useful to religion before and after conversion. But they could contribute nothing to the spiritual development of a person in the absence of faith, and faith was possible only with the regenerating grace of God.

Regeneration was necessary because of the fall. God had created men and women in his own image, but the sin that resulted in the expulsion of Adam and Eve from Eden had corrupted that image. Accordingly, the relationship between God and humanity had been ruptured, so that men and women lived in alienation from God and from their own original human nature. "In our present state," wrote Benjamin Colman, "we are born into sin." A person was in the "natural state an offensive thing to God." Benjamin Wadsworth stated that men and women "deserv'd hell even before we were born." At the beginning of a series of twelve sermons that he published in 1717, Wadsworth wrote, "All mere men since the fall of Adam, are shapen in iniquity and conceiv'd in sin." Wadsworth already had explained the matter in genetic terms several years earlier, when he preached, "Adam was considered a publick person, the head and representative of all his posteritie," but, "by one man's disobedience, many more were made sinners." Nathaniel Appleton advised his readers, "Let us meditate on our miserable estate by nature, duly resent it, and lay it to heart." What "impure, vile, and sinful creatures we are by nature." According to Appleton, "Some men are vain in their imaginations with respect to the natural powers of men, and can't bear to think they are so debased and debilitated by the fall, as they really are." Thomas Foxcroft emphasized that "man's understanding (as well as the other faculties of the soul) is lamentably depraved by the Fall." Foxcroft declared that it was "a truth too palpable and notorious to be disputed" that as a result of the apostasy in Eden, "corruption descends to the whole natural posterity of fallen Adam in all succeeding generations." A person was born into the world separated from God by the vast gulf that had opened as a result of Adam's sin. And for catholicks, as for New England ministers throughout the seventeenth century, no persons, by the power of reason, or the affections, or sheer will, could escape their corrupted state, without supernatural assistance.[2]

Catholick sensing of the enormous distance between God and humanity (tainted by original sin) was informed, paradoxically, by the same literature that contributed to the catholick vision of a delightfully immense and wondrous universe. It was the very emphasis on immensity and, especially, infinity in the universe that was present in the writings of Boyle, Derham, Ray, and Thomas Burnet that both inspired delight and, against the background of Calvinist doctrine in New England, reinforced a sense of distance between God and humanity. The emphasis of scientists such as Boyle on the immense distance between God and humanity has been mentioned. It is also worth noting, however, that in writings such as Burnet's *Sacred Theory of the Earth,* there was in evidence, as Marjorie Nicolson has pointed out, a "paradoxical" response to nature that mixed recognition of order and harmony with perception of chaos. It would seem that a good deal of the English scientific literature was, in fact, susceptible to alternately different interpretations.[3]

Nicolson has argued that in the wake of seventeenth-century scientific (especially astronomical) and physicotheological works, English writers became captivated by the notions of absolute time and absolute space. Terms such as *immense* and *vast,* which became particularly important in discourse about nature, were understood to suggest something as well about the glory of God, who ruled over creation. According to Nicolson, it was the Cambridge Platonist Henry More, whose influence was so strong at Harvard, who "was the first English poet to express, and the first English philosopher to teach the idea of infinite space and an infinity of worlds." More was especially taken with the notion that there were many worlds in the universe, a "plurality" of worlds, and that God in the fullness of his perfection governed these for good: "The centre of each severall world's a Sunne . . . / About whose radiant crown the Planets runne, / Like reeling moths around a candle light; / These all together one world I conceit, / And that even infinite such worlds there be."[4]

Like More, many New Englanders also considered creation to be "vast" and God to be "immense" in his power and glory. They expressed this sense in a variety of ways, and most often through straightforward statements about the vastness and mystery of creation. Another way, perhaps more instructive for what is under investigation here, was through references to very large numbers, and to eternity. Reflection on the nature of time, of course, was not limited to catholick Congregationalists. Judge Sewall, the Westborough pastor Ebenezer Parkman, and the Hollis professor John Winthrop all thought about the nature of time.[5] Indeed, their reflections were often similar to those of catholicks, and this should not be surprising, because meditation on the consequences of the fall and acknowledgment of the enormity of creation—especially, its incomprehensibility—naturally corresponded, for ministers or laypersons regardless of their theological stripe.

Catholicks, in expressing a sense of cosmic vastness, sometimes referred to large numbers, such as "million" or "millions." In fact, a reference to "millions" is usually a sign that a comment on the incomprehensibility of God will shortly follow. Benjamin Colman, in the course of pointing out that weak human faculties were incapable of providing perfect knowledge of God, reflected, as had More, on the plurality of worlds in creation. Colman proposed that "an infinite understanding is visible in the frame and government of the universe." God, as the governor of the universe, naturally possessed an understanding that was itself infinite, "so that supporting millions of worlds he is necessarily and equally in every part and with every creature in them all." Still thinking, it would seem, about incalculable quantities, Colman added that it was possible that "thousands" of kinds of rational creatures who were smarter than human beings might exist among the millions of worlds in the cosmos. Elsewhere, Colman used the more common terminology to describe the inhabitants of all of the various worlds: "How many vast worlds, and millions and millions of living spirits, and moving creatures that have life, has the living God produced and continually preserves." Here Colman said that God could be described only as "infinite essence" and "immense spirit." Colman, in fact, on one occasion observed, "space is so mysterious and inexplicable a thing in nature" that some persons had in fact been "ready to deify it, and to say it is God himself, because immense and never to be searched out." For Colman, this suggested that the faithful should "more and more adore him [God] in his incomprehensibleness."[6]

Wadsworth reminded his congregation of the possibility of spending "millions of years, nay, millions of ages" in hell as punishment for the evil committed during a lifetime, and he recommended that they "mourn for our original sin, our vile depraved nature." Wadsworth, who preached that "God's being is immense and infinite," declared that God was "eternal" and "most high in his knowledge & wisdom," and he asked his congregation: "The sea how large is it? Yet God can hold all of it in the hollow of his hand." In *The Highest Dwelling with the Lowest* (1711), Wadsworth stated that "the being or essence of God, is immense, infinite, it has no bounds or limit." God might therefore make "the brightest displays of his perfections" in the heavens, but God was still "infinitely beyond the bounds and limits" of visible creation and beyond the limits of human knowledge. Thomas Foxcroft argued that "the scriptures do everywhere lead us into the contemplation of nature . . . as the works of God." Foxcroft, who believed that reason was of mighty use in recognizing the hand of God in creation, nevertheless proposed that there were "many mysteries in the divine conduct," and especially in the workings of "divine providence, whereby the vast variety of creatures and things in the universe, are powerfully upheld in their existence."[7]

The consideration of cosmic vastness that included a sense of the absolute or mysterious might have developed in New England under the influence of More, Boyle, Burnet, and other English writers who were fascinated with the "infinite" and might even have been reinforced in Boston-area ministers through their contact with R. Judas Monis, who was appointed to teach Hebrew at Harvard in 1722 and who was well versed in the Cabala. In any event, catholicks believed that the fall of Adam had created an enormous distance between God and humanity. In their consideration of the theological implications of this distance, they drew on the same set of ideas about the enormity of the universe that had informed their response of "delight" to creation. Creation, in its vastness, could be wondrous and cause celebration of the glory of God the governor of the universe. But recognition of the capability of God to govern an infinitely large universe also suggested the gulf between human and divine and the necessity for supernatural grace in the process of reconciliation to God.[8]

Supernatural grace was available to the elect through the covenant of grace, and against the claims of Perry Miller, it can be asserted that catholicks did not abandon the covenant of grace.[9] Foxcroft's papers include several detailed notes on the various covenants. His subject book contained numerous entries under the categories "covenant of redemption," "covenant of redemption different from covenant of grace," and "covenant of works." A series of meditations written on the backs of envelopes was organized around the following theme: "Covenant of grace, different views of it among divines." Foxcroft wrote that the covenant of grace "is also called a new & sound covenant in distinction from the first covenant with Adam." The new "covenant of grace" was "betwixt God and the redeemer & believers in him—So tis often called in distinction from the first covenant of works. This covenant of grace was published and made known to Adam after his fall & has continued in the world in all ages to this day and will to the end of time." In her sermons, Foxcroft explained in more practical terms the necessity for grace in reformation, stressing that the Holy Ghost will visit the sinner, "producing a total change in the moral temper and frame of the soul." "A regenerating change indeed is the fundamental thing," he emphasized, whereby moral rectitude was "restor'd to the soul in a new birth."[10]

Appleton, whom Perry Miller had singled out as a leading example of departure from covenant theology among the Congregationalist clergy, in fact strenuously defended the covenant. Miller cited Appleton's *The Wisdom of God* (1728) as the "best illustration" of the radical omission of covenant theology in the thinking of some early eighteenth-century ministers. Miller claimed that, among other shortcomings, this sermon "never once mentions the covenant." In fact, although new directions are clearly perceptible in the arguments of the book, it nevertheless hardly overlooked traditional Puritan ideas about the covenant. Appleton discussed at length (over two hundred pages) the fall, redemption, and process of conversion and, in fact, made explicit references to the "covenant of grace" and "coventantal engagements to God." Noting the "secret, mysterious, and unsearchable way of the spirit's working this regenerating change in the soul," Appleton called attention to the "most effectual teachings and illuminations" that God "affords to the souls of men, in their regeneration and conversion." Grace was given to correct the deficiencies consequent on original sin, and the ordinance of the Lord's Supper, "is to be considered as a seal of the covenant of grace, as well as baptism, wherein God promises and engages all the benefits of the new covenant to us; so we do herein renew our covenantal engagements to God."[11]

Wadsworth insisted on the necessity for "regenerating grace." He wrote in 1719, "When a person is truly regenerated, or converted, there's a new and holy nature implanted in him." A few years later, he developed this theme in detail, in preaching a sermon on the subject of the "new man of grace." Elsewhere he explained that persons should know God "as your Covenant God." Pemberton stressed in his sermons that persons were entirely dependent on grace for living a godly life, and he emphasized, particularly, the importance of not neglecting covenantal obligations. Colman preached on the importance of faith and reminded his auditors that they were a covenant people. Colman asked a congregation: "Here is something mutual between two parties, God and man; significant to great favour and grace on the part of God, and of special and holy bonds and duty to God on the part of man: Now what can this be but a federal and covenant stipulation?" More precisely, said Colman, it was the "covenant of grace." Colman affirmed elsewhere that there was "an election of grace" so that persons "by a new birth are and shall be made righteous."[12]

Reconciliation to God was made possible by the covenant of grace, whereby the elect were given supernatural assistance in order to overcome the deleterious effects of the fall. There are three aspects of catholicks' understanding of this process of regeneration that we ought to to consider in our seeking to arrive at a sense of catholick thought as a whole. These are (1) the catholick emphasis on the importance of the faculties in conversion, (2) the catholick emphasis on God as a loving parent, and (3) the intense interest of catholicks in the social consequences of conversion.

Catholick ideas about the role of the faculties in conversion were derived from earlier writers. Puritan covenant theologians such as William Ames, William Perkins, Thomas Hooker, and Peter Bulkeley, drawing on a Reformed tradition that had left dangling the threads of argument about faith and assurance, framed an approach to understanding election that proposed the covenant of grace as a relationship between God and humanity that was both absolute and conditional. That is, these theologians believed that the covenant represented, on the one hand, the receiving by persons of free and irresistible grace from a sovereign God, and, on the other hand, the mutual or reciprocal relationship between God and humanity, in which faith and repentance were the conditions for election. Covenant theologians sought to explain, within this framework, that conditional election was not a matter of merit, that it was not a contract providing justification in exchange for good works, but, rather, that God would make use of human faculties in the process of regeneration. In this scheme, it was understood that election came only by the grace of God—the formal cause—but that human integrity to will and act was preserved through necessity for the efficient cause of faith (and repentance). In the "order of nature," it was God who acted first to save the elect, and in the "order of time," individuals repented and believed simultaneously with the infusion of grace. Such a framework for salvation, then, provided ample room for the "persuading" of persons from sin to faith and did not rely on a process that bypassed the faculties.[13]

Some English Puritans and some New Englanders in the seventeenth and eighteenth centuries believed that conversion took place quickly, whereas others thought the process gradual. Catholicks were among the latter.[14] Wadsworth informed his congregation that "there are but some, and probably but few sincere Christians, that can tell the particular time of their conversion. Some can tell it, but probably there are but few that can." Moreover, argued Wadsworth, "tis commonly thought, that those who know, least of the particular time of their conversion, . . . have been best furnish'd with the means of grace, and been kept from scandalous sins." Appleton, in fact, addressing a convention of ministers, specifically warned them not to lead persons into believing that knowledge of the time of one's conversion was necessary to salvation. What is important about this, as far as our understanding of catholick thought is concerned, is that a gradual conversion made more obvious use of the faculties. This was not lost on Appleton, who wrote that "conversion" was the "regular act and exercise of our rational powers put into such a motion by the supernatural grace of God." "Moreover," explained Appleton, "if the work were wrought in an immediate manner, there would not be the use of our natural and rational powers and faculties." Colman made the same claim, writing that "the moral perfections of God must necessarily be communicated to reasonable creatures, and in a degree and measure suitable to their place in the creation of God."[15]

Catholicks, like other Congregationalist ministers, believed that regeneration was characterized by a purification of the will. But catholicks also stressed the importance of the understanding and the affections alongside the will, as key players in the turning of a person from sin to God. Pemberton, Colman, Wadsworth, Foxcroft, and Appleton all believed that the understanding was a key faculty in the process of conversion.[16] As Appleton stated the matter, "The winning of souls is by presenting proper arguments, and perswading them in a rational way to come to Christ," or, stated another way, "not deceiving them as the fowler does the bird, but rather by undeceiving them." But Appleton, as we have seen, also stressed the capability of the affections to enlighten and guide the understanding and the will. Indeed, catholicks sometimes wrote about the understanding as the leading faculty in conversion, but it is clear that they believed, as Foxcroft wrote in describing conversion, that "the understanding is *one* of the introductive powers of the soul" (emphasis mine). In one sermon, Foxcroft could outline the process of conversion as beginning with the understanding "This is, as it were, the outmost gate, or foredoor" to the soul. In another sermon, he could argue, drawing on Pascal, that in fact "It is the heart, & not the reason which has properly the perception of God—. The judgement and the understanding have their proper method: which is by principles and demonstrations. The heart & affections have a different method altogether." For Foxcroft, the affections were one of the "doors of the soul" along with the understanding and the will.[17]

Ministers such as the Mathers, Byles, Checkley, and Gee also believed that the affections had a role in conversion. But, like much of the clergy in the seventeenth century, these ministers (and their theological allies) emphasized what I have called the separating affections in conversion. Their emphasis on "legal terrors" and "fears" in conversion, was, in fact, close to Solomon Stoddard's style of preaching. As Norman Pettit has pointed out, Stoddard was accused by Giles Firmin (a deacon in the First Church in Boston, and later a Presbyterian minister in England) of placing too much emphasis on fear and trembling in repentance in conversion, and not enough on the love of God. The notion of "heart-religion" in the preaching of these ministers was generally reflected in Cotton Mather's statement that "the heart is the special seat wherein the fear of God resides."[18]

Catholick emphasis on the importance of the faculties—including the "connecting" affections—in the process of regeneration was closely intertwined with the belief that God was a loving father, not a judge to be feared. God "treated men as rational creatures," as catholicks (and some noncatholicks) often declared, but, for catholicks, divine compassion was equally important as a characteristic feature of God's commerce with men and women. Indeed, for catholicks, God's compassion and his willingness to lead persons to him by appealing to their rational understanding were two sides of the same coin. Harry S. Stout has argued that in New England in the early eighteenth century, ministers began to picture Jesus as a more sympathetic and beneficent figure than had the second generation. According to Stout, "themes of love and reconciliation were especially prominent in the preaching of Boston's 'liberal clergy,' " or those ministers many of whom I have called catholick. Catholicks saw order and beauty in the world and in the body; they believed in the unity of body and soul and emphasized the utilization of the faculties in the process of regeneration. A view of God as a compassionate and benevolent adopting father was another aspect of the generally hopeful and confident character of catholick theology. It should be noted as well that in their describing the features of a relationship between God and the individual, catholicks likely drew on models available to them from latitudinarian writers.

Latitudinarians believed in original sin and in the idea that a person was not reconciled to God through the performance of good works. Nevertheless, they tended to agree with Tillotson that "this degeneracy is not total. For though our faculties be much weakened and disordered, yet they are not destroyed or wholly perverted." For Tillotson, "natural judgement and conscience doth still direct us to what is good, and what we ought to do." It was worthwhile for preachers to seek to pitch rational "arguments" to their congregations in order to lead them to seek "the blessed Jesus," who, as Simon Patrick explained, was "a person that was very full of love, tenderness and bowels of compassion towards those that deserved nothing." Accordingly, as Stillingfleet argued, the doctrines of Christianity, including the necessity for regeneration, were very persuasive, given "not only the weight of the arguments themselves, but the force they receive from the example" of Jesus. Although they were attentive to the compassion of Jesus, latitudinarians placed more emphasis on his example of charity and on the effectiveness of rationally coherent moral arguments, than on an appeal to the affections. They disapproved of the preaching of "fright and terror" and evidenced what J. Sears McGee has described as "the Anglican strategy" of preaching, which was "to draw men toward conversion by compassionate methods which complemented their natures rather than drag them by harsh ones which were offensive."[19]

Catholick theology did not completely replace fear of God with love of God. Catholicks continued to emphasize the necessity for repentance in conversion, and, like other ministers of their time, they sometimes connected sinfulness with preoccupations of the flesh. The catholick position might best be described as an attempt to balance the traditional (for New England) emphasis on fear of God with preaching that more vigorously emphasized hope. As Stout has written, "this changed orientation did not entail denial of the doctrines of original sin and hell, but it placed them in a broader perspective of hope and deliverance." It was in this spirit that Foxcroft wrote: "Hope and fear must be kept on a ballance. Amazing dread is to be avoided as well as presuming conscience." Wadsworth likewise instructed his congregation not to "give way to overwhelming melancholly, to sinking doubts, fears, dispondencies" in their thinking about salvation. Appleton advised persons to repent with "fear and trembling," but in the same breath he expressed his optimism about salvation in such strong terms as to appear almost Arminian (which he was not): "Don't waste your time in arguing your own incapacity to convert to God, and to believe on the Lord Jesus," but, rather, "make the utmost efforts" and "then there is an infinite probability, that God will grant you his super-natural aids and assistances."[20]

Catholicks understood conversion more as a process by which a person was brought into a loving relationship with God than as the ingraining of trepidation and self-doubt. Colman explained in a letter to a colleague that he did not believe that the "covenant of grace" required belief in a "vindictive & revengeful being." But, unlike English Puritans before them, and Jonathan Edwards, their junior colleague, catholicks wrote little about the process of conversion itself. They stressed the importance of the faculties in regeneration and they often portrayed God as an adopting father. But they were most concerned with the aftermath of conversion, with the bonding of the converted individual to the community of the regenerate. Conversion itself remained for them, as it did for other New Englanders, somewhat mysterious. Catholicks knew that "an 'experimental' knowledge of God was not only reasonable but exhilirating," but they did not claim to know much more about the operations of the Holy Spirit. Appleton believed that "the more wonderful and unsearchable the works of God are, the more readily will he attract the esteem adoration & admiration of his creatures." Conversion, like the experience of God generally, was a beautiful experience, but it was also mysterious: "The way of the spirit is unsearchable. We cannot find out the manner of its operations upon us in the work of conversion. Indeed, the effects of it are plain, and very discernible, but not the manner of its operation." It was the aftermath of conversion, the activity of regenerate persons in the world, that was of more interest to catholicks than any dissection of the process of conversion.[21]

Of course, clergy across a broad spectrum of Protestantism and through several generations had called attention to the importance of the "effects" of regeneration. But catholick interest in the aftermath of conversion ought to be understood, in the context of the history of Congregationalism in and around Boston, as part of a fresh theological perspective. More precisely, catholicks began to articulate an understanding of the aftermath of conversion that had been a part of the thinking of some English Puritans but had survived in America largely as an undercurrent to other doctrinal emphases. The feature of English theology that I have in mind has recently been analyzed by Charles Cohen, who stresses that "the dynamism of Puritan activity and the cohesiveness of their community arose from the psychological foundation laid down by the Lord's mercy in regeneration." According to Cohen, "the affections stimulated by regeneration encouraged affiliation with other similarly engaged people"; indeed, it "promoted group solidarity." Moreover, the affectionate bonding between the saints, which emerged in the group as a consequence of conversion, was possible only through what I have called "connecting" affections. That is, the cooperation among the regenerate in their work in the world could not take place under the influence of a religious sensibility characterized by dread. English Puritans believed that "anguish and dread do not motivate the consistent toil that marks saintly activity. . . . Fear can not sustain work according to Puritan theory." Moreover, they affirmed that the normal context for God's granting grace to persons was, in fact, the communal. As Richard Sibbes explained, "Christ conveys spiritual life and vigor to Christians," inasmuch as they are "united to the mystical body, the church." Affection to God and neighbor following from regenerating grace and growth in holiness through the assembling with the saints were key aspects of Puritan religious life, and they were both firmly planted in the belief that personal piety and public religion were intimately joined.[22]

Catholicks, as we shall see, thought similarly about conversion. But, first we should understand that Puritan ideas about regeneration and the bonding of the saints in love were not transmitted intact directly from old England, through the religion of New Englanders in the seventeenth century, to catholick Congregationalists. The legacy was, in fact, sidetracked along the way. Patricia Caldwell, pointing out the differences between "American" and English conversion narratives, has written that the English "could point to their delight and satisfaction in God," to their joy, peacefulness, cheerfulness, and "above all, their longing . . . to join the congregation of the people of God." The conversion narratives recorded by Thomas Shepard and John Fiske (Wenham and Chelmsford, Massachusetts), between 1637 and 1666, show that in America, on the other hand, " 'effects' were either scarcely thought of, despite the elders prodding, or else deemed so unsatisfying that they were scarcely worth mentioning." American conversion narratives, argues Caldwell, evidence a "constriction of emotion," a condition of " 'deadness' of heart," that arose from the failure of settlers to find some closure between their expectations and the reality of life in the New World. The voices in Caldwell's conversion narratives are "lukewarm and pallid," the product of a "foggy limbo of broken promises, where the human heart was felt to be 'dead and dull.' "[23]

The religious experiences of the first generation might not have been quite as barren of affect as Caldwell suggests. However, it does seem that New Englanders in the seventeenth century were not optimistic that joyful participation in the life of the holy collective would flow naturally from regenerate status. Religious life remained for the most part focused on an understanding of sin and repentance that stressed the importance of the "separating affections," rather than liberation into the satisfying emotional life of a joint project of work and worship with the saints. It is true that the Mathers and Willard, and later Byles and Gee, spoke occasionally of the joy of knowing God. But these ministers sought escape from the world, from the flesh, from time itself, all of which were viewed as impediments to the work of grace. Their references to the joy of the regenerate tended to be descriptions of the life of the godly in heaven, in eternity, not of the bonding of the saints, through intense affection, on earth.[24]

The transmission to the eighteenth century of the English Puritan idea of the aftermath of conversion as a bonding of the regenerate in love was complicated as well by social change in New England in the latter part of the seventeeth century. Social historians have suggested that New England life in that period was characterized by a departure from social control through neighborly "watchfulness." David Thomas Konig, in a study of law and society in seventeenth-century Essex County, argues that the "failure of effective social discipline by means of informal local pressures was another example of how the ideal of the stable, interdependent community that could regulate itself collectively was becoming less of a reality." Konig's analysis of court records in Essex County led him to conclude that the notion of "neighborly regulation of private behavior" (which had its origins in Tudor England) gave way to the idea that persons should not "meddle" in the affairs of others. At the bottom of this change was the emergence of the opinion, among both the public and the court, that there ought to be made a "distinction between the public and private consequences of behavior." Those activities that were not threatening either to the peace or to the safety of the community were viewed as private and were not to be interfered with by persons who might be seeking to root out sin or impurity that they perceived as subversive of the holiness of the community of the spiritually elect.

Konig's picture of the deterioration of social control through watchfulness has been supported by the findings of Roger Thompson, whose study of cases of sexual misdemeanor in the court records of Middlesex County led him to conclude that in the second half of the seventeenth-century "the pioneer ideals of brotherly love were on the wane." Although those ideals did not disappear, they became submerged in the process of the development of town life, at odds with the necessity for more explicit prosecution of miscreants, so that "the towns of Middlesex could hardly rely on ideals of neighborly love and fellowship." In Charlestown and Malden, in particular, "the picture of community life . . . was hardly one of loving neighborliness." It seems that like Konig's communities in Essex County, the towns studied by Thompson began in the seventeenth century to distinguish more sharply in some ways between public and private life. Population growth, the expansion of the economy, and a more powerful English presence in the government all contributed to this development, which has also been explored from a variety of angles by T. H. Breen, Laurel Thatcher Ulrich, and John Demos.[25]

Other scholars, focusing essentially on literary evidence, have offered analyses of seventeenth-century life that correspond generally with the work of social historians such as Konig and Thompson. Agnieszka Salska, after surveying Puritan poetry of the seventeenth century, and especially the writings of Edward Taylor (pastor at Westfield) and Anne Bradstreet—many of which those authors declined to publish—has suggested that the poetry of the period underwent "polarization into public and private modes of expression." Indeed, according to Salska, there occurred in the seventeenth century a "polarization into public and private self." David Leverenz likewise has characterized Taylor's poetry as a "retreat into solitude," symptomatic of "the breakup of shared fantasy and shared community into alienated imaginings." For Leverenz, the preaching of second-generation ministers shows most clearly the "obsessive style, which routinizes emotion by creating a mechanical atmosphere of intellectual exercise rather than emotional expression." According to Leverenz, the division in religion between "public accusation and private solace" in the second half of the seventeenth century is to be understood more precisely as the recognition that public religion was "a dead husk, while vibrant communion was experienced privately." For Increase Mather, Samuel Willard, and others religion became a "search for private solace" juxtaposed to a formal, highly stylized, "rational" public ritualization of guilt.[26]

Leverenz's psychoanalytic analysis is, again, focused on essentially the same issue—a movement toward the separation of public and private in religion—that Norman Pettit explored in his study of the conversion theology of seventeenth-century New Englanders. Pettit argued that after 1675, in the wake of war with the Indians, Boston fires, troubles with England, and other such problems, rigid dogmatism came to dominate public religion. On the one hand, Pettit claimed, "The clergy struggled to preserve the ritual structure of the churches; and indifference to the inner life became more and more pronounced." On the other, there was the rise—largely in reaction to this—of the conversionist preaching of Solomon Stoddard, who, with his rejection of the test of a relation, represented a "return to the sanctity of the inner life, immune from the probings of others." In either case, there was a separation of inner life from public ritual. As Robert Middlekauff has written, New England "culture by the early years of the eighteenth century had relegated religious experience to a private realm."[27]

Catholicks recovered the notion, connected with English Puritanism, of affectionate, religious, social solidarity among the regenerate by encouraging the reunion of personal piety with public religion. Catholick ministers supposed that the regenerate's experience of God was the vision of the immensity and beauty of God, seen in the works of creation and experienced invisibly through the action of grace in the soul. The reforming and enlivening of the faculties, which had been vitiated by the fall, were fundamental parts of that experience. This enlivening included the stirring and enriching of the affections, which, in a regenerate person, made possible the bonding of the faithful in activity in the world.[28]

Catholick understanding of the aftermath of conversion as the union of the saints is reflected in Foxcroft's vaguely Newtonian statements about public worship, quoted earlier, that "the union of many devout souls in a joint presence, mutually raises and enlivens their affections" and that this event is similar to the optical phenomenon in which many different rays of light are intensified into a single beam. Foxcroft explained further that in public worship, there "is a union of the graces of many together, a confluence of pious breathings" that is like "perfume." It was also "like the collection of many waters, emptying themselves out of various rivulets into one common channel." In fact, for Foxcroft, the distance between heaven and earth was most obviously diminished in the activities of the saints as integral parts of the collective. Whether it be through "service to their generation," through their "calling or employment," or, through publick worship, the saints worshipping and working together "do resemble and have communion with the glorious society above, where millions perhaps at once join their melodious songs, and pay their exalted devotions together. By this means there's a *harmony* between heaven and earth; yea, in some sort, a heaven upon earth."[29]

Foxcroft believed that regeneration was the foundation of work in the world. He wrote, "The principle of grace in the saints do's so harmonize with their work, as to incline them to it," and that grace "renders their work daily more and more natural." Harmony with one's work was also harmony with society. "True piety," wrote Foxcroft, "impresses men with a deep sense of the bonds and benefits of society; and so excites them to feel the good of others." Virtue, and especially kindness, was a product of grace. Foxcroft, writing on the "nature of Christian kindness," explained that "it may be consider'd as seated in the heart," but it was also "one part of practical divinity." In fact, morality in general was closely tied to heart, and that included the affections. Rejecting an intellectualized piety and the notion that morality consisted in the cultivation of such, Foxcroft argued that the health of the soul was "not merely intellectual, but moral, and refers not so much to an orderly state of the head, . . . but to the holy frame of his heart, his conscience, will and affections, as well as his understanding."[30] Wadsworth explained that "election is a secret act of God . . . a secret act of his will, that can't be known immediately by men, but only by the fruits and effects of it. 'Tis God's eternal secret proposing in himself, to make such and such persons holy and happy forever, by the union to and communion with Jesus Christ." For Wadsworth, union to Christ meant that a person was also a member of the "mystical body of Christ." As a Christian, a person, then, would find that, bonded to others in the mystical body of Christ, collective life was more rewarding, since "social duties and comforts, are not hindred [*sic*] but furthered by Christianity." The regenerate, "from a principle of love to our neighbors," would live by a code of ethics that included a great many specific things, including giving to the poor, not envying the prosperity of others, showing honor and respect to others, praying for enemies, and, in true catholick fashion, being careful not to "impose our opinions in smaller matters of religion."[31]

Wadsworth, like his colleagues, believed that a Christian must have a godly "walk." The term was defined by Wadsworth as "a metaphor meaning a person's moral course, the usual tenor of our conversation & of our conduct in public." The godly walk was not merely a product of rational reflection on the lessons of Scripture and doctrine, but practical activity flowing from the heart. Wadsworth wrote, "The heart is the spring & fountain of men's thot's, words and actions," so that "from a prevailing principle within, the whole outward behaviour should be conformed." In *An Essay to Do Good* (1710), Wadsworth accordingly preached that "all the actions of the soul," no matter what they were, were to be understood within the category of "moral" action, and he advised his audience that God "sees our outward actions, but he also observes the inward principles from which they flow." Persons therefore were to keep their hearts pure, "not only consider'd in their single capacity as individual persons; but also consider'd as parts or members of any society or community."[32]

Colman expressed his understanding of regeneration as a foundation for the activities of everyday life in typically sensuous imagery. He wrote: "As natural as it is to the sun to shine, or to a living spring to flow, or the the water'd earth by a clear shining after rain to bear; so natural it is unto a principle of grace in the soul to appear in the exercises of holy living." Colman exhulted in "this social nature for worshipping and communicating!" and in the visible beauties of creation: "O what a joy does it give us?" One kind of joy, in addition to the vision of creation, was, for Colman, like Foxcroft, the union of the faithful in public worship. Introducing another sermon, Colman offered a prayer "that many, many of the high and low together, from every worshipping assembly in this great town, may then meet and share in this benediction, and be unto each other, and to their faithful ministers, for a crown of rejoicing." Public worship was an expression of love of God and neighbor, but Colman warned that the "principles of order and worship" were useless if a person were not "gracious in heart." Other activities, of course, also manifested such love and cause for rejoicing that arose from regenerate status. Colman explained that "we unspeakable need one anothers help and service, and unspeakable are the benefits we receive from others in our necessities. The poor serve the rich abundantly, more especially in their sicknesses; and very often do it gratis, for nothing, . . . often (I would wish) from a principle of grace within them, it being all the way they have to express a pious love to God and and their neighbors."[33]

Appleton, preaching before Governor Shirley, addressed the matter of the relation of public and private devotions by way of an excursus on the piety of David and Solomon. With regard to the former, Appleton argued that "altho' David seems to be the composer of the Psalm [72. 1.2.3] under the divine inspiration; yet wee [*sic*] are not to consider it as a prayer of his own meerly for himself, but for publick use, for the people to sing and pray over, in private, but especially in their religious assemblies." Discussing Solomon's use of a prayer taught to him by his parent (Prov. 31.1), Appleton explained similarly that "we may suppose him to make use of this prayer for himself in his private devotions; but especially in public, when he joined with the congregation in the chanting and singing of it."[34]

"Unity," wrote Pemberton, was the "beauty of the world." And the love of God and neighbor that was visible in the activities of the regenerate (such as public worship, service to others, work) was, indeed, one aspect of that beauty. As we have seen, catholicks understood the affections to be of great use in religion, in its private as well as its public dimensions. But the enormous power of love to bond the saints to each other, in the aftermath of conversion, was not derived from a kind of "affection" (in the generic sense) that differed categorically from the affect underlying hate, envy, jealousy, malice, and other destructive, disorderly forms of the "affections" (variously considered). As Appleton explained the matter, "irregular affections" were not "new affections or desires that differ in nature from those that were originally planted in our constitution." Accordingly, catholick recognition of the power of the affection of love was accompanied by acknowledgment of the power of lusts and the dangers that they posed to personal spiritual life and public order. Catholick ministers did not view the human body, by its nature, as a corrupting influence on the spirit. In fact, catholicks believed that a certain amount of indulgence in the pleasures of the flesh was good and could even contribute (as, for example, could music) to the invigoration of piety. Catholicks, however, were keenly aware that "love to God and neighbor" could become love to the world and to oneself. Like other ministers, they believed that a person could become affectionately attached to inappropriate objects (wealth, power, fame) or inordinately attached to appropriate objects (food, drink, sex). When the affections, in general, became "fixed upon improper objects, or carried to an inordinate degree," or when gratification was "pursued in an irregular manner," wrote Appleton, "then they become lusts." Wadsworth likewise warned that "if we inordinately let loose our affections, on any of our outward enjoyments," then trouble would follow. Colman, as we have seen, encouraged laughter but warned against "immoderate mirth" and other forms of "intemperance." It should be noted, moreover, that sins of this sort ("inordinate") came about not essentially as a result of evil flesh's drawing a person into wickedness but, rather, because a person did not remain *actively* engaged in the cultivation of love to God and neighbor. A person blessed with supernatural grace was obliged to nourish the seed of faith and to enlarge it by attendance on the means (prayer, Scripture, public worship, and so on) and through service to others. Sin was understood as the failure of the whole person, body and soul, to respond unceasingly to grace. Such failure left a person increasingly liable to distractions from love to God. Sin was, as Wadsworth explained in his catechism, failure to respond to God: "If we do not love God (fear and trust in him) with all our heart, soul, mind and strength; then we sin by such neglect, Matt. 22. 37. Heb 3.12."[35]

Catholicks, then, like their ministerial colleagues throughout New England, accordingly preached against "lusts." They warned their congregations to fear God and to repent of sinful misdirection of affection toward inappropriate objects. On some occasions, they would strongly and specifically denounce sins of sensuality and "carnality." Such occasions often followed an earthquake, an epidemic of measles, the burning of the meetinghouse, the sudden death of a child, or other such events, at which time—as David D. Hall has written—"fear rose to the surface" of New England life. Unlike Increase Mather, or Mather Byles, or Joshua Gee, however, catholicks remained keenly aware of the power of the affections to order life for good. Catholicks sometimes pictured God as a judge of those who allowed their affections "inordinate" leeway in one form or another. But they did not forget that God was also benevolent. Affirming the beauty and goodness of the body, the capabilities of reason, and the governing of nature by a tender-hearted God, they stressed the importance of the "connecting" affections. The life of the regenerate was not envisioned by them as an intensifying struggle by the individual against the temptations of the world and the flesh. They would not have agreed with Gee when he asserted that "the way of piety," which was "the constant warfare between flesh and spirit," was characterized by the "solitariness of that way." For catholicks, the way of piety certainly demanded self-control and discipline, but it included as well the experience of the beauty of God and creation and the comforts found in union with the saints in a community ordered by love.[36]

To state the matter, again, in terms borrowed from Rudolf Otto: Gee and those who shared his theological ideas were inclined to a view of religion that included a particular stress on the element of *tremendum* and, especially, to the emotional responses of "fear" and "self-depreciation" associated by Otto with that element. Catholicks, on the other hand, although in no way unacquainted with religious fear, tended to offset the paralyzing consequences of fear through their attention to the element of *fascinans,* described by Otto as related to the emotions of "love, mercy, pity, comfort."[37]

In accepting the power of the affections, catholicks took the good with the bad. That is, by emphasizing the importance of the affections in religion, they naturally stressed love of God and neighbor. But they also recognized that any enlivening of the affections ran the risk of generating inordinate or misplaced affection, so that instead of serving to intensify love between godly members of the community, they might, by their sermons, cause social disorder and conflict. This was, of course, precisely the charged leveled against James Davenport and Gilbert Tennent, and George Whitefield as well, during the Great Awakening. Many in New England believed that the preaching of the itinerants, inasmuch as it stirred the affections of those who attended the meetings, also upset the social and ecclesiastical order of New England. Catholicks, as we shall see, did not underestimate the importance of the religion of the "closet." But catholicks were very attentive to the social dimensions of religion. They understood the power of the affections to bind the saints to each other, and they generally envisioned as social the problems that might arise from perversions of the affections.

Catholicks, unlike some other Congregationalist ministers, embraced the entire range of the affections, the "connecting" affections as well as the "separating" affections, as an important component of the religious life. It is important to recognize that Catholicks thus willingly exposed themselves not only to the desirable and beneficial influence of love but also to danger, since perversions of the affections might cause disorder. This does not mean that catholicks simply held their breath and hoped against an outbreak of disruptive paslar persons, should maintain a constant practice of secret prayer. They should enter into their closets, and having shut the door, they should pray, etc., as in Matt. 6.6." Closet duties, as recommended by Foxcroft, included the reading of Scripture, prayer, and various sorts of meditation that formed the foundation for such closet devotion.[44]

In encouraging closet devotions, catholicks were reaffirming the importance of the secret devotional life as practiced by many New Englanders in the seventeenth century. Catholick encouragement of family worship also was a continuation of the devotional practice of previous generations. According to Appleton, Foxcroft, and Colman, the family was a "little society" or "a kind of littler kingdom," something of a middle ground between the individual and the community of the saints, and an important context for worship. Family worship was "a distinct kind of worship from solitary and secret," but it was also a distinct thing from public worship." In family worship, per-
ns prayed, read the Psalms, and engaged together in other kinds of
votional practices, some in the morning, others in the evening.[45]

Catholicks, then, were careful to encourage the cultivation of
er aspects of the religious life besides public worship and the sacra-
ts. Moreover, they warned their congregations against placing too
h spiritual stock in "outward religious performances." Wadsworth
ed, "*We should never concern ourselves meerly with externals in*
on," and Appleton explained, "It is not the outward show, nor
remonies, and circumstantials of religion, that God lays any
upon." Pemberton lamented instances in which "the outward
f religion be preserved, yet there is little close walking with
n spiritual meditation, prayer, and self-examination," and
against "religion degenerated into rituality." Catholicks en-
d public religion, but they were aware that ritual was useful as
s to the faculties, and especially to the affections, only as long
ot constrict and deaden affective piety. For all of their efforts
ing the "sacramental renaissance" of the early eighteenth
tholicks all agreed with Appleton when he preached, "God
the hart even there be no external performance."[46]

eighteenth century, Catholicks shared with other mem-
lergy a concern for the cultivation of secret and family
on Mather, for example, as we have seen, encouraged a
d of secret devotion in *Christianus per Ignem,* and he
of a booklet entitled *Family Religion Urged.* But catho-
e Mathers, Byles, Gee, and some other of the Boston

sion. On the contrary, they endeavored to prevent such an event by emphasizing the importance of ritual, and, especially, of ritual precautions against potentially dangerous consequences of a stirring of the affections. Ritualism is not identical to "routinization," much less so to "intellectualized piety," although the term *ritualistic* is sometimes used (often imprecisely) in connection with references to a vaguely Weberian process of routinization. Ritual can frame a time and a place for minimally structured religious effervescence, as much as it can a time and a place for highly structured, highly elaborated, and comparatively sober forms of worship. In the case of catholick Congregationalists, ritual served both to excite the affections and to guide them in channels appropriate to the purposes of religion. This was not an "intellectualizing" of piety but, rather, an attempt to develop means for the public expression of piety.[38]

David D. Hall has written that as "neighbors fell to quarrelling" and as town life became more complicated near the end of the seventeenth century, ritual—which had been so very important to New England life and which served regularly to restore "fellow feeling"—began to lose its power. Catholicks, responding to this deterioration of ritual just as they responded to the dilution of "neighborliness" in New England society, undertook a program of restoration of ritual, with certain characteristic emphases. It has been suggested that the process of "Anglicization" in New England in the early eighteenth century included the adoption by the Leverett party, in particular, of certain aspects of Anglican ritual. Some of the articles of the Brattle Street *Manifesto* certainly point in that direction. But it was their emphasis on sacramental piety, and especially on the Lord's Supper, that most clearly reflects the interest of catholicks in ritual that both stirred the affections and prevented their causing disorder.[39]

E. Brooks Holifield has argued that there was a "renaissance" of sacramental piety in New England in the early eighteenth century. Catholicks were among the leaders of that renaissance. Pemberton, as early as 1707, was describing the Lord's Supper as a sacrament "for the nourishment of grace." Colman published a "sacramental discourse," a "sermon before the sacrament," in 1728, in which he argued strenuously that persons should participate in the Lord's Supper. The following year, Colman concluded a sermon that was focused largely on the beauty of the body with another recommendation of the Lord's Supper, arguing that it was "an ordinance for us both in body and spirit, as also is baptism," and that "if Christ had not taken flesh and blood, and we were not both flesh and spirit, and to be holy in both and happy in both, this ordinance had not been appointed to us." For Colman, and for other catholicks, the Lord's Supper, in fact, became an instrument of conversion, and part of its nature as a converting ordinance was its capability to move the affections. As early as 1719, Appleton, in a sacramental meditation, had stressed the importance of the Lord's Supper as "a renewal of the covenant between God and us" and a "seal of the covenant of grace," declaring that it was a "means of conversion." "It is an ordinance," Appleton wrote ten years later, that does "stir up our affections, and thereby fit and prepare our hearts for the spirit of God to work upon."[40]

A ritual that so stirred the affections required the observing of certain precautions so that the raised affections would not lead to confusion and disorder. Wadsworth outlined those precautions in his own "sacramental meditation," entitled *A Dialogue between a Minister and His Neighbour about the Lord's Supper* (1724). According to Wadsworth, "Eating and drinking at the Lord's Table is a federal rite, a visible sign or token of a covenant of peace and friendship, and of fellowship and communion between (on the one hand) God in Christ, (and on the other hand) and those who eat and drink at that table." Wadsworth urged Christians to participate in the Lord's Supper "every Lord's Day," but he also made clear that everyone who participated should be at "peace" with his or her neighbors and that "persons distracted or mad" should not attend. Wadsworth's emphasis on being at peace with one's neighbor before attending the sacrament was strongly stated. In effect, it was a ritual precaution against displacement of the power of the sacred from its role in reinforcing fellowship and communion into a mode whereby it became the "bad sacred," manifested as chaos. By requiring as a precaution the settling of quarrels, prior to a person's participation in communion, Wadsworth ensured that emotions would run in the right channels. This protected the integrity of the Lord's Supper as an occasion for enlarging the bonds of love between the participants.[41]

Wadsworth's notion of peace among members of the congregation involved precisely the kind of notion of "neighborliness" that seems to have suffered in eastern Massachusetts in the latter part of the seventeenth century. Wadsworth did not have in mind a superficial exchange of niceties between persons in advance of attending the Lord's Supper. Rather, he expected the genuine resolution of difficulties between persons. Moreover, his sense of neighborliness extended to the importance of neighbors' reproving each other for their bad example or for more serious moral transgressions. Wadsworth wrote

that "the good of the neighborhood or community" required such reproving. He explained that "wise men wont count thee a meddler and a busy-body for it," and asserted that the delivery of a reproc
might very well result in an enriched, closer friendship between neig
bors. This was essentially the view of Thomas Foxcroft as well, v
understood that the "watchman" who led others from their sins a
according to "the eternal rules of compassion."[42]

Alongside their encouragement of sacramental piety, cat
stressed the importance of public worship in general. Persc
were at peace with their neighbors went to the meetinghous
Wadsworth advise them again to "be at peace among yo
And catholicks expected that the experience of public wor
provide an ideal opportunity for the nourishing of that
book that included a preface by Wadsworth, Applet
point that "all private and secret acts of worship" tend
in a person a "devout frame of spirit, but more especi
all acts of public worship." Appleton allowed that
might be used as "helps to conversion, altho' perfo
manner; but they are much more so when they a
assemblies of Christians." Wadsworth set the tone
public worship when he wrote that King David w
God's public worship, on every weekly Sabbat
the House of God (1711), Wadsworth explair
public worship in connection with his view
community: "As they are a people, a society
therefore they should worship God; as a
particular persons in private) they should
fered essentially the same instruction in a
in which he emphasized their public nat
necessity, or in times of persecution, th
administration of baptism or the Lord

This is not to say that catholic
Colman's biographer noted that he
tions and communion with God,"
has strictly requir'd secret and ret
advised persons to "walk closely
relative duties." Colman made
lery company sermon, in whic
gracious woman in the close
than the thunder of the capta
the standard verse of Script

clergy, did not conceive of regeneration essentially as the annihilation of the sinful self—in all of its natural powers and imperfections—but, rather, as the resuscitation of the faculties through grace. God was often envisioned by catholicks as a benevolent father, drawing his adopted children toward him, rather than as a chastising judge. Catholicks did not believe, as did post-Awakening Arminians such as Lemuel Briant or Ebenezer Gay, that justification in God's sight was essentially a matter of morality, built on the detection of natural laws by reason. For catholicks, each person was born corrupted as a result of Adam's sin and for that reason could never be justified before God without saving grace. It was in this spirit that Appleton preached a sermon entitled *The Usefulness and Necessity of Gifts: but the Transcendent Excellency of Grace.*

The Catholick clergy believed that grace enlivened and refined the faculties and in a way so gradual and sometimes so subtle that the time of conversion—the turning from sin to God—could not be precisely known. The turning of a person to God required repentance, especially in the form of weaning of the affections from inappropriate objects, but it involved the experience of delight or joy in God's immensity and majesty as well. Because the religious experience of the regenerate was characterized by continued delight in God, and because catholicks were not inclined to a view of conversion as the annihilation of the self at a particular point in time, it may not be entirely appropriate to speak of the "aftermath" of conversion for catholicks. For catholicks, regeneration was an ongoing process, sometimes involving contrition for sinful habits, sometimes a drawing closer to God in joy, and always a matter of the progressive enlargement of a person's portion of grace. Regeneration also included the intertwining of the individual with the community of the regenerate, and this relationship was characterized by the bonds of affection between persons. For catholicks, personal piety—of an affective sort—and public religion were inextricably bound.[47]

5

The Community of the Regenerate

The catholick clergy believed that the regenerate lived as neighbors, guided by love in their relations with one another. Catholicks also believed, however, that just as religious ritual served both to excite and to channel the affections, so also should social life in general have some measure of structure so that the affection between persons did not become perverted and misdirected into channels that were harmful to the community. Accordingly, they affirmed certain precautions against such an occurrence.

At the foundation of catholick thinking about the individual and society were, as Colman wrote, "the superior laws of revealed religion." Colman summarized these laws as follows: "For we are instructed from the divine oracles: 'To love our nei'bours as ourselves' . . . that we be kindly affectioned one to another in brotherly love, in honour preferring one another." Underlying this teaching, however, was the assumption that a person must love himself or herself in order to love others, since the loving of a neighbor was more or less an extension of self-love. This was precisely the message that Wadsworth wished to transmit when he wrote that God "has implanted in all men, a natural self-love and desire of self-preservation. This is plainly implied in that divine precept, love thy neighbour as thy self. . . . This supposes a self-love which is our duty." Colman, even while preaching against the "hainous nature of the sin of murder," affirmed, "Self-love, and self-preservation, are an invincible principle, and law, implanted by God in the hearts of men." In a letter to a colleague, Colman explained more forcefully that "self-love yet stands in us *next* to the love of God," and that "the first stamp of his blessed image on his intelligent creatures is—*invisible self-love.*" Foxcroft went so far as to identify this principle as an innate passion that guided a person along a course toward perfection: "For self-love is a fundamental principle in human nature. Everything has an innate and invincible *Conatus* or endeavour and propensity towards its own perfection and welfare: And every regular exercise of this natural passion is undoubtedly our proper duty." Catholicks recognized both "self" and "love" in their thinking about the relationship between persons in society.[1]

Affirmation of self-love had not always been a part of the thinking of New Englanders. According to Stephen Foster, the first settlers of the Bay Colony believed that "the self and self-love were two of the results" of the fall. For these New Englanders, "all vice proceeded from self-love, all virtue from self-denial." John Winthrop articulated this notion, writing that "every man is borne with this principle in him, to love and seeke himselfe onely and thus a man continueth till Christ comes and takes possession of the soule, and infuseth another principle love to God and our brother." Thomas Hooker agreed, that in "this vile, vain *Body* of ours," self-love was contrary to virtue. The factors leading to a change of attitude among New Englanders toward self-love are surely various and complicated. It is likely, however, that the growth of a sense of interrelatedness and harmony in cosmic order and the acceptance of life in the flesh as an aspect of that order helped to set the stage for a reappraisal of the notion of the self and with it self-love. In the case of catholicks, there was also the influence of latitudinarian writings, which promoted self-love in a variety of ways. John Wilkins, thinking of cosmic order in general terms, wrote that "everything is endowed with such a natural principle, whereby it is necessarily inclined to promote its own preservation and well-being." Simon Patrick, in a familiar turn of phrase, explained that "God hath made the love of ourselves the pattern whereby we are to love our neighbours." Archbishop Tillotson extended the argument to include the idea of "happiness": "one of the first principles that is planted in the nature of man, and which lies at the very root and foundation of his being, is the desire of his own preservation and happiness."[2]

Catholick Congregationalists for the most part absorbed the spirit of statements such as these and even occasionally suggested, as did Wadsworth, that "man's . . . chief end is God's glory and his own happiness . . . and if they are not the same, yet they are so closely connected that they cannot be separated one from the other." Catholicks, as we shall see, did not overlook the material and emotional benefits derived from activity that was generated by self-love. But it would be inaccurate to depict their point of view as essentially grounded in an expectation of happiness through a merely rational approach to social life. Richard L. Bushman has argued that self-love became, after the Great Awakening, a notion more akin to rational "self-interest" and was often referred to, especially among "rationalist" opponents of the revival, in connection with the desire of the individual for happiness. According to Bushman, "the rationalists who made the satisfaction of human desires the main end of government, seemed to think that self-interest, if enlightened, could be given a free rein and made the very foundation of civil society." But for catholicks, self-love remained largely a religious duty, although the seeds for change that came later are detectable in their thinking. More important, the self-love that served as a point of reference to love of one's neighbors was understood by catholicks to follow from the infusion of grace. Self-love was not naked self-interest by any means, nor was it even (for the most part) the individualistic "pursuit of happiness." Rather, as it was present among the regenerate, it was closely connected to love of God. Without the grace that directed a person toward God, self-love became selfishness.[3]

Those ministers who place a predominant emphasis on God as a judge, on the evil of the body over against the purity of the soul, and on guilt, fear, and shame in spiritual development were less inclined to speak about the bonds of love between persons in society. They also generally took a dim view of self-love. The philosopher John Passmore, commenting on Teresa of Avila's worry that she was not "entirely detached" from the world because of her love for her sister, wrote that "it is loves which make life worth living, which hold us to this world, which illuminate and enliven it. In that sense, love . . . must appear the great enemy to those who wish to deny the world." As I have made clear, I do not believe that ministers such as Joshua Gee, Nicholas Noyes, or Cotton Mather rejected love as an important aspect of Christian life. However, these ministers did conceive of religion largely in terms of the detachment of oneself from the flesh and the world. Thus their cautions against or condemnation of self-love make sense in the context of their thinking. Cotton Mather, discussing the Old Testament aphorism "Do unto others as you would have others do unto you" (rather than the New Testament commandment to love others as oneself), argued, "self-love is the principal venom and effect of our apostacy." Nicholas Noyes, also taking his texts from the Old Testament, connected religious decline in New England with the observation "self-love can blind men's eyes, in what concerns themselves, so as they shall not be able to see the faults in themselves; though they be very quick in seeing faults in others." Joshua Gee made a similar observation, wedged in between a condemnation of the passions and a reminder that life was a war between flesh and spirit: "A principle of self-love will not suffer wicked men to seek and delight in one anothers welfare, any further than will consist with their own private interest."[4]

For catholicks, self-love, as a point of departure for loving action toward one's neighbors, was a religious duty. Self-love and love of neighbor, although not identical, therefore were very closely related one to the other. Catholicks did not offer much in the way of formal definition of this relationship, but in their writings on such matters as commerce and government, some aspects of their thinking can be glimpsed. It is fair to say, however, that catholicks realized that a social order founded simply on "brotherly love" was insufficient for the organization of economic and political life. There are several reasons for this. First, catholicks believed that the regenerate life was characterized by constant endeavoring to draw closer to God and to one's neighbor through the use of the recognized means of grace and through service to others in the world. It was through *activity* in the world that, ideally, the brethren were served. Catholicks understood, however, that self-love could become selfishness when such activity was not undertaken for the glory of God. Just as the stirring of the affections in rituals such as the Lord's Supper required some measure of precaution to ensure that they were not misdirected, so also did the exercise of self-love require some precautions. In the absence of a focus on God, self-love might become distracted into inappropriate forms of activity. (The consequences of this could be particularly serious if self-love up to that point had been growing stronger alongside love of neighbor.) Just as Wadsworth urged the members of his congregation to be at peace with one another before attending the Lord's Supper, so also did catholicks propose that activity in the world be guided by the avoidance of "narrow interest" and by dedication of oneself to the common good.[5]

While emphasizing brotherly love as the guiding influence on social order, catholicks proposed certain precautions against possible perversions of self-love. Such proposals were in many cases reiterations of statements about the necessity for personal dedication to the public welfare that had appeared in the sermons of ministers in the seventeenth-century. In other cases, the stamp of catholick thinking is more clearly detectable. In fact, some scholars, notably T. H. Breen and J. E. Crowley, drawing evidence from the writings of Colman, Wadsworth, Foxcroft, and Pemberton, have argued that catholick statements about government and commerce signal a retreat from the belief that the social order should be (or even could be) founded on religious ideals. Catholicks did not abandon tradition, however. Although there are some new directions apparent in catholick thinking, a strong sense of religious duty and of the importance of piety remained fundamental to the catholick view of social life.[6]

The infusion of supernatural grace into the soul set a person on a course of activity in the world. Charles Cohen has written that the "quintessence of godly love" was for Puritans such as Richard Sibbes not the notion of "an abstracted love and affection, but of love in our places, and callings, and standings, love invested in action." This idea, which was affirmed by Thomas Shepard, developed in the seventeenth century partly as a result of the influence of the Ramist emphasis on practicality and "living well." It was embraced by the catholick clergy and formed a substantial part of the foundation for their preaching on the obligations of the Christian. Practical activity was the end of knowledge of God, and this idea was expressed by catholicks in various ways, with regard to doctrine and piety. Wadsworth, in the course of eulogizing John Leverett, lauded the activities of the deceased and informed the audience: "Practice is the end of knowledge; to understand the best laws and rules can advantage us nothing, if our behaviour be not answerable." Foxcroft made the same point about the relation of knowledge to some practical result. He stated that "there is no doctrine of natural or revealed religion so abstruse and speculative, but some practical application may be made of it." According to Foxcroft, even " 'those mysteries, that seem to be most contemplative and remote from practice' " did in some way tend "to the advancement of practical piety." Colman, in a lecture entitled "Industry and Diligence in the Work of Religion," argued that "a principle of divine grace in the soul" was inextricably bound with "the exercises of holy living."

Pemberton was more explicit in his pronouncements about the matter. Offering the wisdom that each human being was "a creature capable of action, and design," he added that "every man is endowed with active powers." In writing about the soul, Pemberton asserted in 1704 that "activity is of its essence, without which it would cease to be a living soul. Life consists in action." Eight years later he reiterated this opinion: "If the soul does exist it must act; for activity is the nature of it." As far as Pemberton was concerned, the active nature of the soul therefore required that persons find in life some practical activity in which to invest themselves: "The very make and constitution of humanity will infer, that man was designed for action, and sent into the world to have these faculties of operation duly employ'd about some proper business."[7]

One's "proper business" in life was, of course, one's "calling." As Pemberton wrote, "every private Christian" was obliged to undertake, in addition to the general calling to love and serve God, "the work of his own particular calling." Charles Cohen has argued, in fact, that the calling was "an epitome of godly love" and a leading characteristic of the life of the regenerate in a community ordered by love. As developed by English Puritans—who drew on the ideas of Luther and Calvin—the notion of a particular calling included the premise that all activity engaged in by men and women in the world should be undertaken for the glory of God. A particular calling was understood to be a life lived in such a way as to contribute to the common good. The purpose of a particular calling was not to gain individual wealth or status but to serve God and neighbor. Moreover, a calling was not a part-time activity. Fundamental to the conception of the calling was the idea that labor in the world, for the glory of God, was unceasing. As Stephen Foster has written: "Precisely *because* men labored for God and *not* for gold (or status or honor), they had to continue in their callings constantly." A calling thus served in a general way as a framework for activity in the world, guiding the energy and the emotion of the regenerate into appropriate channels. It intertwined love of God with social life, giving direction and shape to the affectionate relationship with one's neighbors. The religious obligation of a calling kept a person pointed toward God in everyday life and thereby helped to prevent the sidetracking of self-love into selfishness.[8]

The constant effort made in connection with one's particular calling was generally referred to as diligence. Catholicks, like other members of the New England clergy, spoke regularly about the importance of diligence as a religious duty. In fact, so numerous are the references to the necessity for diligence and industry in the writings of catholick clergy (and other clergy) that almost any sampling of their work will include them. There are also to be found numerous references to idleness and laziness (or "sloth"), which were perceived as the antitheses of diligence and industry. The religious dimension of the problem of idleness was often present in such references, as in Wadsworth's warning that "idleness is the devils' school." Colman, in recommending a "holy and useful life," asserted that "we come into the world for service, and not to be idle, useless and insignificant in it." Foxcroft preached that divine providence (as formal cause) had caused an earthquake (as secondary cause) in Boston in 1727 at least partly in order "to awake out of that criminal sloth & indolent trifling way of spending their precious time, which multitudes are guilty of." Wadsworth likewise argued the dangers of idleness in a consideration of tavern-frequenting: "How often do Christians occasionally meet with one another, and spend several minutes, half-hours, nay it may be whole hours in needless idle discourse." It would have been much better, said Wadsworth, "if they had spent those precious opportunities" in such a way as to further their "mutual spiritual edification."[9]

Idleness endangered the social order based on love of neighbor by contradicting the obligation to labor constantly in a calling. Another threat to the social order was related to not the absence of acting but misdirected acting, otherwise known as the exercise of a "narrow spirit." Like the warning against idleness, clerical disdain for persons of narrow spirit was not new to the eighteenth century. Catholick clergy repeated the words of their predecessors in condemning it. Typical was Foxcroft's declaration "See the folly and shame of a narrow little soul, a self-seeking spirit, which contracts all your care & tho't within the limits of your own private interest, or party concerns." Opposition to a narrow spirit, and, especially, to "party-concerns," was, of course, a key feature of the catholick view of religion. Party concern and factionalism, whether in society in general or more specifically in government, commerce, or church matters, was selfishness, an absence of concern for the good of the whole. And catholicks were particularly vocal in condemning it in all of these areas. Narrowness, wherever it might be found, was in direct conflict with the catholick spirit. Pemberton, for example, could advise ministers that they "must avoid all actions that will argue them to be under the influence of narrow and stingy spirits." He could also describe the deficient soldier in these terms: "A private spirit, under the government of narrow and stingy principles, is not a martial spirit; it is a blemish on the Man of war." For Pemberton, such persons need not apply to serve in the artillery company: "Such will prefer their own private service before the common tranquility: A man of a private spirit, though very solicitous about the safety of his own cabbine; yet is little thoughtful for the welfare of the bottom, in which his all is embarked."[10]

Private interest was always to give way to public good. Appleton pointed out that "to serve some private interest" was "to gratify a selfish spirit." Foxcroft argued, "True piety gives men a public spirit," and "it teaches them the superlative importance of the public good, above all private interests." "Some there are," said Foxcroft, who "are zealous on the prospect of some secular advantage. Worldly interest is the predominant motive." Such persons should learn that "we must prefer the publick good, before a private interest." It therefore was essential, according to Pemberton, "to get a selfish spirit mortified. For this will clogg us in our" serving our generation "and be a false byas upon us, which will carry us off from our publick views, in pursuit of our private sordid interests." Service to one's generation was achieved through "exposing our private interests to any hazzards," and no private interests were "too dear, nay, not life itself, to part with, for the advantage of our people." As Pemberton wrote, "There is a regular self-love which will calculate all its designs to the public good; but a vicious self-love only to private interests."[11]

Catholicks regularly emphasized the religious aspect of the duty to support the public good (and to avoid selfishness) in work. Wadsworth affirmed to his congregation that when persons are "projecting and contriving how to employ themselves and. . . . how to manage even their outward secular affairs; they should still keep their eye fix'd on God's glory as their end." Foxcroft stressed that "the duties of a man's general, and of his particular calling, may stand well together. A man's general calling, as he is a Christian, does not nullify, but rather confirm his particular calling, and makes it sanctified unto him." It was the "will of God," wrote Pemberton, "that every man's private interest be subordinated for the good of the whole." Pemberton told his congregation to "make the work of religion a man's business in life," and he explained that persons were to "manage secular affairs" so as to make them "subservient to this business."[12]

J. E. Crowley has attempted to chart the development of the rise of a "morally neutral view of work" in America in the eighteenth century. Surveying the decades leading up to the Great Awakening, Crowley, citing as evidence statements made by Colman, Pemberton, and Wadsworth (among other writers in New England and other colonies), argues that there occurred during that time "a loss of confidence in the old social order, an order based on religious ideals." For Crowley, the religious notion of work, of diligent activity in the world carried out for the good of the whole, gave way to the "legacy" of the calling, or a social philosophy that was characterized by "the emphasis on the public good, and the denial of unrestrained economic individualism." In the process, "The concept of the calling lost its religious integrity and the general and personal callings were separated." Colonists continued to believe well into the eighteenth century that morality and work were closely related, but the religious valuation of work, and, in particular, the sense of *religious* obligation to serve the public good and to restrain one's private interest, were lost. Eventually, a morally neutral view of work came to characterize the American attitude toward economic life, although this view was not articulated until after the Revolution.[13]

There were some aspects of catholick thinking (that I will suggest later) that may well have contributed to the eventual deterioration of a sense of religious obligation in economic life (inasmuch as those ideas were appropriated by later writers). Nevertheless, contra Crowley, catholicks themselves remained strongly convinced that social life as love to neighbor was grounded in religion, and, especially, in the regeneration of persons through grace. The concern for public good over private interest, *as a religious obligation,* rather than as a natural law of some sort, is illustrated with particular clarity in sermons by Colman and Foxcroft. In *The Religious Regards We Owe Our Country* (1718), an election sermon, Colman argued that "no man is made only for himself and his own private affairs, but to serve, profit and benefit others. We are manifestly formed for society, and designed by our Great Creator for a mutual dependence on and serviceableness unto each other here in the body." According to Colman, these were the "principles of the Stoicks," which included as well the belief that "we should love all mankind heartily, solicit their interests," and that each person should "exert himself for the public." Had Colman ended with this, then, indeed, we might identify him as a major voice in the transformation of religious duty into rational virtue. However, Colman continued his explanation, calling attention to the "superiour laws of revealed religion." Colman argued that "the *phylanthropy* of our Saviour was more than *humane.* It was a God-like life of love to mankind. . . . And this is his commandement that we love one another, that we love mankind as he has done." Colman noted that the apostles had done this and that their love differed fundamentally from that proposed by the Stoics: "And this they did on those spiritual principles, reasons and motives, which never enter'd into the morals of the heathen, but are peculiar to the Gospel of the grace of God." Paul, in fact, was actually "forced by the love of God to seek the weal of mankind, private and public." Colman then summarized his argument in language that demonstrated quite clearly that by love of neighbor and concern for the public good he had in mind a religious obligation, not a form of social order that was merely rational and ethical. Colman told the governor and the assembly, "Let us not be content to act from a meer human vertue, but from a principle of grace rooted deep in our souls, that what we do for the public may indeed be done for God."[14]

Foxcroft, the following year, proposed a similar argument. Foxcroft was extremely concerned about Christian service in the interest of the common good. In fact, one of the two or three longest lists of citations in his notebook came under the heading "public-spiritedness." That his thinking about this matter followed closely that of Colman was no accident, because his citations on the subjects were drawn in large part from Colman and Pemberton. In *Cleansing Our Way in Youth* (1719), Foxcroft juxtaposed duty to God arising from the "grace of love" to the thinking of the "ethnick philosophers." Foxcroft explained that "the school of nature was never so illuminated, as to be able to teach us our universal duty." He stressed that "purity of intention is a necessary qualification, yea, the very life & soul of a good work." Moreover, this was something that the ancients lacked in their philosophy: "As for the pagan philosophers, they were most notoriously deficient in this matter. In their most refined morals, they never mentioned it. They chiefly recommended vertue, only as the way to honor and ease in the world, or means of pleasure and internal peace." It was not virtue understood as the rational ordering of social life, as the careful regulation of private interest, but, rather, virtue as pure religious morality that Foxcroft expected his listeners to embrace. Accordingly, he explained that as far as "those duties that are moral" were concerned, "the word of God is a most necessary and sufficient guide unto us," providing a system of "moral vertues, such as the best masters of morality in the heathen world cou'd never afford. Their purest ethicks were stain'd with impure mixtures, with corrupt precepts." For Foxcroft, like Colman, the morality that governed social life was rooted in religion and the personal ease or pleasure in the world that might arise from the practice of virtue was not the end of virtue. The intention behind the work—that is, work performed for the glory of God—was what mattered.[15]

This is not to say, however, that catholicks rejected any enjoyment of the fruit of their labors in the world. Catholick understanding of self-love was based on acknowledgment of the connection between love of self and love of neighbor. Grace nourished the growth of communion with God and neighbor, but, as Wadsworth pointed out, in so doing, it contributed at the same time to the spiritual advancement of the individual. Wadsworth preached, "The more we grow in grace and holiness, so much the more profitable it will be for ourselves. God is so good & gracious that he has made a close communion between our duty & interest." Foxcroft advanced this line of thinking by linking it with a high appraisal of life in the world. Foxcroft told a congregation that "life, the life of man, even common and natural life, *especially* when attended with outward comforts, is a valuable good, of great consideration, & high account." Foxcroft was careful to explain that a life restored by grace to communion with God was the highest good, but he argued nevertheless that "human life is a thing of value, *high value,* an excellent good, and especially when brightened with honourable & happy circumstances in the world." Religion, for Foxcroft, contributed directly to the arrival at happy circumstances. Preaching in 1719, he declared that a person who paid close attention to spiritual improvement early in life was likely "to obtain greater blessings in this life, both spiritual and secular." For Foxcroft, temperance and frugality "and the like virtues are the surest method to promote our outward prosperity.—Art thou poor and low in this world? Religion will contribute to your advancement." Wadsworth suggested the corollary of this principle, namely, that lack of attention to one's spiritual well-being could be detrimental to economic life. Wadsworth warned against the dangers of needlessly exposing oneself to temptation: "Ill-company keeping . . . Tends to hinder persons in their worldly business and employment."[16]

Statements that seem to legitimate the enjoyment of worldly comforts that were gained through industry and diligence in one's calling should be seen, however, in the context of more numerous and precise statements encouraging support of the common good. Catholicks generally agreed with Appleton that a man "may indeed have a view to his private interest, to the support and benefit of his family, but then he always subjects his private interest to the public good." In fact, catholicks were keenly aware that commercial life, based on the notion of the calling, could degenerate into purely selfish activity. Catholicks, for all of their advocacy of brotherly love as the guide to social life, concluded that economic relations were to be structured, in some measure, by legal regulations. Holyoke worried about merchants who "deceive in their falsehood as to their merchandize and sale of things. . . . Mammon is their God." Appleton likewise condemned "the Mammon of unrighteousness." Colman worried about the loss of "beauty" in matters of trade asserting, "I am ready to think that the special care for a just medium of trade and commerce belongs to the government of people." Wadsworth, in a sermon entitled *Fraud and Injustice Detected* (1712), condemned "oppresive usury" and selling at an "excessive rate," and he scolded those who "cheat and deceive." He developed particular aspects of this under headings such as "10. When persons detain just wages, or defer the seasonable payment of just debts." Appleton probably took particular interest in this last complaint of Wadsworth, as he was forced to go to court in order to recover a debt of 264 pounds owed to him by Cotton Mather.[17]

Colman's tending toward the view that laws governing trade were needed ought not to be seen in exactly the same way as the call made by Wadsworth for the ritual precaution of "being at peace" before participation in the Lord's Supper. First, Colman's assigning to government the legal regulation of trade differs from the personal and probably less formal initiative to settle quarrels that was recommended by Wadsworth. Colman had in mind the rational-legal organization of social life, not the personal and emotional encounter of persons seeking to overcome impediments to their love for each other. In the second place, those who attended the Lord's Supper—the regenerate—had received grace for love of God and neighbor, whereas many persons in the social world of trade and commerce were unregenerate or unchurched. Colman suggested as much when he observed that there were in New England in the early eighteenth century "more mixt people, and acting on more worldly views, Maxims, and customs." Colman, like other catholicks, seemed to have remained optimistic, for the most part, about the eventual triumph of religion over selfish "customs," however. He did not view New England society as did the Englishman Edward Ward, who observed during his visit to Boston: "But tho' they wear in their faces the innocence of doves, you will find them in their dealings, as subtile as serpents. Interest is their faith, Money their God, and large possessions the only heaven they covet." Catholicks nevertheless proceeded cautiously in their thinking about commerce, arguing the necessity for rules of trade, in part to guide the regenerate but also to restrain the unregenerate.[18]

Although J. E. Crowley has overlooked some important features of the thinking of Colman, Wadsworth, and Pemberton (for example, the religious basis of labor), it nevertheless seems to me that his claim that these ministers contributed in some measure to the "secularization" of economic life—if qualified and softened—is defensible. I would suggest, however, that the logical basis for this claim is found not in the apparent support voiced by Colman and Wadsworth for regulation, or routinization of economic life (although that is relevant), but, rather, in a larger, more central theme of catholick thought. Catholicks, believing in an ordered universe, came to accept the world, the body, and the enjoyment of physical comfort and favorable "circumstances" in advance of other members of the clergy. Their acceptance of life in the body as a part of a plan of order in a universe of interconnected phenomena contributed substantially to their sense of the importance and usefulness of the affections in religion, and, consequently, to their notion of social life as ordered by love. It is ironic that their ideas about the value of life in the body also contributed, probably more than any other part of their thinking, to the emergence of a market society in which rational self-interest was aimed at the accumulation of wealth, and not the glory of God, as its chief end. In fashioning a conceptual foundation for the support of affectionate religion and spiritualized social life, catholicks also contributed indirectly to the emergence of a largely secularized view of at least one aspect of social life. Such a view emerged not in their writings, however, but in the works of later writers, who separated catholick emphasis on religious obligation in social life from an equal emphasis on order and good in creation.

The views of catholicks on government also were rooted in a religious view of society. This is not the belief of T. H. Breen, who has argued that a "court" faction (as opposed to those holding to a "country" ideology), which emerged in the early eighteenth century, deemphasized the religious aspects of government that had been present in early New England. According to Breen, the "court" persuasion was characterized by at least four emphases: (1) a profiling of the character of the good ruler that left only the colonial elite eligible to hold office; (2) an absence of emphasis on the importance of rulers as "the Lord's viceregents on earth," endowed with special God-given talents for officeholding; (3) a lack of concern about whether the ruler was of the elect, because "the state of the magistrates soul was his own business"; (4) a consequent emphasis on "outwardly visible characteristics" such as "education, wealth, and breeding" in identification of the attributes required of a magistrate. The central figures in the articulation of this position, were, according to Breen, Wadsworth ("court minister"), Foxcroft ("court author"), Pemberton ("one of

Boston's more articulate court ministers"), and some other individuals, including Colman. As a way of sketching some aspects of the thinking of catholicks on government, I will address these claims in connection with writings by Wadsworth, Foxcroft, Pemberton, and Colman, suggesting in the process ways in which Breen's analysis is deficient.[19]

Wadsworth preached an election sermon in 1716 and proposed that "very eminent qualifications are needed" for governing. Arguing that "civil government is of divine institution," Wadsworth explained that the two qualifications most desirable in a ruler were "integrity" and "skilfulness." Addressing the matter of integrity first, he described how David had been called from his place as a shepherd "to be a political shepherd to Israel." David was fit for such a position, first of all, because of his piety. Wadsworth argued, "The more any person is after God's own heart, the more inclin'd to fulfill his will; so much the more fit he is to be a ruler." Integrity was a matter of the heart, Wadsworth said, and integrity grew as the heart grew closer to God. David ruled Israel so that "his very soul was indeed ingag'd in it." This was "highly reasonable and needful," because "such a peculiar treasure as God's covenant people were committed to him." David's integrity enabled him to rule over his countrymen in such a way that he was "diligently imploy'd in caring for them, and in promoting their welfare."

Alongside integrity, skill was required of a ruler. David's skill consisted in his "knowledge, understanding, [and] prudence." Wadsworth did not describe skill as a consequence of wealth or breeding. David had been a shepherd before being called to rule Israel. As Wadsworth explained in the course of the sermon, those qualities associated with "skilfulness" enabled a ruler to "consult the good of the whole, the public universal welfare of their people." Arguing that "he that prefers any private advantage to the public good" was a "traitor" to the people, Wadsworth stressed that rulers "should endeavour to prevent what they can, siding, party-making, factions & divisions among" the body politic. The good ruler, for Wadsworth, was qualified for office largely on the basis of "inward," not "outward," characteristics, and his piety, the condition of his soul, was fundamental to the prosecution of his duties as a shepherd to the people. This was entirely appropriate, since government was instituted by God. Wadsworth certainly did not believe that preparation for office, such as an education at the college, was to be overlooked in the judgment of a ruler's qualifications. But in this election sermon, he profiled the good ruler in such a way as to show him in a religious light, not according to the visible evidences of worldly accomplishment.[20]

Ebenezer Pemberton, in his election sermon of 1710, also stressed that rulers "are God's viceregents" and that "all rulers of what degree soever are ordain'd by God." Pemberton stressed throughout the sermon the connection between the ruler's inward state and outward performance, arguing in various ways that it was most desirable that "their external condition may be found in conjunction with the more valuable inherent dignity of a vertuous mind." The "invisible and spiritual image of God" that was desirable in a ruler "consists in righteousness, and all the graces of holiness." Pemberton stressed, moreover, that "external characters of power" were not in themselves sufficient as qualifications for officeholding: "Power and knowledge will not alone constitute a divine greatness; these are to be found to a great degree in the most malignant beings, who are nothing but opposition to the nature and government of God." Since "good rulers are the most lively emblems of God on earth," they "must be god-like in their personal endowments." But rulers also should not forget that they have a great deal in common with the people. In fact, quoting Pascal, Pemberton argued that rulers "are to take a prospect of themselves in their natural condition of infirmity and equality with the rest of mankind." Pemberton thus expressed in this election sermon the view that government was of divine institution, that the ruler was the vice-regent of God, that he was blessed with special endowments, and that the inner condition of his soul was more important to his office than the external characters of his accomplishment. Pemberton certainly expected that education and experience served a person well as preparation for high office. But, like Wadsworth, he acknowledged the usefulness of such qualifications essentially in their conjunction with the "spiritual image of God in the soul."[21]

Thomas Foxcroft's thinking about government is apparent in his funeral sermon for Penn Townsend, a Boston wine merchant who held numerous positions of public trust, as a member of the council, a representative, the speaker of the house, and chief justice of the Suffolk Superior Court. Subtitling his sermon "Mordecai's Character," Foxcroft explained the character of the ruler with reference to the life of that Old Testament leader. Foxcroft made clear at the outset of his sermon that Mordecai rose "from sheep-hook to sceptre," that is, that "this man of God rose from low beginnings in an admirable manner, to the highest preferments." Stressing the movement of Mordecai upward in the social order, Foxcroft detailed this notion as follows: "There's a variety of orders and conditions among men: some moving in a lower, and others in a higher sphere. And sometimes by very observable turns of providence, persons are raised up to a considerable height of dignity and human greatness, that were once of low degree. Mordecai is an instance of this revolution and advancement." As a leader of his people, Mordecai took care to pay the strictest attention to the "public good." Moreover, he was a man of deep piety, and "he doubtless was in his closet daily the Lord's remembrancer for Zion." Drawing an application from this exposition of the character of Mordecai, Foxcroft explained, "True piety gives men a public spirit." According to Foxcroft, "It teaches them the superlative importance of the public good, above all private interests." Foxcroft, then, obviously supposed that a good ruler might indeed come from humble beginnings. Moreover, the good ruler, in serving the public good over his private interest, was guided by piety. Again, the state of the ruler's soul was considered highly relevant to suitability for office.[22]

Colman's election sermon of 1718, to which I have referred, also took as its point of departure the biblical account of the life of Nehemiah, who became the governor of Judea. Urging his audience to "chuse from among your brethren men of piety and virtue," Colman preached at great length on the necessity for love to God and neighbor. Ruling out acquaintance with "soft clothing," "sumptuous living," and "delicious fare" as a character of a good ruler, Colman told Governor Shute that Nehemiah "did not eat the bread of the Governor" but rather called the people to "renew their covenant with God." Although Colman did not expect that his contemporaries should follow Nehemiah's example in every regard, he did propose to his audience that they imitate him in governing the land with an eye "to the interests of God in it." Colman urged his audience: "Let us emulate Nehemiah's piety in this heroic instance of it. And indeed, this is the true heroic vertue and piety, to endeavour in our places to deserve well of mankind, and in the most extensive manner, wherein we can to honour God in the world." Magistrates, like all men and women, were to act "from a principle of grace rooted deep in our souls, that what we do for the public may be indeed done for God." Neither "outward life style" nor "inward" virtue—understood as rational and compassionate treatment of one's neighbor arising from philosophical suppositions—was the foundation of good government. Rather, it was religious piety and a principle of grace in the soul that were desirable in a ruler.[23]

It might be noted that Appleton, in his own view of government, was in agreement with the points made by other catholicks. Preaching an election sermon in 1742, he stated flatly, "I can by no means think of any man fit to be employed in government, that is not a man of prayer." It would be folly, argued Appleton, "to commit any share of government to such who are known as to live without God in the world." Observing that God had given men and women rules by which to live together in society, Appleton explained that even this was not a sufficient basis for government; that is, he argued that a ruler must have more than just a grasp of rules. "It is not sufficient for rulers to have good rules," said Appleton. Rulers must have a "principle of righteousness and holiness in their heart." It was the "righteousness of God in his heart" that enabled the ruler "to imitate the divine pattern."[24]

Catholicks, then, understood the good ruler to be a man of piety, who as God's "viceregent" acted from a principle of grace to protect and enrich the public good. Although this analysis of catholick thinking about government departs substantially from the interpretation offered by Breen, it might be noted that Breen is largely correct in his view that catholicks were to some extent worried about a possible outbreak of "anarchy." But I prefer to state this concern as their acknowledging of the fragility, or unpredictability, of a social order based on a religious worldview that stressed the importance of the affectionate uniting of persons. Just as they supported legal guidelines to economic life, catholicks supported the faithful administration of good laws governing the relations between citizens. But it would be a mistake to see this as their primary emphasis in thinking about government. Rather, they remained committed to a view of social life that rested on the belief that the regenerate, as they grew in holiness and numbers, would be able to live together under the guidance of increasing love. Rules of commerce and laws of government were precautions that were necessary to keep affection running in its proper channels, to prevent self-love from detaching itself from love of neighbor and wandering into selfishness, or the unbridled pursuit of private interest.

The social life of Christians, although it unfolded according to the principle of brotherly love, nevertheless required some measure of guidance in the form of regulations governing economic life and the observance of certain customs in political life. Perhaps most significant, however, among the ways in which catholicks attempted to elaborate and apply the principle of brotherly love to social life was their encouragement to their congregations to imitate the example of others. Exhortation to the imitation of the examples of holy persons had been a standard feature of Christianity virtually throughout its history. In late antiquity, we find as a characteristic feature of Christianity "the holy man as 'Christ-carrying' exemplar." Medieval collections of saints' lives, such as *The Golden Legend,* and later emphasis on the *imitatio Christi,* in books such as the classic attributed to Thomas à Kempis, formed a rich tradition on which Reformers drew, in their own thinking about example. In England, the Anglican minister Jeremy Taylor's popular *The Life of Christ: or the Great Exemplar* was first published in 1649, and many editions followed. English Puritans, sensing a difference between a "pure" Christ and "sensual" humanity, tended to view the notion of a true "imitation of Christ" as a conceit and more commonly looked to the lives of the saints as examples. In New England, some ministers proposed to their congregations the imitation of Christ's life but qualified their encouragements in certain ways. Cotton Mather, whose diary is filled with references to his attempts to imitate Christ, viewed such imitation, according to Robert Middlekauff, essentially as an effort to overcome "the promptings of the flesh." Mather was generally pessimistic about the possibilities for victory in such an engagement, however, so that he "took pains in a number of sermons to remind his church that of course they could not conform to Christ in every respect."[25]

Catholick clergy do not seem to have been as cautious as Mather in recommending the example of Christ to their congregations. Colman, Wadsworth, Foxcroft, Pemberton, and Appleton all stressed that Jesus Christ had been fully human and fully divine and encouraged persons to seek to imitate, as Appleton preached, "the holiness that Christ manifested in his life & conversation." Although in no way overlooking the importance of the atonement of Christ, catholicks tended to be more optimistic than Mather about the possibility for persons to model themselves truly after Christ. Catholick attitudes toward the flesh and the world probably contributed in part to this optimism, but they likely also were influenced in that direction by latitudinarian writers, whose own "optimism," as J. Sears McGee has argued, led them to stress "the ease of imitation of Christ after conversion." Although catholicks would not have agreed that the imitation of Christ was easy, they probably absorbed from latitudinarian sermons a spirit of hopefulness and confidence with regard to human capability to follow in the footsteps of Jesus. Foxcroft, as we have seen, borrowed directly from Tillotson on the subject of the imitation of Christ as love to neighbor.[26]

The proposing of an example was understood by catholicks and other Congregational ministers in New England to serve as an important means of guiding persons in their religious development. Colman wrote in 1702 that examples "do more powerfully incline to practice than bare precepts." Foxcroft declared that "example strikes quick and sinks deep; caries in it a peculiar sovereignity, and a much more controlling power, than dry rules." Wadsworth recommended to his congregation that one way to follow the example of Jesus was, in fact, to be a good example to others. Appleton preached that men should "set good examples before their households," and Foxcroft told his congregation that even "aged persons" and "elder Christians" should endeavor to present themselves as examples to the community. Ministers, of course, were under a special obligation to set good examples.[27] One of the most interesting and suggestive comments on example, however, came from Ebenezer Parkman, who wrote in his diary in 1727 that "example seems to have a far greater influence upon me than precept, since it so gratifies my under powers, my imagination, and curiosity, and thereby captivates my affections." Parkman's observation that example strongly influenced him by stirring his affections is a clue to our understanding the catholick clergy's presentation of example, not in sermons stressing the imitation of Christ but in numerous funeral sermons in which they profiled the deceased as examples of both piety and morality.[28]

Robert Henson, David E. Stannard, and Emory Elliott each have written that funeral sermons in New England became much more "sentimental" after 1700. Henson, arguing that seventeenth-century Puritan funeral elegies described both the love and the zeal of the deceased, claims that "after the turn of the century . . . love ran away with zeal, and some of the elegies took on a sentimental hue." Stannard has argued that after 1720, an "optimistic sentimentality" emerged as the leading feature of "a homegrown variety of American consolation literature." And Elliott, calling attention to the "sudden shift" toward sentimentality in funeral sermons at the turn of the century, has argued that Wadsworth, Appleton, Colman and Pemberton employed "lofty language" and "flowing rhetoric" in their funeral sermons. According to Elliott, social change in the early eighteenth century had made the preaching of a funeral sermon a more complex and often more difficult undertaking, because ministers increasingly were obliged to eulogize a wealthy philanthropist whose election was not obvious. Sentimental rhetoric allowed a minister to sidestep doctrinal matters and to cultivate an emotional response in an audience instead.[29]

Elliot is entirely correct in his claim that catholicks[30] employed in their funeral sermons language that was meant to stir the affections. It is the fact that this language was adopted in connection with an attempt to describe the deceased as an *example* that is most significant, however. Example, as Parkman observed, "captivated" the affections and in so doing instructed in a way that precept normally did not. It is likely that the recommendation of the example of the deceased, given in a funeral sermon, would strike with even greater force on an audience. Catholicks, who generally affirmed the necessity of preaching to stir the affections, exploited the opportunity to speak about a Christian recently deceased by employing language that intensified the affective aspect of the occasion. As ministers, their first duty was to teach the living, not to praise the dead (though, of course, they did not neglect the latter), and teach they did, by holding up to the community the examples of the departed. In this way, the catholick clergy were able to give some definition and direction to the notion of "love to neighbor" on which the social life of the regenerate was based. Moreover, they were able at the same time to fan the flame of that love, to appeal to the emotions of their audiences in such a way as to kindle and to channel their affections.[31]

The "lesson" in the example of the deceased generally was related to the connection between personal regeneration and activity in the world. Usually, this relationship was expressed as a devotion of a person to the public good, arising out of a love to others. Henson's observation that after 1700 identification of the qualities of "tenderheartedness" and "love" in the deceased replaced, in some sermons, references to "zeal" (understood as "indomitable churchgoing") is particularly appropriate in the case of catholicks. Typical of such an emphasis was Wadsworth's declaration after the death of Reverend Thomas Bridge that "nothing is more plainly, frequently, urgently press'd upon them [Christians] in the New-Testament, than that they should do their utmost to live in love and peace," and his assertion that Bridge was a shining example of such love. Again, speaking of Isaac Addington, the former secretary of the province, Wadsworth explained, "He was a great lover of men, studious of peace and good agreement among them (did much to promote it) of a catholick extensive charity." Wadsworth noted as well the numerous unselfish activities of Addington, including his generous donations to charity, but, said Wadsworth, "his piety toward God, rendred him more excellent than anything else." Largeness of heart, purity of heart, and affection to God and neighbor, rather than a strong record of church attendance, were of great importance in catholick funeral sermons. Activity in the world was, of course, also important, but it was understood that such activity blossomed from a principle of grace in the soul, from a pure heart. Catholicks sought to emphasize and explain the piety of the heart and then to suggest ways in which the deceased was guided in everyday activities by such piety.[32]

Catholick emphasis on grace and piety as a foundation for charity can be seen in numerous funeral sermons, beginning with several by Benjamin Colman. In 1723, Colman delivered a sermon "after the funeral of the virtuous and exemplary Mr. David Stoddard," whose "amiable and exemplary life" was examined in view of the text "That ye may be sincere, and without offence till the day of Christ" (Phil. 1:10.). Colman explained first of all that "without offence" meant "being filled with the fruits of righteousness." Colman proposed that "our first and great work is to approve our hearts to God. . . . God looks to the heart and has pleasure in uprightness." Purity of heart was possible only through converting grace: "A blessed regeneration must pass upon us, if we would be without offence in the sight of God or man. Verily, we must be born again, and become new creatures."[33] From "heart-purifying faith" followed the fruits of righteousness, and so, "secondly . . . we should so look to our life and outward conversation as to give no occasion of offence to men, either in our words, actions, or behaviour. We should endeavour this from a pure heart towards God." Moral action consisted in charity toward others and denial of private interest. Stoddard was presented as a model for this kind of Christian life.[34]

In a published funeral sermon for William Harris, who was lost in the smallpox epidemic of 1721, Colman argued the same points. He first introduced the deceased as worthy of imitation. Addressing Harris's wife, Sarah, in a preface to the actual sermon, Colman wrote: "I believe, madam, that you will; desire to imitate the deceased in his silent and secret devotions and charities." Preeminent among such charities was Harris's generous support of the church. But Colman stressed that it was Harris's practice of sending a three-pound note in "the most secret manner to the box at the Old South Church" that was significant. Harris practiced a "singular secresie" in helping the poor and supporting the church, and this, of course, was the epitome of self-denial, refusing even the recognition for one's efforts on behalf of the public welfare. Of course, Colman saw the opportunity to encourage support of the ministry, a constant theme in eighteenth-century preaching, and this may have influenced his phrasing in his concluding his preface (although it certainly did not detract from his chief argument): "These exemplary things in the deceased I have mentioned, for the instruction of the living, the excitation of the rich, and the emulation of the pious."

Preaching on the theme of "righteousness" was common at funerals, because mourners naturally hoped that the deceased would reap in the afterlife the rewards of the righteous. Colman took up this theme as he proceeded in his sermon for Harris. Offering a definition of the term, Colman asked: "Who are the righteous? . . . In a more limited and restrained sense, it sometimes stands for him that is exact, strict and just in his intercourses and dealings with men." Colman immediately qualified this sense of the term by adding, "But for the most part the word righteous is used in the Holy Scripture in a more large and general sense, for one" who "is truly holy in heart and life." It was necessary, then, that the heart be purified in order for one to act virtuously. The "election of grace that by a new birth" persons "are and shall be made righteous" accomplished this, so that "the righteous are so both in heart and life." Colman stressed again that "the righteous are the gracious in inward disposition, and in outward conversation," and observed that the combination of "outward" morality and "inward" justification in the elect was like the combination of Jewish law and Christian grace, in "the harmony of the two testaments."[35]

The connection between purity of heart and the capability for acting morally was made in another way by Colman in a sermon following the death of Samuel Holden of London. Colman praised Holden's diligence, honesty, and prudence in his conducting of his financial affairs, noting that "the Lord blessed him with success, he doubled his stock in a little time; the Lord gave him more because he us'd well what he had." Holden, being devoutly religious, did not only look after his own private interest, however. Colman described his exemplary behavior by first noting that "religion, in its full possession of a soul in superior wordly circumstances, gives a man largeness of heart as the sand of the sea." Suggesting to his audience that piety and worldly wherewithal—the capability to offer on a large scale assistance to the needy—could in some cases nurture each other, Colman told the governor and representatives who were in attendance: "That amidst so many great avocations and encumbrances from the world, the snares and temptations of so many of its glories;

his [Holden's] eyes were not dazles [*sic*] with it as glittering shows, nor his heart taken off, but rather the more settled on the infinitely greater and eternal blessings of heaven; the care of his own soul, the temporal and spiritual good of mankind as far as his influence could reach."[36]

Ebenezer Pemberton, sermonizing after the death of John Wally, who had been a justice of the Superior Court, also distinguished between the "glitter" of earthly accomplishment and purity of heart. Arguing that "we serve our generation by setting them good examples," Pemberton began his sermon by recalling that "it was the glorious character of our great Lord and Master, (while on earth) that he went about *doing good:* And it is the highest attainment of his disciples herein to be followers of him." According to Pemberton, "men may glitter" in "bare power, wealth and honour," but such glory is only "a short flash." Characterizing the Old Testament figure David as one who "served his own generation by the will of God," Pemberton suggested that Wally had done the same for his own generation and that this was "a noble character of a Christian, and his highest wisdom." One way to serve one's generation was "to advance the good and prosperity" of a people, or, stated in another way, "To promote the wealth and riches of a people is to serve them." But, Pemberton observed, "there is the secular, and there is the spiritual prosperity of a people; there are civil and sacred interests, and what tends to promote each of these." And, in fact, these two areas of life were related. Pemberton taught that "the true value and rate of life" was "action." But action could not be separated from a pure heart. Pemberton warned his audience: "Let us see our hearts be right in the service of God. Otherwise what we do will be defective as to principle, spirit and end. And tho' we had done never so much for our generation, yet there will be one thing lacking." In fact, a pure heart produced fruits in all areas of social life. Wally was exemplary because his "works of charity and piety" stood out as a witness to his faith. Pemberton concluded the sermon with a warning against a selfish spirit: "Let us labour to get a selfish spirit mortifyed. . . . When this selfish spirit reigns in us, we shall turn a deaf ear to the loudest calls to attend the service of our generation." The unselfish, those "being lead [*sic*] by the Spirit of God" to act, to serve their generation, were to be emulated: "Their example is for imitation; their diligence, vigour and faithfulness will reproach our sloth and negligence."[37]

The "good example" represented catholick belief in the necessity of a conjunction of purity of heart with visible dedication to the whole of society. In a published funeral sermon for the Harvard benefactor Colonel Francis Foxcroft (the father of Thomas Foxcroft), Nathaniel Appleton—together with the Harvard tutor Henry Flynt, who penned a preface to the sermon—vigorously argued this point. Introducing the sermon, Flynt praised Foxcroft as a man whose "virtues were great and eminent" and whose "high and honourable thoughts of God, and profound veneration of the divine providence" and "grateful affection to his redeemer . . . were exemplary." Appleton, in an argument reminiscent of Colman's comments about William Harris, began the actual sermon by declaring that "altho" righteousness may oftentimes intend some particular vertue, such as justice and honesty in our dealings with one another; yet very frequently we are to understand the whole of religion by it." The whole of religion was, in fact, the giving of honor and praise to God "in our hearts, with our lips, and by our lives." Appleton then explained that there were three kinds of righteousness. One was a "life of piety and godliness," another was "the doing all the duty we owe to our selves", and the last was "the doing justice to our fellow creatures." For Appleton, just as for his colleagues, righteousness—however manifested—began with conversion. A righteous man "has the righteousness of Christ imputed to him. . . . The upright man supposes the *converted* man, who has a gracious change wrought in him, and is effectually turned from darkness to light." Righteousness therefore was "not merely the outward appearance, or possession of religion; it is not merely being given to religious discourse with one another," and "it is not a flaming zeal for any particular forms of worship or discipline." Such things "may perhaps gain us esteem" but "these are not the things that recommend us to God." As Appleton made explicitly clear, "There are no ways pleasing to [God], if they are not accompanied with, or do not proceed from an honest heart." From all of this Appleton concluded that "it is solid unaffected piety, and real vertue" that make one righteous and upright, because "vital piety is the thing that God looks at with pleasure," and where this is absent, "there is only the form of godliness."[38]

This sermon is particularly instructive in that Francis Foxcroft was a member of the Church of England. He nevertheless attended services for many years in the Congregational churches of New England, where he was present "even at the holy table of the Lord." Appleton accordingly noted that Foxcroft "was wont to exercise a catholick charity, and shew respect for all Christians." It probably also was already clear to anyone who heard Appleton's sermon that Foxcroft was a philanthropist. But Foxcroft was not praised as "catholick" merely because he was outwardly generous with his money, or because he sought church fellowship outside his own tradition, or because he acted unselfishly in other ways. Rather he represented the catholick idea of a good example because his visibly unselfish behavior issued from piety, because he was able "to live agreeable to the rules of righteousness," as that term was defined in a broad sense by Appleton.[39]

When John Leverett, the president of Harvard College, died suddenly in 1724, Appleton, Colman, and Wadsworth all preached sermons praising the man, and these were published together in 1724. Appleton began his sermon by asking, "How do you know if a man is a great man?" One way was "upon the account of his outward circumstances." But such an accounting was only of "an inferiour kind of greatness." Appleton reminded his audience, "The rational soul is the principal part" of the human constitution. According to Appleton, "It is that which makes us men. . . . And therefore according to the largeness of a man's soul (its capacities and endowments) may a man be called great. He that has a great soul is a great man, let his outward circumstances be what they will." But the rational soul, which would guide moral response to a particular set of circumstances, was itself shaped by the grace that came with conversion. Appleton stressed that "he therefore that is created anew in Christ Jesus, and that is sanctified throughout . . . is a truly great and excellent man." Those persons who had been given saving grace, said Appleton, were sometimes placed in positions in society that allowed them to do "some great & good things" and to "become so remarkable and conspicuously usefull in the world." It was this "worth and usefulness" in a person, which blossomed from a converted heart and was often so clearly apparent in retrospect after the death of a great man, that Christians should strive to imitate. Appleton added that thoughts of the deceased should leave an impression "of their vertues upon our minds." Leverett's virtues included, especially, his "solid, unaffected piety," his "faith, charity and patience," and his "catholick spirit." Near the end of his sermon, Appleton suggested again the importance of the connection between born-again grace and one's good works. Praising Leverett as a great man, he said: "And as he was thus endowed with gifts and graces; so they manifested themselves in any great and good services that were done by him. He by his diligence and industry, went thro' a great deal of labor and service in the world." Leverett was not only an example of piety but a man who rendered useful service to society.[40]

Thomas Foxcroft's sermon after the funeral of Penn Townsend ("Mordecai's Character") has already been mentioned in connection with Foxcroft's views of the personal attributes desirable in a magistrate. In fact, funeral sermons preached by catholicks (and by noncatholicks) in most cases were connected with the death of a "public figure" who likely had served as a government official at some time. It might be observed, however, that sermons preached by catholicks after the funerals of females generally did not include references to the public good works of the deceased, and there was little suggestion of a love of the brethren in the eulogies for women. On the contrary, after the loss of a female member of the community, catholick ministers were inclined to praise her more for "zeal" than for anything else. In particular, women were portrayed as godly largely in connection with their faithfulness in attendance at public worship. Keeping in mind Henson's observation that prior to about 1700, funeral sermons focused closely on the record of the faithful participation of the deceased in public worship, it would seem that the themes of funeral sermons for females did not change much after 1700—or at least not as much as did those for males. It may well have been that women were not viewed as "public" figures in the same way as were men. Although, as Laurel Ulrich has shown, women exercised a significant influence on the everyday life of the community, they nevertheless, with a few exceptions, were not merchants, government officials, ministers, or college tutors. Their lives were not public in the same sense as were the lives of wine merchants or justices of the Superior Court. As far as funeral sermons were concerned, Catholick ministers seem to have viewed public life essentially in its connection with institutional offices of education, commerce, government, and religion.[41] The differences between sermons for males and females may be attributable in part to this tendency.

In any event, we find Appleton, in his sermon for Colonel Foxcroft's daughter (Mrs. Gerrish), preaching an entirely different kind of sermon than he had for her father. In fact, beyond a reference to her patient suffering, all Appleton could offer in the way of pious public activity of the deceased was notice of her diligent participation in public worship. Colman, in a sermon for Jane Steele, likewise was able only to muster a few words about her Christian suffering and her "public worship of God," including her "exemplary" behavior in "the sanctification of the Lords-Day." Wadsworth's sermon for Anne Dewer was almost entirely lacking in any sort of attention to her public life (though her age, seventeen, may have had some bearing on this). In fact, Wadsworth did not even praise her for church attendance, being able only to note that since she had actively sought membership in the church, she had fulfilled her Christian duty.[42]

The catholick clegy expected that the regenerate would be guided in their social life by the Gospel commandment to "Love thy neighbor as thyself." Underlying this expectation was the belief that true love to one's neighbor was only possible through grace, because love to neighbor, as well as self-love, was always for the glory of God. Activity of any sort undertaken in the world was rooted in a religious view of social life. Nevertheless, catholicks recognized that the affectionate bonding of Christians in community might require some measure of guidance or precaution, since the affections that cemented the regenerate one to the other could be misdirected into channels whereby they might disrupt social life, not order it. Accordingly, catholicks supported certain customs related to political life, and they emphasized the importance of fair trade. They also made use of the funeral sermon as an important way of instructing their congregations in the meaning of love to neighbor. They offered the lives of the deceased as examples for imitation and hoped as well that their own lives might serve as points of reference for Christians who were more powerfully affected by "example" than by "precept."

Conclusion

Fifty years ago, Theodore Hornberger warned that "the Enlightenment in America must not be interpreted too readily as a revolutionary process."[1] This assertion is strongly supported by our investigation of the manner in which the catholick clergy in Boston adopted certain notions that were characteristic of the age of the Enlightenment and at the same time retained theological ideas that represented an older, orthodox religious point of view. Catholicks were drawn to the theories of English writers such as Boyle, Ray, Derham, Tillotson, Stillingfleet, and More but at the same time preserved in their thinking a place for belief in the necessity for regenerating grace. The catholick clergy borrowed from English writers certain ideas about unity, reason, and purpose in nature and endeavored to integrate them into the framework of Congregationalist theology as it had been bequeathed to them by the previous generation. The chief means by which they undertook to accomplish that integration was through their promotion of the affective element in religion alongside the rational-intellectual. That is, Catholicks stressed the importance of an emotional response to the "beauty" of unity and order found in nature, in society, and in God. For catholicks, intellect—perceived as the operation of the faculty of the understanding—was essential to religion, but it was not all-important. The affections played a key role as well.

For those historians who are inclined to view the intellectual history of eighteenth-century America according to the categories of "enthusiasm" versus "reason,"[2] the claim that catholicks (who emphasized affective religion alongside reason) were part of the beginnings of the Enlightenment in America may seem overstated. We should recognize first of all, however, that catholick retention of certain religious ideas as a part of their thinking does not change the fact that they were in the forefront of the American encounter with English scientific theories and philosophy in the early eighteenth century. Second, we should keep in mind Peter Gay's observation that an important part of the Enlightenment was its *antirational* component, which was expressed, in one way, in the defense of passion as a component of human nature. In fact, Gay has argued that the Enlightenment in England—particularly as manifested in the thinking of Francis Hutcheson, Sir Joshua Reynolds, and Edmund Burke—was inclined, by the mideighteenth century, to view beauty as arising solely from passion, independent of intellect. In their stressing the beauty of creation and their promoting the affections, catholicks participated in the beginnings of that part of the Enlightenment that we find in mature form in England in writers such as Hutcheson or Burke, and in America, as Jay Fliegelman has recently shown, in the triumph of the affectional model of authority after 1750.[3]

Catholicks, of course, did not separate the affections from reason. God was the epitome of beauty, love, and reason and the model for their integration. Catholicks continued to value proportion and rational design as aspects of the beautiful in nature. But beauty was at the same time to some extent mysterious, wondrous, and inexplicable. And catholick discourse about the beauty of God and nature and the place of emotion in religion ought to be understood as an attempt to retain an element of the mysterious, perhaps even the antirational, in religion. For catholicks, clearly, this was necessitated by their adherence to the covenant, in which grace operated mysteriously in a person to bring about regeneration. But this necessity does not detract from the fact that catholicks, in their thinking about the affections (including their approval of the role of the senses in arousing the affections), represent an early form of that side of the Enlightenment that came to fruition in what R. S. Crane called the eighteenth-century philosophy of the "man of feeling." In short, catholicks' adoption of theories about unity and reason in nature, together with their unwillingness to abandon a theology of grace, led them to construct, in rudimentary form, a system of thought in which both reason and feeling—the two leading foci of eighteenth-century discourse—were claimed as essential to public and private religious well-being.[4]

Colman, Foxcroft, and Appleton all got along well with those ministers, such as Ebenezer Gay and John Barnard, who represented a rationalist theology in which the affections were relegated to a decidedly minor role and who opposed the revival of the early 1740s. The philosophical agreement between Appleton and Gay, and Colman and Barnard, seems to have been particularly noteworthy.[5] On the other hand, the catholick clergy, in emphasizing the affections, approached the theological position of those who defended the revival. Though catholicks did not identify the affections with the will, as Jonathan Edwards[6] would, they nevertheless generally agreed with Appleton that "when the affections are once stirred up and engaged, they serve very powerfully to inlighten the mind, perswade the will, remove discouragements."[7] It might be observed here as well that the revival, as well as the "rational religion" of the sort associated with Gay, were "catholick" movements in the specific sense that both were inclined to overlook the "smaller things" in religion.

The Great Awakening is usually cited as a crisis in which "reasonable" religion became clearly distinguished from religious "enthusiasm" in New England. Although I do not think that this understanding is entirely correct, I am persuaded that the revival corresponded with a wide range of sudden and dramatic effects of social and cultural change in New England. Catholick theology did not survive the Great Awakening intact largely because the terms on which colonists based their thinking about religion—especially public religion—changed rapidly as New England approached midcentury. Foxcroft, Appleton, and, to some extent, Holyoke continued to preach the catholick theology of the early eighteenth century, but their ongoing contributions to the intellectual life of New England were, after the revival, located essentially in the area of political ideology.[8] Their influence was felt, in religion, in the dialectical theology of Charles Chauncy (Foxcroft's assistant at First Church) and Chauncy's close friend Jonathan Mayhew (West Church).[9] Eventually, their thinking flowed in a more developed form into Unitarianism.

Finally, with the example of catholick ministers in mind, we ought to review the whole business of religion and the Enlightenment in eighteenth-century New England, in order to identify other contexts in which religious ideas and Enlightenment notions of order and reason were creatively mixed. Patricia Bonomi recenty has argued: "An eighteenth-century of 'Enlightenment' skepticism, coming between a 'Puritan' seventeenth-century and an 'evangelical' nineteenth-century simply does not add up."[10] Like the catholick Congregationalist clergy, most Americans in the eighteenth century probably eventually adapted to the Enlightenment, rather than exchanging their religious beliefs for skepticism or atheism or for a form of religion that was entirely foreign to the emotional evangelical religion of the nineteenth century. By studying the Enlightenment as a steady process of change, rather than as the wholesale exchange of one set of ideas for another, we will understand more clearly both the history of religion in eighteenth-century New England and the way in which structures of thought that emerged in the eighteenth century have continued to inform religion in America in the twentieth century.

Notes

Abbreviations

Colman Papers	Benjamin Colman Papers in the Massachusetts Historical Society, Boston
CL	Congregational Library, Boston
Foxcroft, CL	Thomas Foxcroft Notebooks, Congregational Library, Boston
HUC	Harvard University Archives collections
MHS *Coll*,; *Proc.*	Massachusetts Historical Society, *Collections; Proceedings*
NEHGR	*New England Genealogical and Historical Register*
NEQ	New England Quarterly
op.	originally published
Wadsworth, CL	Benjamin Wadsworth Sermon Notes, Congregational Library, Boston
Wadsworth, MHS	Benjamin Wadsworth Diary, 1692–1737, Massachusetts Historical Society, Boston
Wadsworth, HUA	Benjamin Wadsworth, sermon manuscripts, Harvard University Archives
WMQ	William and Mary Quarterly

Preface

1. Ellis L. Motte, Henry Fitch Jenks, and John Homans II, *The Manifesto Church: Records of the Church in Brattle Square . . . 1699–1872* (Boston, 1902). The marriage was performed on September 20, 1700.

2. Henry F. May, *The Enlightenment in America* (New York, 1976), 58, 65, 204, passim; Norman Fiering, "The First American Enlightenment: Tillotson, Leverett, and Philosophical Anglicanism," *NEQ* 54 (1981): 307–44; Theodore Hornberger, "Benjamin Colman and the Enlightenment," *NEQ* 12 (1939): 227–40.

3. Typical is May's assertion: "To believers in progress, rationality, balance, order, and moderation, outbursts of religious emotion were (and are) alarming, disgusting, and inexplicable" (*Enlightenment in America,* 42).

4. Peter Gay, *The Enlightenment: An Interpretation,* vol. 2, *The Science of Freedom* (New York, 1969), 194, 192, 187–207.

5. I have noted in detail, in Chapter 5, throughout the text, and in numerous footnotes, how the interpretations of other scholars have overestimated the degree to which the catholick clergy were responsible for a movement away from a religious view of the world. Two notable exceptions to this trend in interpretation are the analyses of Colman's thought offered by Hornberger ("Benjamin Colman") and by James W. Jones, *The Shattered Synthesis: New England Puritanism before the Great Awakening* (New Haven, 1973). Both of these studies observe that Colman did not break decisively with Calvinism.

6. Perry Miller, *The New England Mind: From Colony to Province* (Boston, 1953), 417–63, 236–49, passim.

7. Philip Greven, *The Protestant Temperament: Patterns of Child-Rearing, Religious Experience, and the Self in Early America* (New York, 1977).

Introduction

1. Josiah Quincy, *The History of Harvard University,* vol. 1 (Cambridge, 1840), 314.

2. These ministers formed the core of catholick Congregationalism as it developed into an intellectual movement, with Brattle, Leverett, and Holyoke making contributions to its development at various times along the way.

3. The thinking of Webb, however, seems to have moved tentatively in a new direction during the Great Awakening.

4. Barnard served as an assistant minister at the Brattle Street Church briefly in 1705, but he does not seem to have developed the taste for affective religion that characterized Colman's thinking.

Chapter 1

1. In addition to the works cited below, see Edward A. George, *Seventeenth Century Men of Latitude* (New York, 1908); John Tulloch, *Rational Philosophy and Christian Theology in England in the Seventeenth-Century* (London, 1874); John F. New, *Anglican and Puritan: The Basis of Their Opposition, 1558–1640* (Stanford, Calif., 1964); G. R. Cragg, *From Puritanism to the Age of Reason* (Cambridge, England, 1966); John Hoyles, *The Waning of the Renaissance 1640–1720* (Hague, 1971), 29–45; Gordon Rupp, *Religion in England 1688–1791* (Oxford, 1986), 5–107; C. F. Allison, *The Rise of Moralism* (New York, 1966); John Marshall, "The Ecclesiology of the Latitude-Men 1660–1689: Stillingfleet, Tillotson, and Hobbism," *Journal of Ecclesiastical History* 36 (1985): 407–25; Norman Fiering, *Moral Philosophy at Seventeenth-Century Harvard: A Discipline in Transition* (Chapel Hill, 1981), 177. On enthusiasm and some responses to it in the seventeenth century see Roland A. Knox, *Enthusiasm:*

A Chapter in the History of Religion with Special Reference to the Seventeenth and Eighteenth Centuries (New York, 1961), 1–8, passim.

2. Barbara J. Shapiro, *Probability and Certainty in Seventeenth-Century England* (Princeton, 1983), 116.

3. Horton Davies, *Worship and Theology in England: From Watts and Wesley to Maurice, 1690–1850* (Princeton, 1961), 52–75 (quote is from p. 73); Hoxie Neale Fairchild, *Religious Trends in English Poetry,* vol. 1 (New York, 1939), 245–46, 253–54, 259; Norman Sykes, *From Sheldon to Secker: Aspects of English Church History 1660–1768* (Cambridge, 1959), 150–51, and *Church and State in England in the XVIIIth Century* (Hamden, Conn., 1962), 390; H. R. McAdoo, *The Spirit of Anglicanism: A Survey of Anglican Theological Method in the Seventeenth-Century* (London, 1965), 159–60; Taylor quoted in J. Sears McGee, "Conversion and the Imitation of Christ in Anglican and Puritan Writing," *Journal of British Studies* 15 (1976): 32; *Trinity Church in the City of Boston, Massachusetts 1733–1933* (Boston, 1933), 35–36; R. Buick Knox, "Bishops in the Pulpit in the Seventeenth Century: Continuity and Change," in *Reformation Conformity and Dissent: Essays in Honor of Geoffrey Nuttall,* ed. R. Buck Knox (London, 1977), 92–114. Barbara Shapiro stresses that latitudinarians viewed passion as a clouding or misshaping of the understanding, and so they frowned on emotion in religion. Their opposition to zeal was a part of their project of "impartial inquiry." Freedom from passion in the mind was the key to good judgment. See Shapiro, *Probability and Certainty in Seventeenth-Century England,* 108–10, 88–89, 104–6, and *John Wilkins 1614–1672: An Intellectual Biography* (Berkeley, 1969), 230–41.

4. Thomas Sprat, *History of the Royal Society of London* (London 1667), 55, 53. Norman Sykes suggested that the "umbrella" of latitudinarianism was spread over a fairly wide range of ideas but that a core can be detected (*From Sheldon to Secker,* 144–46). Joseph J. Ellis thinks that the term *latitudinarian* was originally a derogation, and he suggests as well that it changed in time to a mark of respect, as latitudinarianism became less a vague philosophy and more a practical program of solving ecclesiastical problems (*The New England Mind in Transition: Samuel Johnson of Connecticut, 1696–1772* [New Haven, 1973], 62–64). Shapiro points out that while Wilkins was a latitudinarian, he remained attracted to some aspects of Calvinism. She also comments on the connections among the Royal Society, science, and latitudinarianism (*John Wilkins,* 1–10, 62, 191–250, 228, and *Probability and Certainty in Seventeenth-Century England,* 112–14). On Stillingfleet and Glanvill see also Tulloch, *Rational Theology in England in the Seventeenth Century,* vol. 1, chaps. 5, 7.

5. Edward Stillingfleet, *Irenicum* (London, 1662), preface, 65, 69, 70; *A Rational Account of the Grounds of Protestant Religion* (London, 1665), 298. Stillingfleet discussed the matter of canon and catholicity in *A Discourse Concerning the Nature and Grounds of the Certainty of Faith in Answer to J. S. His Catholick Letters* (London, 1688). He addressed the matter of transubstantiation as a religious ceremony in a meeting "held with some gentlemen from the church of Rome, April, 1676" in *A Relation of a Conference Held about Religion* (London, 1676). Gilbert Burnet, the strongly anti–Roman Catholic bishop of Salisbury, coauthored the latter work.

6. Shapiro, *Probability and Certainty in Seventeenth-Century England,* 109ff.; Richard S. Westfall, *Science and Religion in Seventeenth-Century England* (Ann Arbor, Mich., 1973), 175; Joseph Glanvill, *Catholic Charity* (London, 1669), 31, 15, 29, 14; *The Vanity of Dogmatizing* (London, 1661), 104, 117, 135; *Essays on Several Important Subjects in Philosophy and Religion* (London, 1676), chap. 4, 17, 20, 21. Umphrey Lee discusses Glanvill together with other writers of the time in the context of the tension

between enthusiasm and philosophy in *The Historical Backgrounds of Early Methodist Enthusiasm* (New York, 1967). Glanvill's own writing on the theme of philosophy and enthusiasm is focused in *Philosophia Pia* (London, 1671).

7. Simon Patrick, *A Brief Account of the New Sect of Latitude-Men* (London, 1662), 7–9; *Two Sermons One against Murmuring the Other against Censuring* (London, 1689), 37, 46, 57, 63; *Sermon Preached at the Funeral of John Smith* appended to John Smith, *Select Discourses* (London, 1660), 517.

8. Simon Patrick, *A Discourse Concerning Prayer: Especially of Frequenting the Daily Publick Prayers* (London, 1686), 127, 129; Tulloch, *Rational Philosophy and Christian Theology in England in the Seventeenth-Century,* vol. 1, 440.

9. Shapiro, *John Wilkins,* 30–60, 62–64, 262n; John Wilkins, *Sermons Preached upon Several Occasions* (London, 1682), 394, 400, 426–27, 413, 415–16; *Of the Principles and Duties of Natural Religion* (London, 1675), preface, 9–10; *A Discourse Concerning the Gift of Prayer* (London, 1653), 1–25. Following some Puritan writers, Wilkins in 1693 referred to zeal as a "mixed passion," which could yield beneficial or detrimental effects (*Ecclesiates, Or a Discourse Concerning the Gift of Preaching* [London, 1693], 280–81).

10. John Tillotson, *Sermons Preached on Several Occasions* (London, 1671), 147, 151, 152–53, 127, 129 (see also 137–38, 185, 191, 211, 219, 282); *Sixteen Sermons* 2d ed., vol. 2 (London, 1700), 356, 360, 362–63, 366, 367–68, 374–75; *Sermons and Discourses,* 2d ed., vol. 3 (London, 1687), 425, 445. According to Norman Fiering, William Byrd II, of Westover, wept on reading some of Tillotson's sermons in May 1710 ("The First American Enlightenment: Tillotson, Leverett, and Philosophical Anglicanism" *WMQ* [1981], 344 n. 62). Of Whichcote, Tillotson wrote: "He had attained so perfect a mastery of his passions, that for the latter and greater part of his life he was hardly ever seen to be transported with anger" (*Sermons and Discourses,* 2d ed., vol. 3, 244–45). In a sermon preached before the House of Commons in 1678, Tillotson illustrated the "pretence of zeal for God and religion" with reference to Jesus' rebuke of the apostles James and John for their heated discussion with Samaritans who would not receive Jesus with hospitality (*Sermons and Discourses,* 2d ed., vol. 3, 5–8). William M. Spellman has recently argued that Tillotson was more concerned with piety than scholars have allowed but nevertheless claims that Tillotson for the most part emphasized practical as opposed to speculative aspects of Christian theology (William M. Spellman, "Archbishop John Tillotson and the Meaning of Moralism," *Anglican and Episcopal History* 56 [1987]: 405–22). The standard introduction to Tillotson is Irene Simon, ed., *Three Restoration Divines: Barrow, South, Tillotson* (Paris, 1967). A useful brief profile of Tillotson's sermons is Norman Sykes, "The Sermons of Archbishop Tillotson," *Theology* 58 (1955): 297–302.

11. Harry S. Stout, *The New England Soul: Preaching and Religious Culture in Colonial New England* (New York, 1986), 127, 128–47; T. H. Breen, *The Character of the Good Ruler: A Study of Puritan Political Ideas in New England* (New Haven, 1970), 221; David Grayson Allen, *In English Ways: The Movement of Societies and the Transferral of English Local Law and Custom to Massachusetts Bay in the Seventeenth Century* (Chapel Hill, 1981), 3–160; Richard Bushman, "American High-Style and Vernacular Cultures," in *Colonial British America,* ed. Jack P. Greene and J. R. Pole (Baltimore, 1984), 345–83; Bernard Bailyn, *The Ideological Origins of the American Revolution* (Cambridge, Mass., 1967); Robert Blair St. George, "Style and Structure in the Joinery of Dedham and Medfield, Massachusetts, 1635–1685," *Winterthur Portfolio,* vol. 13, ed. Ian M. Quimby (Chicago, 1979), 1–46; Philip Greven, *Four Genera-*

tions: Population, Land and Family in Colonial Andover, Massachusetts (Ithaca, N.Y., 1970; *The Protestant Temperament: Patterns of Child-Rearing, Religious Experience, and the Self in Early America* (New York, 1977). A useful, wide-ranging study of models of British colonization is Jack P. Greene, *Pursuits of Happiness: The Social Development of Early Modern British Colonies and the Formation of American Culture* (Chapel Hill, 1988), esp. 7–80. For Massachusetts, see John M. Murrin, "Anglicizing an American Colony: The Transformation of Provincial Massachusetts" (Ph.D. diss., Yale University, 1966), esp. 28–45.

12. Ellis, *New England Mind in Transition,* 55–87; Herbert and Carol Schneider, eds., *Samuel Johnson: His Career and Writings,* vol. 1 (New York, 1929), 11. Samuel Johnson wrote that his exposure to the "new learning," particularly as it was made available to him through the Jeremiah Dummer donation of books to Yale in 1714, transformed his thinking (ibid., 2:186); J. William T. Youngs, Jr., *God's Messengers: Religious Leadership in Colonial New England, 1700–1750* (Baltimore, 1976), 37–38. When William Brattle left Harvard and was ordained and installed at the First Church in Cambridge, the ceremony did not include the traditional "laying on of hands" (John Langdon, Sibley, *Biographical Sketches of Graduates of Harvard University,* 1678–1689, vol. 3 [Cambridge, Mass., 1885], 200). A study detailing some attempts made in the colonies to limit enthusiasm is David S. Lovejoy, *Religious Enthusiasm in the New World* (Cambridge, Mass., 1985).

13. Samuel Sewall, "Letter Book of Samuel Sewall" *Collections of the Massachusetts Historical Society* 2, 6th ser. (1888): 144; Samuel Eliot Morison, *Three Centuries of Harvard 1636–1936* (Cambridge, Mass., 1964), 46. An excellent analysis of the changes in the Harvard curriculum, with an emphasis on the rise of moral philosophy (and the decline of the art of divinity) at Harvard, is Norman Fiering, *Moral Philosophy at Seventeenth-Century Harvard.* But Fiering's argument ought to be considered alongside the advice that the Marblehead pastor John Barnard (H.C., 1700) gave to an assembly of ministers in 1738: "Ever subject philosophy to divinity. Philosophy is but the result of humane understanding, and reasoning; Divinity, I mean what turns upon revelation, flows directly from the divine mind, and therefore . . . philosophy be . . . but as an hand-maid unto divinity" (*The Lord Jesus Christ* [Boston, 1738], 28). On the other hand, one description of the Harvard curriculum by a visitor from England in the eighteenth century includes no reference to "divinity" at all: "The tutors there instruct their pupils in logick, natural and moral philosophy, metaphysicks, geography, astronomy, arithmetick and geometry, & c." ("A Brief Relation of the Plantation of New England," *Massachusetts Historical Society Collections* 3d ser., 1 [1825]: 100–101). An exception to the general rule that Leverett's students did not defect to Anglicanism is Henry Newman (H.C. 1687), who converted to Anglicanism in England and later became secretary to the Society for the Propagation of the Gospel. Samuel Myles was the son of the Baptist minister John Myles, who was ejected from England by the Act of Uniformity in 1662 and, after immigrating to New England, eventually became pastor of Boston's First Baptist Church. After graduating from Harvard in 1684, just before the appointment of Leverett, Samuel left for Oxford, returning to Boston as the rector of King's Chapel in 1689 (Samuel Eliot Morison, *Harvard College in the Seventeenth Century* (Cambridge, Mass., 1936), 2:558; Frederick Lewis Weis, *The Colonial Clergy and the Colonial Churches of New England* [Baltimore, 1977 (op. 1936)], 148).

14. Murrin, "Anglicizing an American Colony," 34; Colman to White Kennett, Dec. 17, 1725, and Nov. 1712, and to persons in Ireland (address missing) Mar. 17, 1736, Colman papers, MHS; Colman quoted in Josiah Quincy, *The History of Harvard*

University (Cambridge, Mass., [?], 1840), 1:233; Ebenezer Turell, *The Life and Character of the Reverend Benjamin Colman, D.D.* (Boston, 1749), 95.

15. Benjamin Colman quoted in Clayton H. Chapman, "Life and Influence of Reverend Benjamin Colman, D.D., 1673–1747" (Ph.D. diss., Boston University, 1948), 87; Henry Newman to Mr. Taylor (of the Society for the Propagation of the Gospel), Mar. 29, 1714, Newman papers, MHS. As pastor of the Second Church in Boston, Increase Mather was often absent from the daily affairs of the college, which was across the Charles River in Cambridge.

16. Arthur D. Kaledin, "The Mind of John Leverett" (Ph.D. diss., Harvard University, 1965), 243, 244, and "summary." Kaledin quotes the phrase "true catholick church" from Leverett.

17. The term *temperament* recently has been used more or less interchangeably with *mentality* or even *culture*. I use the term in the sense proposed by John Owen King III as a reference to "psychological style," and this is largely in keeping with the meaning of Philip Greven as well (King, *The Iron of Melancholy: Structures of Spiritual Conversion in America from the Puritan Conscience to Victorian Neurosis* [Middletown, Conn., 1983], 1, 81, 330–31; Greven, *Protestant Temperament,* 4, 12–18).

18. Michael G. Hall, *The Last American Puritan: The Life of Increase Mather 1639–1723* (Middletown, Conn., 1988), 285. The curriculum description given here is from the description given by Benjamin Wadsworth in his *Diary,* Harvard University Archives, 27–28. A thorough survey of the seventeenth-century Harvard curriculum is in Morison, *Harvard College in the Seventeenth Century,* 1:139–284; see esp. 252–263 for a description of the curriculum in metaphysics and moral philosophy; On Ramus see Walter J. Ong, S.J., *Ramus, Method, and the Decay of Dialogue: From the Art of Discourse to the Art of Reason* (Cambridge, Mass., 1958). On Ramus in New England see Perry Miller, *The New England Mind: The Seventeenth Century* (Cambridge, Mass., 1939), 116–78. On Ames and Ramus, Keith L. Sprunger, "Ames, Ramus and the Method of Puritan Theology," *Harvard Theological Review* 49 (1966): 133–51. On Ames and Ramus in New England, Miller, *New England Mind,* and the translation and excellent commentary by Lee W. Gibbs, *William Ames: Technometry* (Philadelphia, 1979). A perceptive and informative discussion of Burgersdyck and Heereboord at Harvard, and analysis of the relation of Cartesian thought generally to Puritan writers in the development of the Harvard curriculum, is in Fiering, *Moral Philosophy at Seventeenth-Century Harvard,* 10–103, 165–76.

19. Norman Fiering, "The First American Enlightenment: Tillotson, Leverett, and Philosophical Anglicanism," *New England Quarterly* 54 (1981): 336. Fiering points out the popularity of Tillotson in other colonies beside eastern New England and stresses especially the appeal to reason in his sermons. Murrin, "Angelicizing an American Colony," 28; John Barnard, *A Call to Parents* (Boston, 1737), 13, 34; Clifford K. Shipton, *Biographical Sketches of Those Who Attended Harvard College* (Boston, 1873–1975), 4:107, 504; *A Catalogue of Curious Valuable Books Belonging to Ebenezer Pemberton* (Boston, 1717) includes these other titles (or abbreviated titles): Stillingfleet's *Origine Opera, Reformations Justified,* and *Idolatry of the Church of Rome;* Patrick's *Of Repentance, The Truth of the Christian Religion, Select Psalms,* and *Divine Arithmetick;* Wilkins's *A Discovery of a New World* and *On Natural Religion; Harvard College Catalogus Librorum Bibliothecae* (Boston, 1723) includes, as does the Pemberton list, other latitudinarian writers such as Chillingworth and Burnet; Quincy, *History of Harvard University* (Cambridge, Mass., 1840), 1: 314–20; John Hancock, "Commonplace Book," Houghton Library, Harvard University, 28; "Diary of John Quincy Ad-

ams," *Proceedings of the Massachusetts Historical Society* 14 (1902): 416. The archives of the First Church in Cambridge, where William Brattle (1696–1717) and Nathaniel Appleton (1717–1784) served, include a book of sermons by Stillingfleet and a copy of Wilkins's *Natural Religion* (London, 1683). The latter seems to have come into the possession (in 1723) of Thomas Blowers (H.C. 1695), who was born and raised in Cambridge but served a congregation in Beverly.

20. In many instances Foxcroft listed the name of an author, followed by the title of the sermon or book. This was almost always true of his references to other New England writers, such as Solomon Stoddard and the Mathers, and of the exceedingly numerous allusions to Pemberton and to Wadsworth. Sermons by New England's ministers, which were published individually rather than in collections, required title references. Sometimes, however, beside the author's name Foxcroft wrote only a volume number, together with some page numbers. For some books, notably the volumes of collected sermons by Anglican writers, which were published in England, a volume and page number were all that were necessary to locate the source. The references to works by latitudinarians lack titles and therefore sometimes appear to the modern reader so vague as to make positive identification of the title impossible. However, in some cases, the combination of subject heading and volume and page numbers leads clearly back to the source.

21. The Foxcroft notebook is with his manuscript sermons in the Congregational Library, Boston. The entries in the book probably date from the second decade of the eighteenth century to 1762 or so. Under the heading "justifications of religion" Foxcroft cited "Stillingfleet—serm p 42" and "Bp Wilkins—p. 391." He also cited "Tills. vol 2 pp 447, 465 coll V. ser. 9." The *third* volume of Tillotson's *Sermons and Discourses* (London, 1687), the ninth sermon, preached before the king at Whitehall, was on the topic of the importance of the examples of princes and governors but did not include the page numbers cited by Foxcroft. The reference to Wilkins is clearly to *Sermons Preached upon Several Occasions* (London, 1682), because it begins on 391 and because another sermon in the collection, on the theme of "bad company," is cited by Foxcroft elsewhere in his notebook. The Stillingfleet sermon is from *Sermons Preached on Several Occasions* (London, 1673) and begins on p. 42. Foxcroft's citation of the Tillotson sermon under the heading "example of Christ" identifies Tillotson, "vol. 3." This is in all likelihood from the third volume, second edition, of *Sermons and Discourses* (London, 1687), sermon 2. The quotation is from p. 39, but see also 48–49. Foxcroft wrote to Samuel Johnson: "I often disputed for episcopacy . . . and leaned pretty much to the Church of England," but "I was not so perfectly satisfied in all the terms of conformity as ever to imagine I should actually take orders" (Foxcroft to Johnson, Aug. 12, 1726, quoted in Shipton, *Biographical Sketches* [1944], 6:47).

22. Thomas Foxcroft, *A Discourse Preparatory to the Choice of a Minister* (Boston, 1727), 60–61. It is my impression that Congregational ministers, in the course of delivering a sermon, were more inclined to call to the attention of their audiences books of those writers who were known for their devotional guides and manuals than works of more refined and complex theological or philosophical substance. The former writers included Thomas Doolittle, known for *A Treatise Concerning the Lord's Supper* and *A Call to Delaying Sinners;* Matthew Henry, author of *Communicants Companion;* Richard Baxter; and John Flavel. Boston booksellers stocked literally dozens of works by these writers. See Worthington Chauncey Ford, *The Boston Book Market 1679–1700* (Boston, 1917), 85, 112, 118, 140, 141, 155, 160, 161, 164, passim. An informative and perceptive discussion that suggests common interests and reading of ministers and

laypersons is in David D. Hall, *Worlds of Wonder, Days of Judgment: Popular Religious Belief in Early New England* (New York, 1989), 21–70.

23. Increase Mather quoted in Morison, *Harvard College in the Seventeenth Century,* 542–43 (see also 541); Perry Miller thought that the break between Mather and Leverett took place in 1696, when Leverett and the Brattles did not side with Mather in his protest against a charter clause granting visitation rights to the governor and council (*New England Mind,* 237–38). Morison thought that the tutors "joined with the Mathers in defeating the proposed charter of 1696" (541).

24. Increase Mather, *Autobiography,* ed. Michael G. Hall (Worcester, Mass., 1962), 327–28; Cotton Mather, "Important Points Relating to the Education at Harvard College . . ." quoted in Arthur D. Kaledin, "Mind of John Leverett," 236; Norman Fiering, commenting on Cotton Mather's view of the course charted for the college by Leverett, writes: "Cotton Mather died in 1728, to the end a trustee of the old ways" (*Moral Philosophy at Seventeenth Century Harvard,* 41; Cotton Mather's library contained at least two volumes by Stillingfleet and Tillotson's *Discourse against Transubstantiation* (London, 1685). See Julius H. Tuttle, "The Libraries of the Mathers," *Proceedings of the American Antiquarian Society* new series, 20 (1910): 350–51. See also Norman Fiering, "Transatlantic Republic of Letters: A Note on the Circulation of Learned Periodicals to Early Eighteenth-Century America," *WMQ* 33 (1976): 642–60, and T. G. Wright, *Literary Culture in Early New England, 1620–1730* (New Haven, 1920), 159–216; Edward Holyoke to George Whitefield, Feb. 20, 1744, 8, MHS; Sewall "blotted against" Easter, Christmas, Valentine's Day, and other "Anglican" days on Holyoke's almanac (*The Diary of Samuel Sewall 1674–1729,* ed. M. Halsey Thomas, vol. 1 [New York, 1973], 599). The Calef incident is described in Miller, *From Colony to Province,* 249–254. John Barnard, "Autobiography of the Reverend John Barnard," *Collections of the Massachusetts Historical Society* 3d ser., 5 (1856): 215. Youngs, *God's Messengers,* mistakenly has Holyoke's describing Barnard as "catholick," rather than vice versa (81); Joshua Gee made his comment to Whitefield (Shipton, *Biographical Sketches,* 6:181); Wadsworth's falling and rising fortunes in connection with Harvard are described in Shipton, 4: 85ff. Nathaniel Appleton, a strong supporter of the new curriculum, thought that the curriculum at the time of Leverett's death was even better than when he was a student (ibid., 87). A complete discussion of the troubles of the college in this regard is in Morison, *Harvard College in the Seventeenth Century,* 489–536.

25. Morison, *Harvard College in the Seventeenth Century,* 537ff.; Shipton, *Biographical Sketches,* 4:108. Two hundred fifty of Willard's sermons were collected and published as *A Compleat Body of Divinity* (Boston, 1726). Ernest Benson Lowrie (*The Shape of the Puritan Mind* [New Haven, 1974]) sees Willard as more influenced by the currents of rationalistic religion than were the Mathers.

26. John Higginson (1660–1708) immigrated from England and was educated by Thomas Hooker before assuming his responsibilities at First Church in Salem. Nicolas Noyes (H.C. 1667, d. 1717) was his colleague at First Church. James Allen was ejected from England for nonconformity in 1662 and six years later was installed at First Church in Boston. See Weis, *The Colonial Clergy,* 105, 153, 19. The history of First Church in Boston is particularly interesting in that after losing one of the strongest voices for covenant orthodoxy in James Allen (d. 1710), it called to the pulpit, only seventeen years later, the young Charles Chauncy, who would make for himself a reputation as a vigorous defender of rational religion and who contributed substantially to the eventual emergence of Unitarianism in New England.

27. "Wadsworth Diary 1692–1737," MHS. Some of the document (but not the account of his journey) is in cipher. However, a key to the cipher is located inside the cover; Murrin, "Anglicizing an American Colony," 45; "Harvard College Records," in *Publications of the Colonial Society of Massachusetts* 16 (Boston, 1925), 563; Josiah Quincy, *The History of Harvard University* (Boston, 1840), 1:365–76, 560–74; quoted in Shipton, *Biographical Sketches,* 5:603.

28. Carl Bridenbaugh, *Mitre and Sceptre: Transatlantic Faiths, Ideas, Personalities, and Politics* (New York, 1962), 59; Turell, *Life and Character of the Reverend Benjamin Colman, D.D.,* 1–43. Larzer Ziff thinks that Mrs. Rowe's influence on Colman was important and that it was through her that Colman developed a kind of "sentimentality" in his character (*Puritanism in America: New Culture in a New World* [New York, 1973], 274–76). Rowe's sentimentality is discussed in Hoxie Fairchild, *Religious Trends in English Poetry,* 1:136–40. I discuss sentimentality in Chap. 6.

29. Ellis L. Motte, Henry Fitch Jenks, and John Homans II, *The Manifesto Church: Records of the Church in Brattle Square . . . 1699–1872* (Boston, 1902), 3–5; Samuel K. Lothrop, *A History of the Church in Brattle Square, Boston* (Boston, 1851), 1–64; Henry Wilder Foote, *Annals of King's Chapel,* vol. 1 (Boston, 1882), 89–93; J. Nelson to Benjamin Colman, May 20, 1699, Colman papers, MHS; T. H. Breen, *The Character of the Good Ruler: A Study of Puritan Political ideas in New England, 1630–1730* (New Haven, 1970), 94–95. An analysis of the founding of the Third Church in Boston is in E. Brooks Holifield, "On Toleration in Massachusetts," *Church History* 38 (1969): 188–200. On problems arising from changing perceptions of the authority of ministers see David D. Hall, *The Faithful Shepherd: A History of the New England Ministry in the Seventeenth-Century* (New York, 1974), 176–278.

30. Motte et al., *Manifesto Church,* viii.

31. Marian Card Donnelly, "New England Meetinghouses in the Seventeenth-Century," *Old-Time New England* 47 (1957): 91. Compare with the styles in Dolores Bacon, *Old New England Churches* (New York, 1906), frontispiece, 4, 33, 50, 86. Those who broke off from the New North Church in a dispute over the choice of a minister and formed the New Brick Church for a while referred to their new church as "the revenge Church of Christ" (*Historical Notes of the New North Religious Society* [Boston, 1802], 14–15). Cotton Mather, *Diary of Cotton Mather,* vol. 1 (New York, 1957), 329–30, 332, 326.

32. *The Diary of Samuel Sewall,* 1674–1729, ed. M. Halsey Thomas (New York, 1973), 2:873; letter from John Higginson and Nicholas Noyes, Dec. 30, 1699, Colman papers, MHS; Samuel K. Lothrop, *History of the Brattle Street Church Boston* (Boston, 1851), 29; Motte et al., *Manifesto Church,* 12–13, and the reference to the "uncomfortable church meetings" (1699–1704) during which the meaning of the voting clause was discussed (12). The minister chosen to assist Colman was William Cooper (H.C. 1712). David D. Hall discusses ministerial concern about "democracy" in *The Faithful Shepherd: A History of the New England Ministry in the Seventeenth Century* (New York, 1972), 207–218. Willard quoted in, ibid., 212. Increase Mather, "To the Reader," in Samuel Torrey, *An Exhortation unto Reformation* (Cambridge, Mass., 1674).

33. Higginson and Noyes letter, Colman Papers, MHS; Baird Tipson, "Invisible Saints: the Judgment of Charity in the Early New England Churches," *Church History* 44 (1975): 470. Tipson suggests that the interest of church purity was second to confirmation of individual *certitudo salutis* (469–70); Patricia Caldwell has suggested that in early New England, it was difficult for a person to fail the "test" of a relation (*The Puritan Conversion Narrative: The Beginnings of American Expression* [New York,

1983], esp. chaps. 2, 3); Edmund Morgan, *Visible Saints: The History of a Puritan Idea* (New York, 1963); Thomas M. Davis and Jeff Jeske, eds., "Solomon Stoddard's 'Arguments' Concerning Admission to the Lord's Supper," *Proceedings of the American Antiquarian Society* 86 (1976): 14. David D. Hall, commenting on changing ideas about church membership in New England, writes: "The immigrants had believed that the truly 'catholic' church was invisible and insisted that the form of the visible church was particular covenanted congregations." By the end of the seventeenth century, there had emerged an understanding of the church that was catholic and visible (*Faithful Shepherd,* 225).

34. J. William T. Youngs, Jr., suggests that Connecticut Valley churches were dispensing with the test of a relation in the late seventeenth century (*God's Messengers,* 83). David D. Hall observes that as early as the 1680s, some churches in the Boston area had replaced the requirement of a public relation before the congregation with the practice of relation given in private to a minister, which then was read to the congregation. Hall refers specifically to the advent of this practice at the Old South Church, First Church Charlestown, First Church Cambridge, and the church in Watertown (*Faithful Shepherd,* 205). David Flaherty thinks that from 1660–1700, male candidates gradually were given the option of making a relation in private, a courtesy that had been extended to women for some time. He suggests that this was in fact the case at First Church Boston, by the late seventeenth century (*Privacy in Colonial America* [Charlottesville, Va., 1972], 145–47). A. B. Ellis reads the church records differently, claiming that a public relation was required at First Church in Boston as late as 1712 (Arthur B. Ellis, *History of the First Church in Boston, 1630–1880* [Boston, 1880], 171). Williston Walker argued that public relations "still continued in extensive use at the close of the first quarter of the eighteenth century, and were favored by conservatives like the Mathers." He adds, however, that private examinations increasingly took the place of public tests after 1725 or so (*A History of the Congregational Churches in the United States,* 3d ed. [Boston, 1894], 219ff.). John M. Bumsted, after an extensive review of New England church records, concluded that it is not possible to identify accurately a trend in the disappearance or reaffirmation of the requirement of a relation in the early eighteenth century ("The Pilgrim's Progress: The Ecclesiastical History of the Old Colony, 1620–1775" [Ph.D. diss., Brown University, 1965], 348 n. 28, 79–84). It is probable that in most churches, there was some disagreement, and continuing discussion, about the practice. Of a "general meeting" at the First Church in Boston, on June 9, 1730, the records report, "The mater of relations; long debates upon it." After a long night, it was voted that certain persons could be "admitted without obliging them to comply with the said custom" of a relation (*The Records of the First Church in Boston 1630–1868,* ed. Richard D. Pierce, Publications of the Colonial Society of Massachusetts, vol. 39 [Boston, 1961], 159, 158). Shipton thought that Foxcroft supported the removal of the requirement of a relation at First Church (*Biographical Sketches,* [1942], 6:51). It might be noted that Pemberton was considered a "liberal" by some persons because he readmitted sinners to the church covenant before the elders could examine them publicly (Shipton, *Biographical Sketches,* 4:110). The church at Cambridge removed the requirement of a relation in 1697 (Stephen Paschall Sharples, *Records of the Church of Christ at Cambridge in New England 1632–1830* [Boston, 1906], 121–22).

35. Lothrop, *History of the Church in Brattle Street Boston,* 21–28; Increase Mather, *The Order of the Gospel* (Boston, 1700), 131, 117–136. The Brattle Street Church responded to Mather's book with *The Gospel-Order Revived* (New York,

1700), which was probably written by Colman but was published in New York because, according to its supporters, the Mathers had influenced Boston publishers not to accept it (Kenneth Silverman, *The Life and Times of Cotton Mather* [New York, 1984], 153). Teresa Toulouse, " 'Syllabical Idolatry': Benjamin Colman and the Rhetoric of Balance," *Early American Literature* 18 (1983–84): 259, and *The Art of Prophesying: New England Sermons and the Shaping of Belief* (Athens, Ga., 1987), 56–63. On Rowe and Watts, see Fairchild, *Religious Trends in English Poetry,* 1:120–34.

36. Philip Greven has argued that acceptance of diversity "in church and community" was a feature of the "moderate" Protestant temperament (*Protestant Temperament,* 256–61).

37. Benjamin Wadsworth, *Mutual Love and Peace among Christians* (Boston, 1701), 5, 12–13, 18.

Chapter 2

1. T. H. Breen, *The Character of the Good Ruler: A Study of Puritan Political Ideas in New England, 1630–1730* (New Haven, 1970), 87–133. For population growth in New England see Daniel S. Smith, "The Demographic History of Colonial New England," *Journal of Economic History* 32 (1972): 165–83. On commercial growth and social change see Bernard Bailyn, *The New England Merchants in the Seventeenth Century* (Boston, 1955); Carl Bridenbaugh, *Cities in the Wilderness: The First Century of Urban Life in America, 1625–1742* (New York, 1938). Jack P. Greene, in *Pursuits of Happiness: The Social Development of Early Modern British Colonies and the Formation of American Culture* (Chapel Hill, 1988), provides some models of growth of other British colonies along the eastern seaboard and Caribbean (on New England see 7–80). See also the essays in Jack P. Greene and J. R. Pole, eds., *Colonial British America: Essays in the New History of the Early Modern Era* (Baltimore, 1984), and especially those by Jacob Price ("The Transatlantic Economy" [18–42]), Gary B. Nash ("Social Development" [233–61]), James A. Henretta ("Wealth and Social Structure" [262–89]), and David D. Hall ("Religion and Society: Problems and Reconsiderations" [317–44]). Recent studies challenging or extending the conclusions of earlier researchers about the extent of social dislocation or tension in the late seventeenth and early eighteenth centuries are Stephen Innes, *To Labor in a New Land: Dependency, Exchange, and Community in Seventeenth-Century Springfield* (Princeton, 1983), and Christine Leigh Heyrman, *Commerce and Culture: The Maritime Communities of Colonial Massachusetts 1690–1750* (New York, 1984). T. H. Breen and Stephen Foster argue that from 1630 to 1684 "the Bay Colony avoided significant social and political disorder," and they comment on the effect of the charter revocation on this peace ("The Puritans' Greatest Achievement: A Study of Social Cohesion in Seventeenth-Century Massachusetts," *Journal of American History* 60 [1973]: 6, 20ff.). Philip F. Gura stresses the diversity of religion among the first generation (*A Glimpse of Sion's Glory: Puritan Radicalism in Seventeenth-Century New England, 1620–1660* [Middletown, Conn., 1984]). Increase Mather, *The Day of Trouble* (Cambridge, 1674).

2. The literature on declension (pro and con), and on the jeremiad, is extensive. Perry Miller explained the jeremiad with regard to the federal theology, in a context of declension, in *From Colony to Province: New Culture in a New World* (New York, 1973), 19–146. Sacvan Bercovitch stresses the importance of the jeremiad for the

development of American literature ("Horologicals to Chronometricals: The Rhetoric of the Jeremiad," in *Literary Monographs,* vol. 3. [Madison, Wis., 1970], 1–124). Frank Shuffleton downplays terror as a feature of the jeremiad but stresses church purity (*Thomas Hooker 1586–1647* [Princeton, 1977]). Harry S. Stout, commenting on how wars, calamities, and natural disasters served a purpose to the doomsayers, observes: "By always living within the *fear* of desertion [by God] without ever conceding the *fact* of desertion, the clergy could rein in a wayward people carried along by the centrifugal pulls of the wilderness" (*The New England Soul: Preaching and Religious Culture in Colonial New England* [New York, 1986], 80). David D. Hall suggests that congregations might have paid increasingly less attention to ministers preaching jeremiads. Hall's excavation of popular religion in New England also indicates that declension may not have been as far-reaching as Miller (and others) had believed. Hall also stresses the perceived distance between church and world (*Worlds of Wonder, Days of Judgment: Popular Religious Belief in Early New England* [New York, 1989], 138, 139–140, 148–49, 163, passim). Of the recent studies focused on social history, Patricia U. Bonomi (*Under the Cope of Heaven: Religion, Society and Politics in Colonial America* [New York, 1986]) argues against the theory of declension; Roger Thompson, on the other hand, concludes that declension was "a reality rather than the myth recent scholars have depicted" (*Sex in Middlesex: Popular Mores in a Massachusetts County, 1649–1699* [Amherst, Mass., 1986], 194. Also see Williston Walker, *The Creeds and Platforms of Congregationalism* (New York, 1893), 428.

3. See A. W. Plumstead, *The Wall and the Garden: Selected Massachusetts Election Sermons 1670–1775* (Minneapolis, 1968), 3–37. Hall, *World of Wonders, Days of Judgment,* 167–68, 71–116, and "Religion and Society: Problems and Reconsiderations," in Jack P. Greene and J. R. Pole, eds., *Colonial British America: Essays in the New History of the Early Modern Era* (Baltimore, 1984), 336. William Bradford, *Of Plymouth Plantation 1620–1647,* introduction by Francis Murphy (New York, 1981), 73. Impressions of early non-Puritan immigrants and visitors were generally more positive. See William Wood, *New England's Prospect,* ed. Alden T. Vaughn (Amherst, Mass., 1977; originally published in London in 1634); Thomas Morton, "New English Canaan or New Canaan," ed. Charles Francis Adams (Boston, 1883; originally published in 1637, probably in Amsterdam); Emmanuel Altham to Sir Edward Altham, March 1623/24 in *Three Visitors to Early Plymouth,* ed. Sydney V. James (Plimoth Plantation, 1963), 37. Michael Wigglesworth, "God's Controversy with New England," *Proceedings of the Massachusetts Historical Society* 12 (1871–73): 83; Richard Slotkin, *Regeneration through Violence: The Mythology of the American Frontier, 1600–1860* (Middletown, Conn.: 1973), 77. For discussion of a sense of the mysterious and magical in nature, see Jon Butler, "Magic, Astrology, and the Early American Religious Heritage," *American Historical Review* 84 (1979): 317–46.

4. Hall, "Religion and Society: Problems and Reconsiderations," in Greene and Pole, eds., *Colonial British America,* 336; Jonathan Mitchell, *Nehemiah on the Wall* (Cambridge, 1671), 28. The sermon was preached in 1668. Samuel Danforth, *Errand into the Wilderness* (Cambridge, 1671); Samuel Willard, *The Only Sure Way to Prevent Threatened Calamity* (Boston, 1682); Urian Oakes, *A Seasonable Discourse* (Cambridge, 1682) and *New England Pleaded With* (Cambridge, 1673). In the former sermon, Oakes stresses that God has not forgotten the "zeal" of those who "came after him into this wilderness" (24). Cotton Mather, *The Way to Prosperity* (Boston, 1689); Nicolas Noyes, *New-England's Duty and Interest* (Boston, 1698); John Higginson, *The Cause of God* (Cambridge, 1663), 10; Increase Mather et al., *A Course of Sermons on*

Early Piety (Boston, 1721), 13. The book is a collection of eight sermons preached by different ministers at the Boston Thursday lecture. Mather preached on 1 Chron. 29:19: "What the pious parent wishes for."

5. Jacques LeGoff, "Le desert-forêt dans l'Occident médiéval," in *L'imaginaire médiéval: Essais* (Paris, 1985); Mircea Eliade, *Patterns in Comparative Religion* (New York, 1958), chap. 5; Charles Hambricke-Stowe, *The Practice of Piety: Puritan Devotional Disciplines in Seventeenth-Century New England* (Chapel Hill, 1982), 258–59. David D. Hall, in an analysis that suggests the appropriateness of the theories of Victor Turner to this context, recently has called attention to the importance of role reversal in rituals of repentence among New Englanders (*Worlds of Wonder, Days of Judgment* 168ff., and Victor W. Turner, *The Ritual Process: Structure and Anti-Structure* [Ithaca, N.Y., 1969]). Richard Slotkin thinks that the "captivity narrative was a primary vehicle for the American Puritan's mythology." Something of the tension between wilderness conceived as "good" and as "bad" is represented in Slotkin's statement, made in the course of his discussing the captivity narrative, that Puritans feared both a " 'marriage' of the English and 'American' cultures and a symbolic cannibalization of Indians by whites" (*Regeneration through Violence,* 100, 101, and 101–4).

The historian of religions Jonathan Z. Smith has argued, that "Chaos *only* takes a significance within a religious world view. Chaos is a sacred power; but it is frequently perceived as being sacred 'in the wrong way.' " According to Smith, the ancient Israelite perceived the wilderness in this way, that is, "The wilderness or desert was not seen as neutral ground, but rather as sacred land." But the wilderness was sacred in the "wrong way," and so, it was "the demonic land, the wasteland, the dangerous land." The wilderness, and those things associated with it, were powerful as well as dangerous. Indeed, the myth of New England's founding and mission, which constantly was recounted to audiences in the jeremiad, was meaningful only because it was juxtaposed to the constant danger of the wilderness. The power of the sacred, as explained in the sermon, consisted as much in the "bad sacred," namely, the chaos of the wilderness, as in the "good sacred," or the creation of a godly order out of that chaos. See *Map Is Not Territory: Studies in the History of Religion* (Leiden, 1978), 97, 109.

For a discussion of Anglican perception of those things that were neither good nor bad, see Bernard J. Verkamp, *The Indifferent Mean: Adiaphorism in the English Reformation to 1554* (Athens, Ohio, 1977).

6. J. Rodney Fulcher, "Puritans and the Passions: The Faculty Psychology in American Puritanism," *Journal of the History of the Behavioral Sciences* 19 (1973): 138; David Leverenz, *The Language of Puritan Feeling: An Exploration in Literature, Psychology and Social History* (New Brunswick, N.J., 1980), 209. Both of these studies, and Leverenz's in particular, are quite useful, but the authors, in the course of arguing for "rationality" in Willard's thinking, run the risk of understating the emotion in Willard and others of his generation (though I would agree with both Leverenz and Fulcher that there is ample reason to claim that there is less in the way of "connecting" affections in Willard and in the others whom they treat). Robert Middlekauff, "Piety and Intellect in Puritanism," *WMQ* 22 (1965): 467–68, and *The Mathers: Three Generations of Puritan Intellectuals 1596–1728* (New York, 1971), 171–72. Rudolf Otto, *The Idea of the Holy: An Inquiry into the Non-Rational Factor in the Idea of the Divine and Its Relation to the Rational,* trans. John W. Harvey (New York, 1958), 12–24, 31–40.

7. St. Thomas Aquinas, *Summa Theologiae,* Latin text and English trans., Blackfriars (New York and London, 1964), 1a. 78. 1; 1a. 79, 1; 1a. 79, 2; 1a. 81, 3; 1a2ae. 77,

1. The connection of the sensitive appetite to the material world is clear in assertions such as "The sense appetite, as a material faculty, inheres in a bodily organ" (1a2ae. 77, 1).; J. Rodney Fulcher, "Puritans and the Passions," 125. Fulcher stresses that the faculty psychology that descended from Aquinas (with additions made by French and English writers) to seventeenth-century Puritans was plagued by problems conceiving the relationship between body and soul, as well as the various "faculties" of the soul. According to Fulcher, "a notion of self-as-whole was finally introduced into American Puritanism by Jonathan Edwards" (125); H. M. [*sic*] Gardiner, Ruth Clark Metcalf, John G. Beebe-Center, *Feeling and Emotion: A History of Theories* (Westport, Conn., 1970, op. 1937), 106–118. See also Etienne Gilson, *The Christian Philosophy of St. Thomas Aquinas* (New York, 1956), 200–248, and *Reason and Revelation in the Middle Ages* (New York, 1966); Anthony Levi, S.J., *French Moralists: The Theory of the Passions, 1585–1649* (Oxford, 1964), 7–27.

8. Perry Miller, *The New England Mind: The Seventeenth Century* (Cambridge, Mass., 1939), 244–45, 251, 190–91; Fulcher, "Puritans and the Passions," 124, 127–36, 130; Edward Reynolds, *A Treatise of the Passions and Faculties of the Soule of Man* (London, 1640). Umberto Eco has detailed the ways in which Aquinas himself viewed the body and the world favorably, even as "beautiful" (*The Aesthetics of Thomas Aquinas,* trans. Hugh Bredin [Cambridge, Mass., 1988, op. 1970]). Miller claims that the English Puritan John Preston, among others, distinguished between a "sensuall" appetite, "which apprehends things conveyed to the senses," and a "rationall appetite" (Preston quoted in Miller, *New England Mind,* 252). Miller's emphasis on the focus of Puritan theology on reason and its capabilities is challenged by John Morgan, *Godly Learning: Puritan Attitudes toward Reason, Learning and Education,* 1560–1640 (New York, 1986), 44–46. The Puritan difficulty in coming to terms with life in the body, in the world, is well illustrated by Edmund P. Morgan, *The Puritan Dilemma: The Story of John Winthrop* (Boston, 1958), and, with reference to church membership and discipline, *Visible Saints: The History of a Puritan Idea* (New York, 1963). Thomas Shepard is quoted in Leverenz, *Language of Puritan Feeling,* 188; see also 187–90. Puritans often used *passions* and *affections* interchangeably. Many scholars in the past fifty years (e.g., Fulcher, "Puritans and the Passions," 131, 135, 137) have echoed, in various ways, the comment made by M. M. Knappen, regarding the tension in Puritanism between the freedom and responsibility of the will and the necessity, for salvation, of irrestible grace: "The Puritan writing theology gave to God all the responsibility, and, therefore, all the glory for man's salvation. But in the pulpit, as in popular writing, he was delightfully inconsistent, putting the burden on the individual" (*Tudor Puritanism: A Chapter in the History of Idealism* [Chicago, 1939], 392).

9. David D. Hall recently has argued that popular religion in New England in the seventeenth century (which was, he has explained, *not* separate from the clerical tradition) was "an incessant striving to defeat evil in the world and oneself" and was organized, essentially, around rituals and rhetoric of repentance. Colonists accordingly opposed "purity" to "uncleanness." But in their ritual, they "arranged to their own liking the boundary between purity and danger"; this was particularly true of public worship: "Purity and danger converged on the meetinghouse: both were somehow intermingled in perceptions of the passage from the 'world' into the 'church.' " According to Hall, "ambiguity, or the possibility of seeing things two different ways, was endemic" in religion in New England. I agree with much of what Hall has argued, but I would add here that the willingness to employ the affections in the process of repentance ought to be seen as both a separation from the world and a simultaneous submer-

gence of the person into worldly chaos (described by William Perkins, and other English Puritans, as the misery of doubt and disorientation that marks the early stages of regeneration). In this sense, purity and danger were "commingled" in the process of repentence itself. See Hall, *Worlds of Wonder, Days of Judgment,* 6, 121, 163, 184ff., 242, 163. Other recent studies stressing repentance in the religious life of English Puritans or seventeenth-century New Englanders are Charles Lloyd Cohen, *God's Caress: The Psychology of Puritan Religious Experience* (New York, 1986), and Charles Hambricke-Stowe, *The Practice of Piety.* On the general topic of the dialectic between "order" and "chaos" in culture see Victor W. Turner, *The Ritual Process: Structure and Anti-Structure* (Ithaca, N.Y., 1969).

Andrew Delbanco recently has argued that in the late 1630s New England ministers began to retreat from a rhetoric that was designed "to incite holy intoxication into a 'benummed' people." According to Delbanco, when "the cry was raised against the reign of 'things,' " a concept of sin as appetite, or desire itself, rather than the settling of desire on an inappropriate object, became common. (*The Puritan Ordeal* [Cambridge, Mass., 1989], 204–5).

10. Seymour Van Dyken, *Samuel Willard, 1640–1707: Preacher of Orthodoxy in an Era of Change* (Grand Rapids, Mich., 1972). Leverenz thinks that Willard retained in his *Compleat Body of Divinity,* as that work took shape over many years, a sense of "paternal distance" between God and the individual, a sense of God as a judge, rather than as a pitying father. I agree with Leverenz's own judgement of Willard's thought: "What appears to be a tender comfort to modern readers is actually an atrophy of feeling, an excess of mind" (*Language of Puritan Feeling,* 214, 203, 217, 142, 139, 219, 200). Emory Elliott has argued that both the second and third generations in New England suffered from a sense of guilt and shame, and he relates this to child-rearing practices and an internalized sense of failure arising from a perceived destruction of the errand by forces of historical change. For Elliott, Willard, who cultivated rationalistic approaches to theologizing, was less inclined than Oakes and the Mathers to urge on his audiences fear of God's wrath (*Power and the Pulpit in Puritan New England* [Princeton, 1975], 7–11, 165, 158–172). Philip Greven, stressing Willard's view of the cosmos as rationally ordered, places him among "moderates" such as Charles Chauncy (the eighteenth-century minister of First Church). In spite of his "rationality," Willard stressed guilt and separation in his sermons, and he was not comfortable with life in the physical world. It seems to me that he is in fact closer to the "evangelical" temperament described by Greven. I do, however, take Greven's point about the rationalistic flavor of Willard's theology. Indeed, it may have been just that that made him a good compromise "acting president" at Harvard after the removal of Increase Mather (*Protestant Temperament,* 9, 199–203, 226–36). Harry S. Stout sees Willard as a voice in support of the covenant, within the context of colonial political turmoil, rather than against the background of his childhood. Commenting on sermons preached in the immediate aftermath of the loss of the charter and the arrival of the troublemaking Governor Andros to Massachusetts, Stout writes of Willard (and Nathaniel Gookin [H.C. 1675]): "Sermons like Gookin's and Willard's showed how carefully ministers avoided pulpit commentary on explosive political issues, concentrating instead on the salvation of the soul. By selecting texts that spiritualized adversity and focused attention on eternity, ministers hoped to direct the people's immediate fears" into revival, and away from rebellious crusades (*New England Soul,* 113–14). Ernest Benson Lowrie argues, "What was troubling Willard most" was "the fact that in New England 'forwardness and zeal for God is almost out of date,' " though Lowrie also stresses the

rationalistic aspects of Willard's thought (*The Shape of the Puritan Mind: The Thought of Samuel Willard* [New Haven, 1974], 230). James Jones sees Willard as a somewhat liberal defender of orthodoxy, but "the irony of Willard's ministry is that as an antidote to the declension he could only recommend the same emphasis on duty and will that he knew was the cause of it" (*The Shattered Synthesis: New England Puritanism before the Great Awakening* [New Haven, 1973], 75). A good discussion of the Puritan notion of "legal fear" (as in the theology of William Perkins) and its importance in the abasement of the individual in the process of conversion is in John Owen King, *The Iron of Melancholy: Structures of Spiritual Conversion in America from the Puritan Conscience to Victorian Neurosis* [Middletown, Conn., 1983], 29–36.

11. Samuel Willard, *A Compleat Body of Divinity* (Boston, 1726), 798, 802, 803. Willard also described the "closing" affections, of which love was the most important, and from which desire, hope, and joy derived (744). It seems to me, however, that they figure considerably less into his scheme of repentance. (Willard, *Only Sure Way,* 31–32.) Willard seems to have been familiar with the ideas of William Fenner, the English Puritan author of the influential *Treatise of the Affections.* Fenner had taught that "zeale is the highest strain of all the affections," and that it was critically important that a person "give God the zeale of our affections." Zeal, for Fenner, was not a single affection but, rather, an intensity of affection generally, without regard to distinctions among hatred, shame, compassion, and so on. It is obvious from the context of the sermon that Willard did not use the term in this sense, however. He instead had in mind zeal as a "separating" affection. Willard referred to Fenner in his commonplace book, which is in the Harvard University Archives. A useful discussion of Fenner and the possible role of his book at Harvard is in Fiering, *Moral Philosophy at Seventeenth-Century Harvard: A Discipline in Transition* (Chapel Hill, 1981), 157–65, and 159 n. 29 for the reference to Willard's commonplace book. William Fenner, *A Treatise of the Affections* (London, 1642), 141, 142, 152, 3, 153.

12. Increase Mather, *Heaven's Alarm* (Boston, 1681), 12; *A Call to the Tempted* (Boston, 1723/24), 15; *Some Sermons wherein Those Eight Characters* (Boston, 1718), 148, 80, 79. In this sermon Mather refers to zeal as a "mixt affection." This follows English Puritan discussion of the affections, but it is clear that Mather, while apparently accepting the mixed nature of the affections, leans hard to the side of "separating" affections. For a perceptive discussion of the place of love (and zeal) in the affections understood as "mixt," see the analysis of English Puritan thought in Cohen, *God's Caress,* chap. 4, esp. 130–33. *A Plain Discourse* (Boston, 1713), 48, 49–50; *Awakening Truth's Tending to Conversion* (Boston, 1710), 36. There is also a limited discussion in this sermon on the person's turning to Jesus Christ in conversion, but there is no recommendation that this be done in connection with the affections. Rather, Mather seems to stress the intellectual consent given to truth. *A Course of Sermons on Early Piety,* sermon by Increase Mather, 22ff. Also note: "Hence we see, men ought not to set their hearts inordinately upon their children" (10). Michael G. Hall discusses Mather's millennial hopes (*Last American Puritan,* 271–79).

13. Urian Oakes, *A Seasonable Discourse* (Cambridge, 1682), 17; *New-England Pleaded With* (Cambridge, 1673), 33, 11; *The Sovereign Efficacy* (Boston, 1682), 29. John Higginson, *A Testimony, To the Order of the Gospel* (Boston, 1701), 9 (this was written in response to the Brattle Street manifesto); *Our Dying Saviour's Legacy* (Boston, 1686), 198, 66. Higginson, like most other ministers, did not rule out the role of affections in moving the person toward Christ, but this aspect was deemphasized in relation to separation from sin. Nicholas Noyes "May 28th, 1706. To My Worthy

Friend, Mr. James Bayley . . . A Poem" (Boston, 1707), broadside. Judge Sewall knew from Noyes that the end of the world was imminent (*The Diary of Samuel Sewall, 1674–1729*, ed. M. Halsey Thomas [New York, 1973], 1:501).

14. Clifford K. Shipton, *Biographical Sketches of Those Who Attended Harvard College,* vol. 5 (Boston, 1873–1975), 466. Shipton emphasizes Webb's preaching about declension, lusts, and the horrors of hell. John Webb, *Some Plain and Necessary Directions* (Boston, 1741), 74. Webb was more likely than his elders to refer to God as a compassionate father, as he did in passing herein (27). See also (together with pages from preceding quotations from these sermons) *The Duty of a Regenerate People* (Boston, 1734), 15, 12, 24, 26, and *Christ's Suit to the Sinner* (Boston, 1741), 12–14, 27; *The Greatness of Sin Improved* (Boston, 1734), app. but also 26 on compassion; *The Young Man's Duty Explained* (Boston, 1718), 11, 12, 25. Webb told those mourning the early death of William Waldron (H.C. 1717; first pastor of the New Brick Church) that the deceased demonstrated exemplary "zeal" in his preaching "against the sins of the times" (*The Duty of Ministers* [Boston, 1727], 20). Webb prevailed over John Barnard for the position in 1714. Webb's sermons include numerous references interrelating the devil, the world, and lusts and passions.

15. Shipton, *Biographical Sketches,* 6:179–80; John Eliot, *Biographical Dictionary* (Boston, 1809), 215–16; Joshua Gee, *The Strait Gate* (Boston, 1729), 68–69, 67. Gee registered approval of those who "think our saviour, by the narrower afflicted way, has a special reference to the opposition of the world" (42). Gee also inveighed against those who would rely on "modes and forms" in religion (46). *Israel's Mourning* (Boston, 1728), 15.

16. Mather Byles, *The Visit to Jesus by Night* (Boston, 1741), 23; *A Discourse of the Present Vileness of the Body* (Boston, 1723), 2, 3, 6, 8; *Repentance and Faith* (Boston, 1741), 52; *The Glories of the Lord* (Boston, 1740), 27.

17. Sewall, *Diary,* 1:76; Samuel Checkley, *The Death of the Godly* (Boston, 1727), 1; *Murder a Great and Crying Sin* (Boston, 1733), 15, 5, 6, 19–20. Harry S. Stout remarks on Checkley's description, in detail, of the terrors of hell and his jeremiadlike laments about New England's sins (*New England Soul,* 226, 249).

18. Silverman describes some ways in which Increase influenced Cotton Mather (Kenneth Silverman, *The Life and Times of Cotton Mather* [New York, 1984], 24–52, 156). Mitchell Breitwieser has argued that Cotton Mather understood "Enlightenment modes of describing the world" to be antithetical to piety and that he sought in *The Christian Philosopher* to negate the power of the Enlightenment and to reassert piety. According to Breitwieser, "The government of Enlightenment by piety . . . is the government of Cotton Mather by the voice of Increase within him" (Mitchell Robert Breitwieser, *Cotton Mather and Benjamin Franklin: The Price of Representative Personality* [New York, 1984], 109–10).

19. Greven, *Protestant Temperament,* 66–67. For Greven, persons of "evangelical" temperament viewed their bodies as "loathsome corruption and pollution." Cotton Mather, *Diary of Cotton Mather,* 2:119; *Conversion Exemplified* (Boston, 1703), 1. Writing in 1726, Mather imagined "the destruction of a world whose ordeals and traps, at least, he had grown to hate, 'a World,' he said 'which is not a *Paradise* (nor is like to afford one) but is an horrid and howling Wilderness; A Land of Pits and of Droughts, and fiery flying Serpents' " (Silverman, *Life and Times of Cotton Mather,* 414–15).

20. Robert Middlekauff, "Piety and Intellect in Puritanism," *WMQ* 22 (1965), 460; Cotton Mather, *Piety and Equity, United* (Boston, 1717). All of the sermons were

published in Boston, except *The Greatest Concern in the World.* I read the second edition, published in New London in 1718. Mather often refers to "heart" in his sermons. But his emphasis is generally on the apprehension of revealed truth and its power to turn the sinner to God, rather than on the actual inflammation of the emotions. (Preaching on the doctrine of predestination, Mather declared, "This admirable truth shall not go out of our hands, until we feel it make a most heart-melting impression on our hearts" [*Free Grace, Maintained & Improved* (Boston, 1706), 7].) It seems that Mather would trust the "closing" or "connecting" affections only when the self—and its fleshly, worldly inclinations—had been overcome. In fact, in the process of conversion, feeling of any sort (including separating affections) was suspect. Robert Middlekauff, writing about Mather's emphasis on the "annihilation" of the self in conversion, observes: "Cotton Mather's 'method' [of conversion] was not intended to produce feeling—if guilt, sorrow, humility, repentence, contrition are all sorts of feeling—but rather to yield debasement and dependence" (*Mathers,* 236). Mather apparently had no shortage of love toward his family (David Levin, *Cotton Mather: The Young Life of the Lord's Remembrancer 1663–1703* [Cambridge, Mass., 1978], 298–300). As a way of underscoring the fact that Mather's thought is hard to decipher, I note two studies (with which I disagree) that suggest that Mather in fact supported the excitation of the affections: Eugene E. White, *Puritan Rhetoric: The Issue of Emotion in Religion* (Carbondale, Ill., 1972), 31–32; Joyce Irwin, "The Theology of 'Regular Singing,' " *NEQ* 51 (1978): 189–90. Mather was not alone in his apparent dismissal of the affections as an important part of conversion. Ebenezer Parkman (H.C. 1721), minister at Westborough for nearly sixty years, recorded in his diary his covenant renewal, in 1729. There is no mention of the role of the affections in an otherwise detailed account. Parkman did write: "He that is Christ's hath crucified the Flesh, with the affections and lusts. Have I?" (*The Diary of Ebenezer Parkman 1703–1782,* ed. Francis G. Walett [Worcester, Mass., 1974], 34–38).

21. David D. Hall, *The Faithful Shepherd: A History of the New England Ministry in the Seventeenth-Century* (New York, 1974), 276–77. Mather's rebuttal is entitled "A Collection of Some of the Many Offensive Matters, Contained in . . . *The Order of the Gospel Revived*" (1701). Colman is usually identified as the author of *The Gospel Order Revived,* but there is no clear and final testimony as to his part in writing it. According to Arthur B. Ellis, First Church became friendly toward the Brattle Street Church as early as one year after the founding of the latter, but some differences remained for as long as ten years (Arthur B. Ellis, *History of the First Church in Boston, 1630–1880* [Boston, 1880], 166). The First Church rejected Colman's *Gospel Order Revived* but did not condemn those who embraced it: "Wee doe herein declare our utter dislike thereof, tho wee doe not condemn those who conscientiously practice otherwise" (*Records of the First Church in Boston,* 99–100). E. Brooks Holifield suggests that by 1718 Increase Mather changed some of his views on toleration. Holifield also points out that the identification of factions in Boston church politics in the seventeenth century is difficult, because of exceptions to "party" behavior ("On Toleration in Massachusetts," *Church History* 38 [1969]: 188–200; see 198 on Increase Mather).

22. A good discussion of the Heads of Agreement is in Hall, *Faithful Shepherd,* 223–25. See Middlekauff, *Mathers,* 218–30; Silverman, *Life and Times of Cotton Mather,* 138–46, 303, 368, 329–31; Stout, *New England Soul,* 128–30. Cotton Mather, *Manuductio* (Boston, 1726), 128; *Ratio Disciplinae Fratrum Nov-Anglorum* (Boston, 1726), 86–89. Daniel Neal, *The History of New England* (London, 1720), 610.

Kenneth Silverman, as well as David Levin and Robert Middlekauff, have suggested that Mather's active support for Christian union in the late seventeenth century was fueled by his belief that the Second Coming was near (he calculated the year to be 1697), and that he wished to effect a reformation before it dawned. In fact, Mather often looked beyond life in the world to existence among the saints in heavenly society. In *Bonafacius* (1710), which described ways in which persons might do good in the world, Mather, following the calculations of the English scientist William Whiston, announced his eagerness to see the fall of the Anti-Christ (and the coming of Jesus Christ), in 1716. Indeed, Mather, for all of his practical "do-good" and his interest in science, might be understood, as Mitchell Breitwieser has suggested, as an "observer," not as a "user" of creation. See Middlekauff, *Mathers,* 231; Levin, *Cotton Mather,* 293, 135; Silverman, *Life and Times of Cotton Mather,* 303; Cotton Mather, *Bonafacius: An Essay upon the Good* (Boston, 1710), xvii; Breitwieser, *Cotton Mather and Benjamin Franklin,* 109–10.

23. Harry S. Stout remarks on "the tendency of third-generation ministers to record and 'idealize' their past." I agree with Stout that the third generation believed that "if they did not know their history they did not know God." But I agree with him as well that the third generation "altered the major categories of New England's ongoing errand," so as to make a place within the errand for ecumencial endeavors, among other things (*New England Soul,* 136, 129).

24. On Rowe and Colman see Larzer Ziff, *Puritanism in America,* 274–76; Teresa Toulouse, *The Art of Prophesying: New England Sermons and the Shaping of Belief* (Athens, Ga., 1987), 57–60. Miller, *From Colony to Province,* 462–3, 269. I do not think that Wadsworth was "unemotional," however (463). Miller refers to Wadsworth elsewhere as "ultra-conciliatory" (*Jonathan Edwards* [Westport, Conn., 1949], 20). Michael G. Hall also calls Colman a "peacemaker" (*Last American Puritan,* 298), and William B. Sprague describes him as "pre-eminently a lover and promoter of peace" (*Annals of the American Pulpit* [New York, 1857], 226). An example of Wadsworth's peacemaking activities was his contribution to the published discussion of the founding of the Brattle Street Church. Wadsworth elected to travel the high road of conciliation, rather than join in the war of words (with the Mathers, Higginson, Colman, and others). Wadsworth intimated in *Mutual Love and Peace among Christians* (Boston, 1701) that the heated discussion about the new church should be softened with open-mindedness and recollection of a sense of the bonds of Christian love between persons.

25. Ziff, *Puritanism in America,* 268. Ziff added that the test of a relation "was certainly too tastelessly personal and would have to go." Bruce E. Steiner, "New England Anglicanism: A Genteel Faith?" *WMQ* 27 (1970): 133. The most recent study to stress that the founders of the church were wealthy merchants is Bonomi, *Under the Cope of Heaven,* 62, 68, 93.

26. Bruce Tucker, "The Reinterpretation of Puritan History in Provincial New England," *NEQ* 54 (1981): 488, 489, 485–86; "The Reinvention of New England," *NEQ* 59 (1986): 318, 328. Tucker thinks Foxcroft did not see continuity with England in 1730 but eventually came to stress it ("Reinterpretation," 496). I think that Foxcroft (like other catholicks) began his project of reconciliation with England by making adjustments in his thought directly related to church matters and that it was through such adjustments that he fashioned for himself a basis for examining the larger considerations of trans-Atlantic politics. Tucker is primarily concerned with the long-term political implications of adjustments to the new charter, whereas I am specifically interested in the development of new religious ideas within a changing social and

political environment. On Andros, see Breen, *Character of the Good Ruler,* 141–160. Stout comments on the effects of Andros's presence in New England on Congregationalist mission (*New England Soul,* 111–23). The second generation's view of religion within the Anglo-American world might be generally described, following Jonathan Z. Smith, as a "locative vision of the world," that is, as an emphasis on *place,* and, especially, on place as representative of a closed, or static, experience of the world. Smith proposes in opposition to this the "utopian vision of the world (using the term in its strict sense: the value of being in no place)," in which "beings are called upon to change their limits, break them, or create new possibilities." The eventual catholick response to the new charter—*as compared to* the worldview of the second generation, or of Webb, Byles, et al.—lies closer to the "utopian" vision than to the "locative." See *Map Is Not Territory,* 100–101. Also useful, especially on the seventeenth century, is Alexander Koyre, *From the Closed World to the Infinite Universe* (Baltimore, 1957).

27. Arthur D. Kaledin, "The Mind of John Leverett" (Ph.D. diss., Harvard University, 1965), 242, 229, and Leverett quoted, 241. For the symbol ♡ in Leverett's writings, see his "Commonplace Book, 1680–1711," MHS. On Colman see especially Toulouse, *Art of Prophesying,* 46–74; Ziff, *Puritanism in America,* 273–279; Miller, *Jonathan Edwards,* 17–22. Stout, *New England Soul,* 157. Michael Hall offers the surprising opinion "The men who started Brattle Street Church admired a cool, disengaged, tolerant approach to religion and church worship," and he juxtaposes this to the "hot and passionate" piety of Increase Mather (*Last American Puritan,* 319). If Hall is right, then the undertakers of the Brattle Street Church made a very serious miscalculation in wooing Colman back across the Atlantic to take up duties as their pastor. Colman was indeed tolerant, but he was not "cool" and was certainly not "disengaged."

28. Thomas Foxcroft, *Ministers, Spiritual Parents* (Boston, 1726), 49; Thomas Foxcroft Notebooks, CL. Among Foxcroft's notes are several long prayers (undated) that he wrote. One of these, a prayer to be said in the morning, while including a reference to God's judgment of humanity, stressed essentially God's mercy and love. Another also stressed the closing affections, in phrases such as "We bless thee for our creation & preservation in all the blessings of *this life,* but above all for thine inestimable love" (emphasis added). Foxcroft's use of "set formes" such as these prayers would not have sat well with Increase Mather (as noted previously). Robert J. Wilson III identifies Foxcroft as "the principal leader" of those who were "moving away from rational preaching and back toward a more emotional faith" (*The Benevolent Deity: Ebenezer Gay and the Rise of Rational Religion in New England, 1696–1787* [Philadelphia, 1984], 68).

29. Isaac Newton, *Opticks: Or, A Treatise of the Reflections, Refractions, Inflections and Colours of Light* (bk. 1, pt. 2, prop. 5). Though the book was not published until 1704, Newton's theories about light and color were known as early as 1672, as a result of a paper on the subject that he sent to the Royal Society. Thomas Foxcroft, *The Character of Anna* (Boston, 1723), 35. There is no evidence to suggest that Foxcroft had actually read Newton, but the *Opticks* was listed in the Harvard catalogue of 1723. According to Charles B. Giles, Colman, while in Bath, read Newton's *Principia,* Locke's *Essay,* and works by Richard Bentley ("Benjamin Colman: A Study of the Movement toward Reasonable Religion in the Seventeenth Century" [Ph.D. diss., University of California at Los Angeles, 1963], 147–69).

30. Benjamin Wadsworth, *An Essay on the Decalogue* (Boston, 1719), 13; *Men Self-Condemned,* (Boston, 1706), 50; Sermons preached at the Brattle Street Church, Nov. 4, 1711, and Nov. 18, 1711, RBR Ms. drawer 7, Congregational Library; Sermon

preached Mar. 30, 1712, "Twenty-three Manuscript Sermons," Harvard University Archives. Wadsworth told his congregation in 1708, "A sense of the love of Christ does produce holy affections in us correspondent unto the love of Christ" (Thomas Foxcroft Notebooks, Congregational Library, Feb. 13, 1708). Ebenezer Pemberton, sermon preached Mar. 28, 1697, in "Hunting and Gibbs. Sermons. 1696/Richard Brown, Notes to Sermons, 1696," MHS; "Sermons June 13, 1708–April 3, 1709," 101.205 MHS (see especially sermons preached by Pemberton in fall 1708 and Jan. 7, 1709); Sermon preached Mar. 24, 1709 (public fast), Thomas Foxcroft Notebooks, Congregational Library. Nathaniel Appleton, sermon preached late October or early November 1718, in Ebenezer Parkman, Notes of Sermons, 1718–1722, MHS; *The Wisdom of God* (Boston, 1728), 282–83.

31. Benjamin Colman, *A Sermon at the Lecture in Boston, after the Funerals of . . . William Brattle . . . and . . . Ebenezer Pemberton* (Boston, 1717), 12–13; *The Hope of the Righteous* (Boston, 1721), 11; *Souls Flying* (Boston, 1740), 26; *Early Piety Again Inculcated* (Boston, 1720), 33. Colman seems to have been warmly affectionate to the members of his own family, as well as to his friends. According to his son-in-law, "He was most complaisant, tender, and affectionate" to each of his three wives and was "singularly affectionate and kind" to his friends. His letter of concern to his daughter after the earthquake reflects some of his fatherly affection (Ebenezer Turell, *The Life and Character of the Reverend Benjamin Colman, D.D.* [Boston, 1749], 210, 215; "Letter from Benjamin Colman to his Daughter, Mrs. Jane Turell," *NEHGR* 15, no. 4 [October 1861]: 316–17).

32. Lee W. Gibbs, *William Ames: Technometry* (Philadelphia, 1979).

33. Cassirer, *The Platonic Renaissance in England,* trans. James R. Pettegrove (New York, 1970), 60–61, 149–50; McAdoo, *Spirit of Anglicanism,* 102; Norman Sykes, *From Sheldon to Secker: Aspects of English Church History 1660–1768* (Cambridge, 1959), 144–46; G. R. Cragg, *From Puritanism to the Age of Reason* (Cambridge, England, 1966), and Cragg, ed., *The Cambridge Platonists* (New York, 1968), 28. See also G.P.H. Pawson, *The Cambridge Platonists and Their Place in Religious Thought* (New York, 1974), who, like Cassirer, sees tensions beneath the surface of their thought.

34. Benjamin Whichcote, *Select Sermons* (London[?], 1698), 381, 68; McAdoo, *Spirit of Anglicanism,* 83–84. On piety in More see John Hoyles, *The Waning of the Renaissance 1640–1740* (Hague, 1971), 30–44. On their rejection of predestination see Sykes, *From Sheldon to Secker,* 144, and Clarence Gohdes, "Aspects of Idealism in Early New England," *Philosophical Review* 39, no. 6 (November 1930): 551. McAdoo (*Spirit of the Renaissance,* 96, 101, 102, 106), Barbara Shapiro (*John Wilkins 1614–1672: An Intellectual Biography* [Berkeley, 1969]), 144), and Daniel Walker Howe ("The Cambridge Platonists of Old England and the Cambridge Platonists of New England," *Church History* 57 [1988]: 472) comment on how their religion resembled the mysticism of Plotinus. For the opinion that the Cambridge Platonists, and especially More, approved of emotion, or a "noble enthusiasm" in religion, see Fiering, *Moral Philosophy at Seventeenth Century Harvard,* 177; Gohdes, "Aspects of Idealism," 551; Lee, *The Historical Backgrounds of Early Methodist Enthusiasm,* 85ff.

35. Norman Fiering, *Moral Philosophy at Seventeenth-Century Harvard* (Chapel Hill, 1981), 251, 47 n. 77 ("Whatever the case may be concerning the inner affinities between New England Puritanism and Cambridge Platonism, the success of More's ethics in New England is undeniable" [251, and, on the popularity of More's ethics in America, see 252 n. 33]). Harvard College, *Catalogue Librorum Bibliothecae; A Cata-*

logue of Curious and Valuable Books Belonging to Ebenezer Pemberton; Howe, "Cambridge Platonists," 472; Franklin B. Dexter, "Influence of the English Universities in the Development of New England," *Proceedings of the Massachusetts Historical Society* 17 (February 1880): 341, and see the chart on 352; Gohdes, "Aspects of Idealism in Early New England," believed that the "Cambridge Platonists fared better in America than in England," and he argued that Cudworth (and Glanvill) served as sources for American ideas about witches (552, 546).

36. Ralph Cudworth, *A Sermon Preached before the Honourable House of Commons* (London, 1647), 5, 61, 34. The phrase "bowels of compassion" appeared in English sermons of the seventeenth century, and in New England sermons as well. Cudworth, *The Union of Christ and the Church in a Shadow* (London, 1642), 1, 6.

37. Henry More, *An Explanation of the Grand Mystery of Godliness* (London, 1660), 513, 51, 538; *Enthusiasmus Triumphatus* (London, 1662), 3–6, and passim; *An Antidote against Atheism,* 3d ed. (London, 1662) contains arguments about the beauty of the human body, and creation in general, and wonder stories (see bk. 2, esp. chaps. 7–12, and bk. 3 [wonder stories]). Fiering (*Moral Philosophy*) stresses More's desire to preserve religious enthusiasm and compares him in this regard to Shaftesbury (177). McAdoo (*Spirit of Anglicanism*) describes the latitudinarians as similar to Cambridge Platonists "minus the sense of wonder and the genius" (158).

38. Basil Willey, *The Eighteenth-Century Background: Studies on the Idea of Nature in the Thought of the Period* (London, 1961 [op. 1940]), 4. For an excellent discussion of the perception of beauty in nature in the seventeenth century among English scientists and poets, but especially Thomas Burnet, see Majorie Hope Nicolson, *Mountain Gloom and Mountain Glory: The Development of the Aesthetics of the Infinite* (Ithaca, N.Y., 1959). The Harvard Library in 1723 listed Ray's *The Wisdom of God in Creation* (London, 1709), Thomas Burnet's *Sacred Theory of the Earth* (London, 1697), and numerous volumes by Boyle, including theological and philosophical works and reports of specific experiments with earth, air, fire, and water (*Catalogus Librorum Bibliothecae*). Pemberton owned the Burnet, William Whiston's *A New Theory of the Earth* and "sermons at Boyles lecture," and William Derham's *Physical Theology* and *Astro-Theology* (*A Catalogue of Curious Valuable Books . . .*). Thomas Foxcroft, under the heading "Works of God" in his notebook, included references to Ray and Derham (Thomas Foxcroft Notebooks, Congregational Library). Charles Morton, who emigrated to Charlestown in 1686 and became a kind of unofficial tutor to Harvard students, wrote a textbook that introduced them to scientific explanations for events that had usually been considered "supernatural" in origin, such as earthquakes and comets (see Fiering, *Moral Philosophy,* 207–38; Morton, *Compendium Physicae, Publications of the Colonial Society of Massachusetts* [Boston, 1940], 33). Boyle's connection to New England was financial as well as intellectual. Funds from his estate were used to buy books and pay salaries—including President Leverett's—at Harvard, and Colman's series of lectures at Bath (for which Colman had to come to terms with some of the new science) were founded in 1691 according to the terms of Boyle's will ("Harvard College Records," *Publications of the Colonial Society of Massachusetts,* 15:264, 290, 395, 401; 16:455, 500, 511, 522, 529, 540; William T. Youngs, Jr., *God's Messengers: Religious Leadership in Colonial New England, 1700–1750* [Baltimore, 1976], 157 n. 75; Giles, "Benjamin Colman," 147–69). Cotton Mather recognized his debts to "the industrious Mr. Ray, and the inquisitive Mr. Derham" (*The Christian Philosopher: A Collection of the Best Discoveries in Nature, with Religious Improvements* [London, 1721], 3). Robert Middlekauff (*Mathers*) points out that Cot-

ton Mather read Robert Boyle's *Usefulness of Experimental Natural Philosophy* (1663) in the 1680s and borrowed heavily from it. In spite of this debt, I do not think that Mather ever really came to trust or to feel safe in the world.

It was not necessary for New Englanders to read Newton in order to comprehend the "Newtonian world." Willey proposed that Derham's and Ray's works were "representative of the period of the Newtonian illumination" (Willey, *Eighteenth-Century Background,* 27). Whiston was the first person to present Newton's theories to a popular audience (which included the Newtonian spokesman-to-be Alexander Pope) in his popular lectures at Button's coffee house in Covent Garden (James E. Force, introduction to *Astronomical Principles of Religion, Natural and Reveal'd* by William Whiston [New York, 1983], 38, 5).

39. Barbara Shapiro, *Probability and Certainty in Seventeenth-Century England* (Princeton, 1983), 88. Richard S. Westfall argues generally the same interpretation of the virtuosi (Richard S. Westfall, *Science and Religion in Seventeenth-Century England* [Ann Arbor, Mich., 1973]). Robert Boyle, *The Christian Virtuoso,* in *Philosophical Works of the Honourable Robert Boyle, Esq.,* ed. Peter Shaw, M.D., vol. 2 (London, 1725), 242, 239, 275, 246. Harry S. Stout in discussing the New England ministry's adoption of the rhetoric of "delight" in creation associates it primarily with Tillotson. Tillotson actually emphasized sober morality more than delight, or other emotional experiences of the "sublime" (*New England Soul,* 133).

40. Joseph Glanvill, *Essays on Several Important Subjects in Philosophy and Religion* (London, 1676), chap. 5, "The Agreement of Reason and Religion"; Edward Stillingfleet, *Rational Account of the Grounds of the Christian Faith* (London, 1662), 367. Stillingfleet argued that one of the "pretences of the atheists of our age" was a claim for "the inconsistency of the beliefs of scripture with the principles of religion" (from the preface). John Wilkins, *Of the Principles and Duties of Natural Religion* (London, 1675), 18, preface; *Ecclesiastes, Or a Discourse Concerning the Gift of Preaching* (London, 1693), 174, 177, 178ff.

41. John Tillotson, *Sermons Preached on Several Occasions* (London, 1671), 3, 98ff., 184, 194; *Sermons and Discourses,* 2d ed., vol. 3 (London, 1687), 73, 72, 84. Tillotson constantly emphasized the importance of a good argument for reinforcing belief in Christianity. He wrote, "Nothing ought to be received as a divine doctrine and revelation without good evidence that it is so: that is, without some argument sufficient to satisfie a prudent and considerate man" (77). The best arguments were related to the excellence of Christian morality: "The miracles of it [Christianity] are the great external evidence and comprehension of its truth and divinity; but the morality of its doctrines and precepts, so agreeable to the best reason" are the "things which our religion glories in as her crown and excellence" (*A Sermon Preached Nov. 5, 1678* [London, 1678], 1–2).

42. I suggest further influences in chap. 3.

43. Stout, *New England Soul,* 133.

44. Religious language emphasizing beauty and light in creation had been popular, within the mainstream of Christian theology, at least since Aquinas, who, as Umberto Eco has shown, incorporated such notions into the foundation of his aesthetics (*The Aesthetics of Thomas Aquinas,* trans. Hugh Bredin [Cambridge, Mass., 1988, op. 1970]).

45. Benjamin Wadsworth, *The Great and Last Day of Judgment* (Boston, 1709), 106; *Twelve Single Sermons* (Boston, 1717), 106; Nathaniel Appleton, *The Wisdom of God* (Boston, 1728), 212; *Faithful Ministers of Christ* (Boston, 1743), 22; Benjamin

Colman, *A Brief Dissertation* (Boston, 1735), 8; *Early Piety Again Inculcated* (Boston, 1720), 11. Examples of Foxcroft's references to the "light of nature" and "the father of lights" are in *Ministers, Spiritual Parents* (Boston, 1726), 21, and *The Day of a Godly Man's Death* (Boston, 1722), 108. According to Harry S. Stout, expressions such as "the Father of Lights," "Great Governor of the Universe," and "Supreme Architect" were rare in the seventeenth century (*New England Soul,* 133). Perry Miller thought that Colman's *A Humble Discourse of the Incomprehensibility of God* (Boston, 1715) was a "masterpiece" and "a principal vehicle . . . for the popularization of the new science" (*Jonathan Edwards,* 18). The sermon contained assertions about the visibility of God in "the frame and government of the universe" but, especially, numerous statements about the vastness and beauty of the universe (with a liberal sprinkling of references to "millions," "thousands," and infinity [iv, 6, 7, 27–28, 29, 30, 33ff.]). The sermon is a good example of the "aesthetics of the infinite" in the seventeenth and eighteenth centuries, described by Marjorie Hope Nicolson (*Mountain Gloom and Mountain Glory*). Deception and self-deception, which Congregationalists knew about from the warnings of seventeenth-century Puritans, were possible even with light and darkness. Appleton, in writing about the need for missionaries to the Indians, declared that the Indians were severely lacking in exposure to Christian doctrine, "unless what some of them have by the Romish missionaries, which light is but darkness" (*Gospel Ministers* [Boston, 1735], i).

46. Benjamin Colman, *Early Piety Again Inculcated,* 10–11; *The Government and Improvement of Mirth* (Boston, 1710), 115; Thomas Foxcroft, *The Voice of the Lord* (Boston, 1727), 3; Benjamin Wadsworth, Sermon preached Aug. 13, 1721, Thomas Foxcroft Notebooks, Congregational Library. Wadsworth wrote, "God makes the brightest displays of his glorious perfections" in the heavens (*The Highest Dwelling with the Lowest* [Boston, 1711], 4–5).

47. Benjamin Wadsworth, *An Essay to Do Good* (Boston, 1710), 27; Sermon preached Aug. 5, 1722, Thomas Foxcroft Notebooks, Congregational Library; Nathaniel Appleton, *Faithful Ministers of Christ* (Boston, 1743), 39, 22; Benjamin Colman, *God Deals with Us as Rational Creatures* (Boston, 1723), 7, 8. Colman believed that "would men but open their eyes and see, wou'd they give their minds to contemplate God in his works, wou'd they use their reason and survey the same things that daily occur to them," they would discover God's will (*Humble Discourse,* 42). More concisely, Colman informed Governor Shirley in 1741, regarding the works of creation, "We have minds and eyes to observe 'em, and memories to retain 'em" (*The Lord Shall Rejoice* [Boston, 1741], 18). Appleton, preaching on "how the wicked will be punished after death," informed his audience that "natural light will in a great measure teach us this"; that "reason will tell us that the wicked & ungodly do those things that are very offensive and hatefull to the pure eyes of God" (Sermon preached Oct. 17, 1725, in Solomon Prentice, *Notes on Sermons 1724–1726,* Harvard University Archives).

48. Benjamin Colman, *Faithful Pastors* (Boston, 1739), 4. Compare with Wadsworth, *The Well-Ordered Family* (Boston, 1712), 5, which has a slightly different focus. Foxcroft, *Character of Anna,* 15–16. See also Edward Wigglesworth, *Two Lectures on Romans IX.18* (Boston, 1741), Harvard University Archives. Foxcroft, under the heading "subjects for meditation," wrote the following on the back of a letter: "Of God his being and perfections, which are inseparable and the same. God is being of infinite [proportions?]. Evidence of the existence of such a being from scripture and reason" (Letter from James Cary et al., Apr. 2, 1730, Thomas Foxcroft Notebooks, Congregational Library). This was before Joseph Priestley's discovery (1774) of "dephlogis-

ticated air," or oxygen, and for many the invisible air that persons breathed remained mysterious and even dangerous. At the end of the seventeenth century, Cotton Mather believed that the air was populated by "hideous droves of thos wicked spirits, being fallen angels" (*Addresses to Old Men* [Boston, 1690], 53). Increase wrote twenty years later, "The air is the devil's territory" (*Meditations upon the Glory of the Heavenly World* [Boston, 1711], 91), and Mather Byles, twenty years after that, asked: "How many sins enter at the eyes? . . . Pass in at the ears, forever open to the vanity of empty and corrupted air, and drag him on to excess and intemperance" (*Discourse on the Present Vileness of the Body,* 2–3). John Hancock (H.C. 1689), of Lexington, wrote, "There is even a rule in the Kingdom of Darkness, and a prince of the power of the air" (*Rulers Should Be Benefactors* [Boston, 1722], 7). After the first decade of the eighteenth century, catholicks were inclined to view the air as mysterious but not necessarily evil, and, in fact, by the 1730s, Colman was writing that the air, "as the wondrous work of God, accompanying the light, which how should it [light] glare, or be visible at all, but thro' a vehicle of Air" (*Brief Dissertation,* 9). Cotton Mather claimed to be quoting the English poet Edmund Waller when he gave a somewhat positive valuation of the air in *The Christian Philosopher: A Collection of the Best Discoveries in Nature, with Christian Improvements* (London, 1721), 69. On air as mysterious but not dangerous see Foxcroft, *The Voice of the Lord* (Boston, 1727), 11–12; Wadsworth, *The Great and Last Day of Judgment,* 59. Also, compare Foxcroft, *Cleansing Our Way in Youth* (Boston, 1719), 6, and *A Practical Discourse Relating to the Gospel Ministry* (Boston, 1718), 16, 24–25, with *A Discourse Concerning Kindness* (Boston, 1722), 31. Note also Mather's third-hand recounting of the story of the "ship in the air" (*Magnalia Christi Americana,* bk. 1 [New York, 1967, op. 1702], 84). Samuel Moody in 1746 copied into his Harvard notes an excerpt from Derham's *Physico-Theology* commenting on the mysterious phenomenon of having to breathe more at high altitudes (*Commonplace Book 1746,* Harvard University Archives).

49. According to Greven, moderates "responded both to their physical selves, and to the self as a whole in ways which differed profoundly from the intense mistrust and hostility felt by evangelicals. Instead of feeling a need to reject the appetites of the body and the passions of the self, instead of waging constant and total warfare against the impulses and desires of their natures, moderates accepted the appetites and passions that allied them with the animal world as essential aspects of their humanity, indispensible for the preservation and pleasures of the self" (*Protestant Temperament,* 206).

50. Thomas Foxcroft, Sermon preached Sept. 3, 1719, Thomas Foxcroft Notebooks, Congregational Library; Appleton, *Wisdom of God,* 379; Wadsworth, *Great and Last Day of Judgment,* 8; Colman, *The Holy Walk* (Boston, 1728), app. (no pagination).

51. Benjamin Wadsworth, *The Benefits of a Good, and The Mischiefs of an Evil, Conscience* (Boston, 1719), 58; Nathaniel Appleton, *The Origin of War Examin'd* (Boston, 1733), 11. Colman, *The Faithful Ministers* (Boston, 1729), 5; *A Humble Discourse,* 43, 33, 36; *Early Piety Again Inculcated,* 12–13, 3–4; *The Lord Shall Rejoice* (Boston, 1741), 22. For Colman's views see also *The Credibility* (Boston, 1729), 17, 18, 19. The increase in the wearing of wigs around 1700 may have been partly related to the emergence of a more positive view of the body. Judge Sewall was strongly opposed to wigs and chose to remain wigless and a widower, rather than accede to the demand of a would-be spouse that he adopt the practice (*Diary of Samuel Sewall,* 2:964, 967n). Sewall apparently thought it sufficiently important as to note (approvingly) in his diary

that all of the pallbearers at the funeral of John Higginson "wore their own hair" (611). Sewall's views on wigs are summarized in *Publications of the Colonial Society of Massachusetts* 20 (1918): 109–28. T. H. Breen thinks that in the late seventeenth century, "many New Englanders regarded wigs as an outward sign of inward corruption" (*Character of the Good Ruler,* 141–42). Colman, Wadsworth, and Pemberton each wore a periwig at least some of the time. John Barnard sported a long wig, sword, and black clothes while traveling in England, but in the New World, during the Port Royal expedition, his wig took a bullet ("Autobiography of the Rev. John Barnard," *Collections of the Massachusetts Historical Society* 3d ser., 5 [1856]: 205; Shipton, *Biographical Sketches,* 4:504, 84).

52. Foxcroft, *Voice of the Lord,* 3; Colman, *Early Piety Again Inculcated,* 14; Geoffrey Nuttall, *The Holy Spirit in Faith and Experience* (Oxford, 1946); Wadsworth, *Men Self-Condemned,* 39–40; Appleton, sermon preached Apr. 11, 1725, in Solomon Prentice, *Notes on Sermons 1724–26,* Harvard University Archives. See also Miller, *New England Mind,* 191 and 181–206. On Edwards see Norman Fiering, *Jonathan Edward's Moral Thought and Its British Context* (Chapel Hill, 1981), 287–89, 299, and *Moral Philosophy,* 140–42, 141 n. 74; Roland Andre Delattre, *Beauty and Sensibility in the Thought of Jonathan Edwards* (New Haven, 1968); Conrad Cherry, *Nature and Religious Imagination from Edwards to Bushnell* (Philadelphia, 1980), 56. Cotton Mather's familiarity with (and perhaps disapproval of) Descartes is suggested in his statement "Tho' it may be disputed, whether this be the first proposition, whereof any man can be certain, as a new philosophy has taught us, I think therefore I am; yet it is no new divinity to teach, that as men think so they are" (*Christianus per Ignem* [Boston, 1702], 7). Mather's view of Henry More was more clearly lacking in enthusiasm: "Be more of a Christian, than to look on the *Enchiridion* of [Henry More] as, Next the Bible, the best book in the world" (*Manuductio,* 27; quoted in Fiering, *Moral Philosophy,* 239). I agree generally with Fiering in his opinion that there was an affinity between Cambridge Platonism and New England Puritanism, and his argument for the appearance in New England by the late seventeenth century of a kind of moral philosophy that emphasized the affective element in human nature and in moral knowledge. It seems to me, however, that although traces of this philosophy are detectable in catholick thought, it did not emerge clearly in New England until the work of Jonathan Edwards.

53. Mather Byles, "The Best Rule of Self-Examination," Sermon appended to *Repentance and Faith* (Boston, 1741), 42. Gee, *Strait Gate,* 35. Hall, *Last American Puritan,* 170. The Puritan problem of discovering providences in a mechanical world is described in Maxine Van de Wetering, "Moralizing in Puritan Natural Science: Mysteriousness in Earthquake Sermons," *Journal of the History of Ideas* 43 (1982): 404–20. A discussion of "carnal reason" focused on Michael Wigglesworth's ambivalence toward the natural world is " 'Ladders of Your Own': The Day of Doom and the Repudiation of Carnal Reason," *Early American Literature* 19 (1984): 42–67. Robert Daly stresses Wigglesworth's uncompromising rejection of the natural world but argues that Puritans in seventeenth-century New England were not bound by their theology to a negative view of the flesh (*God's Altar: The World and the Flesh in Puritan Poetry* [Berkeley, 1978]). Samuel Checkley condemned murder as against "the light and law of nature" but was more concerned with the unrestrained passions that caused murder (*Murder a Great and Crying Sin,* 7). In trying to make sense of the death of George I in 1727, Checkley argued that chance and fortune did not rule the world but, rather, God, as governor of the world and efficient cause, worked through

secondary causes according to his plan (perhaps an odd claim to make in connection with an English king who could not understand English and so absented himself from meetings of his ministers). Checkley made no claim for human capability through reason to detect God's hand or order, however (see *The Duty of a People* [Boston, 1727], 12; for Checkley, the world that year remained "full of trouble, our days in it few and evil" [*The Death of the Godly* (Boston, 1727), 1]). John Webb stated that government officials should be guided by "the laws of nature" as well as "the light of divine revelation." Webb seems to have moved closer to the catholick camp during the Great Awakening, inasmuch as he spoke of God's compassion for the sinner he adopts, but he continued to stress human depravity and an evil world as the realm of Satan (*The Government of Christ* [Boston, 1738], 28; *Some Plain and Necessary Directions,* 27, 41–42, 79). Ebenezer Gay, in Hingham, was a leading advocate of rational religion in New England, and, as Robert J. Wilson III points out, he had a "tendency to separate the rational faculties from the emotions" (*Benevolent Deity,* 172). An example of Gay's view that the passions were opposed to the rational faculties is *Minister's Insufficiency* (Boston, 1742), and his emphasis on reason is clear in his Dudleian Lecture delivered at Harvard, *Natural Religion as Distinguish'd from Revealed* (Boston, 1759). James Jones thinks that Gay and Lemuel Briant reduced religion to the moral life lived under the eye of a benevolent God, "without even the lip service" that other ministers sometimes "paid to inward piety" (*Shattered Synthesis,* 137, 131–42). An example of Briant's emphasis on human capability to know moral law through reason and his dismissal of emotional preaching is *The Absurdity and Blasphemy of Depreciating Moral Virtue* (Boston, 1749). John Hancock, Jr. (H.C. 1719, d. 1744), the father of Governor John Hancock, was related by marriage to the Harvard tutor Henry Flynt and preceded Briant at the First Church in Quincy (Braintree). He was, like Briant, not disposed to emotional religion but suspected the flesh in a way that Briant did not (*A Discourse upon the Good Work* [Boston, 1743], 16, 19; *The Danger of an Unqualified Ministry* [Boston, 1743], 9, 10, 28; *The Examiner, or Gilbert against Tennent* [Boston, 1743], 10–11, and his condemnation of the Brattle Street support of the revival, 8; *The Instability of Humane Greatness* [Boston, 1738], 24; Hancock bragged that forty-nine children of First Church had graduated from Harvard, in *A Memorial of God's Goodness* [Boston, 1739], 34). John Hancock the elder (H.C. 1689) was similar to the later John Webb, in that he preached about "the light of nature" and was not entirely opposed to "heart religion" but worried about the decay of religion and the "carnal security" of New Englanders. Like his son, he was one of the area's most outspoken supporters of the college. See *Rulers Should Be Benefactors,* 7, 23; *The Lord's Ministers* (Boston, 1735), 8; *The Prophet Jeremiah's Resolution* (Boston, 1734), 3, 19, 20, 25–26; *A Sermon Preached at the Ordination of Mr. John Hancock* [*Jr.*] (Boston, 1726), 9, 17, 29–30, 31. John Barnard of Marblehead was closer to catholick thinking than probably any other of the area ministers, but he retained more than a healthy dose of concern about emotional religion, as confirmed by his response to Whitefield's visit to the area. See "Autobiography of the Reverend John Barnard," *Collections of the Massachusetts Historical Society,* 3d. ser., 5 (1856): 229–30; *A Call to Parents* (Boston, 1737); *Two Sermons: The Christians Behaviour* (Boston, 1714), 5, 32–33; *The Peaceful End of the Perfect and Upright Man* (Boston, 1714, 1–2; *The Throne Established* (Boston, 1734), 9, 18–20, 33, 35; *The Lord Jesus Christ* (Boston, 1738), 11, 29–30; *The Hazard and Unprofitableness* (Boston, 1712), 27. John Higginson and Nicholas Noyes, Letter to Brattle Street Church, Dec. 30, 1699, MHS.

Chapter 3

1. Ebenezer Pemberton, *A Christian Fixed in His Post* (Boston, 1704), 12; Thomas Foxcroft, *The Blessings of a Soul in Health* (Boston, 1742), 3; Benjamin Colman, *A Humble Discourse of the Incomprehensibility of God* (Boston, 1715), 37; Nathaniel Appleton, *The Wisdom of God* (Boston, 1728), 388; Thomas Foxcroft, *The Day of a Godly Man's Death* (Boston, 1722), 5. Catholick descriptions of life in heaven included references to the quality of social life there and to seemingly sensory experiences. Foxcroft envisioned heaven as a place where the saints would have the "brightest visions" and "shall eat of the hidden manna, and drink of the river of pleasure which flow's [*sic*] at God's right hand" (*Cleansing Our Way in Youth* [Boston, 1719], 57; *A Discourse on the Great Happiness* [Boston, 1720], 12). Just after death, the soul went to the "hades of the happy," which was for "separate spirits" (Ebenezer Pemberton, *A True Servant of His Generation* [Boston, 1712], 20; *The Divine and Original and Dignity of Government* [Boston, 1710], 60). Body and soul were reunited on the last day, because, as Colman argued, the saints, while on earth, "worship God with their bodies in holy manner; they labor and work for God with their bodies, and they suffer for Christ with their bodies," so "will not God glorify them in body and spirit?" (*The Credibility* [Boston, 1729], 19, 24, 26–28; see also *A Devout and Humble Inquiry* [Boston, 1715], 20; Appleton, *The Wisdom of God,* 380–83). The social or public character of heavenly life is mentioned in Foxcroft, *Discourse on the Great Happiness,* 19; *Divine Providence Ador'd* (Boston, 1727), 22; Ebenezer Pemberton, *A Funeral Sermon on . . . Samuel Willard* (Boston, 1707), 13, and appended to the sermon, Colman's "A Poem on Elijah's Translation."

2. Increase Mather, *Meditations upon the Glory of the Heavenly World* (Boston, 1711), 58, 82, 69. Mather believed that the resurrection body would be unlike the carnal body (148–49). Joshua Gee, *The Strait Gate,* (Boston, 1729), 53.

3. Henry More, *The Immortality of the Soul* (London, 1659), 457, 267, 266, 265. Magnetism was the subject of much discussion in the late seventeenth century, among scientists and among theologians who wished to use it as evidence of how detectable but still largely mysterious forces operated within the universe.

4. Norman Fiering, *Moral Philosophy at Seventeenth-Century Harvard: A Discipline in Transition* (Chapel Hill, 1981), 274. For Fiering, the "confluence" of body and soul, will and intellect, and so forth, "was symptomatic of the transitional state of moral psychology in the last half of the seventeenth century." Moreover, in "More's theory of the passions . . . there is evidence that the special qualities of the regenerate state were generalized into a universal image of human nature" (274). Fiering suggests that for More, "interior emotions," a class of emotions that humans shared with angels, were emotional "bridges" to heaven (272–74).

5. Charles Morton, "A System of Ethicks" in Ebenezer Williams, *Commonplace Book 1707–1708,* Harvard University Archives, 6–7. Morton's "Pneumaticks" was quite obviously indebted to Descartes through Heereboord, as noted by the author in asides such as "proved by Heereboord following [Des]Cartes in his 4th and 5th Meditation[s]" ("Pneumaticks, Or a Treatise of the Rev'd Mr Charles Morton about the Nature of Spirits" in Williams, *Commonplace Book,* 10). *The Spirit of Man* (Boston, 1693), 15. Morton also discussed in detail the "mixt body in generall & its affections" and pneumaticks in "A Synopsis of Naturall Philosophy According to the Method of the Antients but Improved & Augmented with the Notions of Later Philosophers" (1680), sec. 3, 11, 28, Harvard University Archives. The tutor William Brattle's *Com-*

pendium of Logick, also in use at Harvard, included assertions such as "the affections or passions, as love, hatred, joy, greif [*sic*], hope, fear, and their species," did "result from conjunction of thinking being and extended substance" (Obadiah Ayer, "Notes on Brattle" [1708], 25, Harvard University Archives. Besides the thorough discussion in Fiering (*Moral Philosophy,* 207–38), see Samuel Eliot Morison, *Collections of the Colonial Society of Massachusetts* 33 (1940): preface. Fiering has argued that Morton held "strictly to the belief that the assumed analogy between God and man was real, and that it was not only possible to make deductions pertaining to both based upon knowledge of one or the other spirit, God's or man's, but necessary and right to do so" (216).

It might be noted that for Morton, the observation of nature was an important method by which a person might know God. Morton wrote, "Objective and acquired knowledge of God's existence is from the world the creation or book of nature." For Morton, the scrutiny of nature according to reason made God visible: "The invisible things eternall power & Godhead are clearly seen by the things that are made saith the apostle (Rom 1–20) the direction to this head of arguing rather than the testimony of the Scriptures . . . that it is the eye of our understanding exercising right reason & and using the spectacle of the creatures" ("System of Ethicks," 7, 19).

6. William Fenner, *A Treatise of the Affections* (London, 1642), 4–5, 3, 8, 6, 112, 114–25; Charles Lloyd Cohen, *God's Caress: The Psychology of Puritan Religious Experience* (New York, 1986), 35–36, 39. Norman Fiering calls Fenner's *Treatise* "possibly the most significant work on the passions that emerged from English Puritanism" (*Moral Philosophy,* 159). Fiering argues that the term *will* in Fenner "no longer means anything like rational appetite but is simply another term for heart or love and is not strictly an intellectual faculty at all" but, in fact, is understood as "the seat of the passions" (ibid., 161). Fiering, in seeking to show the emergence in the seventeenth century of a groundwork for eighteenth-century sentimentalist ethics, stresses emotional sensibility in Fenner. I am more interested here in Fenner's notion of the susceptibility of the affections to preaching or to other means. Norman S. Grabo has observed that Fenner believed it necessary to "employ natural means for raising and exciting the affections" ("Puritan Devotion and American Literary History," in *Themes and Directions in American Literature: Essays in Honor of Leon Howard,* ed. Ray B. Browne and Donald Pizer [Lafayette, Ind., 1969], 10). The affections were for Fenner much like a channel or pipe through which grace flowed (*Treatise,* 53–68). Perry Miller argued that New England Puritans in the seventeenth century believed that "logic was a corrective of sinful passions, and regeneration would take the form of reinvigoration of rational discourse." According to Miller, they thought that the passions could deceive the understanding and were to be kept chained to right reason (Perry Miller, *The New England Mind: The Seventeenth Century* [New York, 1939], 262–63). Miller, and numerous scholars following him, have commented on the influence on Puritan faculty psychology of *The French Academie,* a late sixteenth-century work by Pierre de la Primaudaye, and *A Treatise of the Passions and Faculties of the Soul of Man,* by Edward Reynolds, eventual bishop of Norwich. Both works cast a suspicious eye on the affections (see Rodney Fulcher, "Puritans and the Passions: The Faculty Psychology in American Puritanism," *Journal of the History of the Behavioral Sciences* 19 [1973]: 128–32). Eugene E. White correctly observes, however, "The Puritans also 'suspected' the intellect, though not to the same degree as the emotions" (*Puritan Rhetoric: The Issue of Emotion in Religion* [Carbondale, Ill., 1972], 200 n. 13).

7. Benjamin Wadsworth, *The Benefits of a Good, and the Mischiefs of an Evil,*

Conscience (Boston, 1719), 12; Foxcroft, "vid. Fenner, Treat of the Aff's" in Subject Notebook, Thomas Foxcroft Notebooks, Congregational Library; Solomon Stoddard, *The Defects of Preachers Reproved* (New London, 1724), 24–25, 13; *The Safety of Appearing at the Day of Judgement* (Boston, 1729), 98. Stoddard's own fear that religion in New England was declining is clear in *The Danger of Speedy Degeneracy* (Boston, 1705), 6–7, 10, 13, 18–28. In *The Efficacy of the Fear of Hell* (Boston, 1713), Stoddard stressed the importance of the fear of hell as necessary to turn persons from sin, and he also sprinkled the argument with reports of declension (e.g., 198). A discussion of Stoddard's view of the affections that stresses Stoddard's rejection of prevailing ideas about the faculties is James G. Blight, "Solomon Stoddard's *Safety of Appearing* and the Dissolution of the Puritan Faculty Psychology," *Journal of the History of the Behavioral Sciences* 10 (1974), 238–50. Eugene E. White also discusses Stoddard's faculty psychology and suggests the primacy of emotion for Stoddard in the process of persuasion. See "Solomon Stoddard's Theories of Persuasion," *Speech Monographs* 29 (1962): 235–59, and *Puritan Rhetoric,* 29, 33–40. A survey of Stoddard's theology focused on the stages of conversion is Thomas A. Schafer, "Solomon Stoddard and the Theology of Revival," in *A Miscellany of American Christianity: Essays in Honor of H. Shelton Smith,* ed. Stuart C. Henry (Durham, N.C., 1963), 328–61. Fiering suggests that Fenner's *Treatise of the Affections* was known to other New Englanders (*Moral Philosophy,* 159 n. 29).

8. Benjamin Colman, *The Government and Improvement of Mirth* (Boston, 1710), 26, 27–30, 34, 48, 30, 139, 150, 152, 149, 153. Colman described the relationship between the body and the mind as a "union so strict and intimate" with a "sympathy on both sides so tender," but he claimed as well that the soul, in seeking union with God, was inclined to "higher objects" rather than to limited "sensitive joyes." But it is clear that Colman believed that the operation of the senses contributed substantially in this world to the well-being of the soul (104, 100–101). Colman's analysis of the effect of Psalm singing on the affections is especially significant because it predates by about fifteen years some of the arguments of those who proposed a "new way" of singing in the controversy that broke out in Massachusetts in the early 1720s. The proposals for a style of psalm singing, as they were introduced about 1720, stressed singing by note, rather than in the traditional way, or "lining out," in which the congregation repeated a line (or two lines, or the following half-line) after it had been sung by a deacon. Joyce Irwin has argued that the new style of singing was attractive to those persons who had absorbed some elements of the "Rationalism, Pietism, and baroque learning" that had made its way to New England in the eighteenth-century ("The Theology of 'Regular Singing,' " *New England Quarterly* 51 [1978] 176–92). Her example of the influence of "Baroque" ideas about the effect of music on the affections is *The Sweet Psalmist of Israel* (Boston, 1721), by Thomas Walter (H.C. 1713), who was the minister to a church in Roxbury and the nephew of Cotton Mather. Walter's seeming adoption of the notion that the pleasant impressions of music on the ear could produce affections suitable to a religious use might have come to him during the period of time (up to about 1720), when he had wandered from his uncle's orbit into a friendship with the Anglican John Checkley. However, by all other accounts, he was orthodox, being the author of several published defenses of orthodoxy and of Cotton Mather. I do not see much in the way of "Enlightenment rationalism" in Walter's *The Scriptures the Only Rule* (Boston, 1723) (Irwin "Theology of 'Regular Singing,' " 185 n. 21). On Walter see Perry Miller, *The New England Mind From Colony to Province* (Cambridge, Mass., 1953), 334–35, 468–69, 473; and Clifford K. Shipton, *Biographical Sketches of those*

who attended Harvard College in the classes 1713–1721, vol. 6 of *Sibley's Harvard Graduates* (Boston, 1942), 18–24. Irwin's thesis itself makes sense, but I think her choice of Walter as an example needs to be qualified, and I also note Silverman's claim that the unpublished sermon (1721) by Cotton Mather on singing, from which Irwin draws further evidence, was in fact not written by Mather. Furthermore, I agree with Silverman that Mather only "paid lip service" to the "musical and aesthetic side of singing" and that he instead emphasized "the exegetical and devotional aspects" (Kenneth Silverman, *The Life and Times of Cotton Mather* [New York, 1984], 454n.). The singing controversy is described in Ola Winslow, *Meetinghouse Hill 1630–1783* (New York, 1952), 150–70.

9. Appleton, *The Wisdom of God,* 282; Cotton Mather, *The Accomplished Singer* (Boston, 1721), 14–15, 23. A few years earlier, Mather had prepared a commentary on the Psalms that would be of assistance in a person's deriving a lesson from them (*Proposals for Printing by Subscription "Psalterium Americanum"* [Boston, 1718]). Laura L. Becker thinks that the singing controversy can be understood as a battle between ministers who wished to change the singing and laymen who resisted change ("Ministers vs. Laymen: The Singing Controversy in Puritan New England, 1720–1740," *New England Quarterly* 55 [1982]: 79–95, 86). I think that for some ministers, such as Mather, the adoption of regular singing might indeed have been for the purpose of more carefully ordering and disciplining worship. However, the Brattle Street Church adopted the practice in 1699, and, given the spirit of the undertakers of the church in that year and the articles of the *Manifesto,* it is unlikely that the church was seeking to impose a greater discipline on worship (see John M. Murrin, "Anglicizing an American Colony: The Transformation of Provincial Massachusetts" [Ph.D. diss., Yale University, 1966], 37–39). Perry Miller thought that the new way was "part of the effort on the part of orthodox leaders to get the people to sing in unison so that their thoughts and feelings might thereby become more ordered" (*From Colony to Province,* 469). In the first half of the eighteenth century, only a small proportion of churches adopted the new way (Cyclone Covey, "Puritanism and Music in Colonial America," *WMQ* 8 [1951]: 378–88; Harry S. Stout, *The New England Soul: Preaching and Religous Culture in Colonial New England* [New York, 1986], 159). On other kinds of singing (folk, broadside, with dancing) in colonial Massachusetts see *Music in Colonial Massachusetts 1630–1820,* vol. 1, *Music in Public Places,* Publications of the Colonial Society of Massachusetts, vol. 53 (Boston, 1980). John Cotton approved of persons' singing any sort of spiritual songs, including ones that they composed, in private. In public, Cotton allowed only for the singing of Psalms (*Singing of Psalms* [London, 1650, op. 1647]). The distinction made by Cotton between what was fit for public versus private singing is significant.

10. Appleton, *Wisdom of God,* 279; Sermon preached Nov. 20, 1720, and the series ending Feb. 19, 1721, in Ebenezer Parkman, *Notes on Sermons 1718–1722,* MHS.

11. Clifford K. Shipton, *Biographical Sketches of those who attended Harvard College in the classes 1701–1712,* vol. 5 of *Sibley's Harvard Graduates* (Boston, 1937), 602; Appleton, Sermon preached Jan. 3, 1720, Ebenezer Parkman, *Notes,* MHS; *God, and Not Ministers* (Boston, 1741), 30, 18. Appleton, like Colman, did not object to the drinking of alcoholic beverages but only to excessive or "unseasonable" drinking (Sermon preached Feb. 20, 1720, Parkman, *Notes*). Robert J. Wilson follows Perry Miller (*From Colony to Province*) and Joseph Tracy (*The Great Awakening: A History of the Revival of Religion in the Time of Edwards and Whitefield* [Boston, 1845]) in associat-

ing Appleton theologically with Charles Chauncy and the Hingham Association of Ebenezer Gay. Wilson correctly identifies Appleton as "the embodiment of catholic toleration," and Wilson is right in seeing a measure of similarity in theological innovation in all of these men. But Appleton did not drift quite as far from "pure Calvinism" as Wilson suggests. In *The Clearest and Surest Marks* (Boston, 1743) Appleton registered his disapproval of the excesses of the revival (but not nearly as vociferously as did Charles Chauncy in *Seasonable Thoughts on the State of Religion in New-England* [Boston, 1743]). But he proposed at the outset of the sermon that persons may "widely differ in some points from each other" and still be true Christians, and he argued as well that the "extreme" of being unprepared to acknowledge the Holy Spirit "in all his gracious influences and operations upon men's hearts" was "as dangerous and fatal as the other" extreme of violently disordered affections arising from a lack of knowledge (206–7). Such a statement places Appleton very close to both Chauncy and Gay in that it expresses a distaste for "extremes," but in the context of Appleton's other writings, and particularly his defense of the covenant, it should be seen as an unwillingness to give up emotional religion. (See Robert J. Wilson III, *The Benevolent Deity: Ebenezer Gay and the Rise of Rational Religion in New England, 1696–1787* [Philadelphia, 1984], 64, 109, 100–101.) I mention specifically in chap. 5 Perry Miller's profound misreading of Appleton as a leading figure in the rejection of the covenant among some third-generation ministers.

12. Benjamin Wadsworth, *Five Sermons* (Boston, 1714), 30; "Wadsworth Diary 1692–1737," MHS; "Memoir of the Reverend Benjamin Colman" *NEHGR,* 3 (1849): 121n.; Wadsworth, Sermon preached Apr. 19, 1696, "Nineteen Sermons, 1696–1704," and Sermon preached Feb. 10, 1712, "Twenty-three Manuscript Sermons, August 19, 1711–April 27, 1712," Harvard University Archives.

13. Thomas Foxcroft, *The Character of Anna* (Boston, 1723), 35; *Cleansing Our Way in Youth,* 174; *A Practical Discourse Relating to the Gospel Ministry* (Boston, 1718), 36, 24–25, 26.

14. Foxcroft, *The Day of a Godly Man's Death,* 108; *Cleansing Our Way in Youth,* 59, 61, 71, 72–73; *Character of Anna,* 23, 37.

15. Pemberton, Sermon preached Dec. 2, 1711, Thomas Foxcroft Notebooks, Congregational Library. "Sermons June 13, 1708–April 3, 1709," MHS, contain examples of Pemberton's warnings against lukewarmness. *A Funeral Sermon . . . Samuel Willard* (Boston, 1707), 49. Stout, *New England Soul,* 148–65. Holyoke's nickname derived from his weight of 235 pounds (Shipton, *Biographical Sketches,* 5:275). Holyoke, *Obedience and Submission* (Boston, 1737), 28.

16. E. Brooks Holifield, *The Covenant Sealed: The Development of Puritan Sacramental Theology in Old and New England* (New Haven, 1974), 168. Among some congregational ministers, such suspicion survived in force. Even in 1729, the Reverend Ebenezer Parkman of Westborough, rebuked himself for "heart uncleanness and adultrie, thro The Eye—Pictures, etc; The Ear—Songs, etc." (Diary, Sept. 1729, 36).

17. Michael Clark, " 'The Crucified Phrase': Sign and Desire in Puritan Semiology," *Early American Literature* 13 (1978/79): 289, 290. Clark observes that the dialectics involved in Puritan hermeneutics was "as fragile as it was complex; it could not last" (291). William K. B. Stoever also has pointed to the fragile dialectics in Puritanism (William K. B. Stoever, *A Faire and Easie Way to Heaven: Covenant Theology and Antinomianism in Early Massachusetts* [Middletown, Conn., 1978], 188); however, I think that his claim that Puritans in early New England approved of corporeal images when they were used in relation to divine things (5–6) needs clarification. See Robert

Middlekauff, "Piety and Intellect in Puritanism," *WMQ* 22 (1965): 469–70, and the Oakes quotation on 469; Baird Tipson, "The Routinized Piety of Thomas Shepard's Diary," *Early American Literature* 13 (1978): 76–77, 67. I accept Clark's criticism (" 'Crucified Phrase' " 293 n. 18) of Robert Daly's claim (*The World and the Flesh in Puritan Poetry* [Berkeley, 1978]) that Puritans were not opposed to sensuous imagery. Clark's argument has something in common with Charles Hambricke-Stowe's view "Meditation was the natural outcome of reading in that the substance of the exercise often emerged from the passage read" (*The Practice of Piety: Puritan Devotional Disciplines in Seventeenth-Century New England* [Chapel Hill, 1982], 161–75; quote on 161). Clark generally follows Norman S. Grabo in the latter's suggestion that Puritan thinking about meditation substituted words for visual images (Grabo, "Puritan Devotion and American Literary History," in *Themes and Directions in American Literature: Essays in Honor of Leon Howard,* ed. Ray B. Browne and Donald Pizer [Lafayette, Ind., 1969], 11, 21). Clark, in identifying Richard Baxter's book on meditation (*The Saints Everlasting Rest* [1650]) as a departure from previous Puritan ideas about the natural world, follows Louis L. Martz (*The Poetry of Meditation* [New Haven, 1962]). Lynn Haims has argued that the Puritan need to visualize the holy, frustrated by injunctions based in Calvinism, found some measure of satisfaction in "covert forms" of expression ("The Face of God: Puritan Iconography in Early American Poetry, Sermons, and Tombstone Carving," *Early American Literature* 14 [1979]: 15–47). See also Fiering, *Moral Philosophy,* 188.

18. Holifield, *Covenant Sealed,* 194–97. See also Holifield, "The Renaissance of Sacramental Piety in Colonial New England," *WMQ* (1972): 33–48. Holifield bases his conclusions on a sampling of writings by Wadsworth, Colman, Edward Taylor, Stoddard, Willard, and the Mathers, among others. I agree with his general conclusions, but I think that he overlooks some differences in the theologies of these ministers, and, consequently, his analysis misses some important points. In particular, I do not think that the practice of "spiritualizing the creatures," as proposed by Mather, ought to be understood as a significant departure from the earlier, seventeenth-century attitude of suspicion toward the senses, the corporeal image, and the affections. For Holifield, Cotton Mather's *Christianus per Ignem* (Boston, 1702) and *Agricola* (Boston, 1727) are typical of the guides to meditation on the events of everyday life, or "spiritualizing the creatures," that appeared in England after 1650 and in New England after 1700. It is obvious that Mather intended in these books to encourage the observation of inanimate physical objects as well as creatures as part of a technique of meditation. In *Christianus per Ignem,* he borrowed from "the incomparable Robert Boyl" the idea "of making occasional reflections, full of devotion and morality, unto the meanest of objects." In Mather's hands, Boyle's investigation of nature became a technique of meditation made up of three parts, which, together, formed a "certain triangle." The technique consisted in "first, going forth to observe the properties of the creatures themselves; then coming back to advise ourselves, with instructions brought from them; and lastly, darting up to him that sitteth in the heavens, our petitions." Mather did not assign a role in this process to the affections, however. In his summary in verse of the relationship, during meditation, between the world of the senses and the faculties, the affections are absent: "The touch, the taste, eye ear, and smell, / matter provide for musing well. / Invention, judgement, memory, / and conicience [*sic*] have a faculty, / to make all praise him that made all." But, if Mather indeed was following, as he claimed, the lead of Boyle in devising his technique of meditation, then this should not in fact be surprising. Boyle, as we have seen, understood the investigations of the

Christian virtuoso essentially as a program leading to comprehension of "abstract truths," and not in any way related to an exciting of the "passions." Mather, like Boyle, did not wish to stir the affections, but, rather, sought—perhaps by the hermeneutic described by Clark—the truth of Scripture and sound doctrine. Indeed, Mather's "triangular" method suggests just the sort of disjuncture between image and significant sign (always relating to God) that Clark suggests was present in the meditations of earlier Puritans. In fact, Mather's "triangular" method was not a triangle at all, but rather, in spatial terms, a right angle (or right triangle minus the hypotenuse). In the scheme that he describes, God was not connected directly to the object of meditation (no hypotenuse). It would seem that as far as meditation was concerned, God was connected only indirectly to the observed world, through the (regenerate) person. Such a scheme seems to correspond in some ways to seventeenth-century Puritan devotional exercises as described by Fiering; that is, that meditation was a technique for discovering signs of regeneracy. Mather did write that the "second part" of meditation was "to affect ourselves." But he gives no indication that by this he intended that "affections" were to be excited. See Mather, *Christianus per Ignem,* 13, 186–87, 14, 2, 9. For Boyle see chap. 2.

Mather's *Agricola,* written twenty-five years later, was modeled not on Boyle's writings but on the popular books of the English Puritan John Flavel of Devon. Flavel's *Husbandry Spiritualized* (1699) proposed that observation of the creatures husbanded by the shepherd or farmer could serve as a foundation for meditation. This "spiritualizing the creatures," however, was not specifically aimed at raising the affections. Flavel contrasted "carnal hearts," "carnal joys," and the "sensual way" to the "transcendency" of "spiritual joys." Indeed, Flavel at one point in the book wrote: "The wheels of my affections being oiled with carnal delight, runs so fast, that they have need most times of trigging. Here I rather need the curb than the spur." Flavel's suspicion of the affections is clearest, however, in *Keeping the Heart,* a book popular enough in New England to warrant its publication in Boston in 1702. In this guide to ways for "keeping the heart from sin" Flavel stressed the importance of the fear of God, declaring, "By this fear of the Lord it is that men depart from evil." Flavel may have been referring to the "holy fear" or "reverent fear" that Charles Cohen has suggested was characteristic of regenerate life—as opposed to the fright experienced by the unregenerate—among English Puritans (Cohen, *God's Caress,* 101, 122–23, 131–33). Nevertheless, Flavel warned in no uncertain terms of the dangers of the affections, stressing their capability to disrupt and undermine the spiritual life: "He that will keep his heart must have the eyes of his soul awake and open upon all the disorderly and tumultuous stirrings of his affections; if the affections break loose and the passions be stirred, the soul must discover and oppress them." See Flavel, *Husbandry Spiritualized,* 7th ed. (London, 1705, op. 1699), 199, 42, and the poem juxtaposing Christ to the world (37–38); *Keeping the Heart* (Boston, 1720), 11–12.

19. Benjamin Wadsworth, *The Great and Last Day of Judgement* (Boston, 1709), 54.

20. Cotton Mather is the primary figure in Robert Middlekauff's analysis ("Piety and Intellect in Puritanism" *WMQ* 22 [1965]: Nathaniel Appleton, *Isaiah's Mission Consider'd* (Boston, 1728), 16; Benjamin Colman, *Government and Improvement of Mirth,* 122; *The Lord Shall Rejoice* (Boston, 1741), 3; *Early Piety Again Inculcated* (Boston, 1720), 10–11.

21. Appleton, *Wisdom of God,* 282–83. It is worth noting that although some twentieth-century scholars may identify "joy" as an "aesthetic" response to perceived

beauty, it was considered a passion by the seventeenth-century English writer Edward Reynolds (Fulcher, "Puritans and the Passions," 130).

22. Of course, in Colman's case, the reading of Scripture sometimes was aimed directly at raising the affections. This, again, was a form of the "syllabicall idolatry" that Increase Mather had accussed Colman of fostering.

23. Tipson, "Routinized Piety," 75, 66; Middlekauff, "Piety and Intellect," 460; Brown quoted by William T. Youngs, Jr., citing the diary of Israel Loring, in *God's Messengers: Religious Leadership in Colonial New England, 1700–1750* (Baltimore, 1976), 62. Mather came close to the thinking of catholicks in some ways, but, for all of his emphasis on piety and the occasional references to the importance of the heart, he differed from catholicks in his ideas about the passionate, or affective, side of religion. Mather certainly was close to catholick thinking in his belief that God "will deal with us as rational creatures"; in his occasional references, late in life, to the usefulness and beauty of creation; and in some other ways. But Mather remained suspicious of the affections. For Mather's remarking on the usefulness of the body see *The Christian Philosopher: A Collection of the Best Discoveries in Nature, with Christian Improvements* (London, 1721), 222, and *The Wonderful Works of God* (Boston, 1690), 25; on reason and religion (though not as strongly stated as in Colman's writings), see *Reasonable Religion* (Boston, 1700) and *A Letter to Ungospellized Plantations* (Boston, 1702), 12–13; on piety, see *Malachi: Or, the Everlasting Gospel* (Boston, 1717), 2, 7–12, and *The Resort of Piety* (Boston, 1716), 22–24.

One *possible* exception that I have found with regard to Mather's thinking about the affections is from *The Christian Philosopher.* In his discussion of the human capability to hear, he wrote that some philosophers and scientists had reported "strange things of the Power which Musick has over the Affections" (252). But I think that his usage of the term *affections* here is in the generic sense intended by Charles Morton when he taught, in his physics notes, that the "affections of Naturall Bodies include Quantity, Place, Time & Motion" ("A Synopsis of Naturall Philosophy," 14). This interpretation is supported by the fact that Mather gave as examples of "strange things" the breaking of glasses by the voice, the pain experienced by wounded sailors at the concussion of a cannon shot nearby, and those "who at some notes of music are unable to hold their water" (252).

24. Letter to George Whitefield, Feb. 20, 1744, 3, 12f., MHS.

Chapter 4

1. Here again is the similarity to Philip Greven's Protestants of "moderate" temperament. According to Greven, moderates acknowledged "the persistence of sin and evil in the world, which they saw as the result of some degree of depravity in human nature," but "they also felt confident that human nature contained much good and promise as well." The moderate view of human nature was thus characterized by "less fear and more optimism" than the view of their evangelical counterparts. Catholicks conform closely to Greven's profiling of the "moderate" in these regards, but catholicks seem to have taken a bit more seriously the matter of original sin. See *The Protestant Temperament: Patterns of Child-Rearing, Religious Experience, and the Self in Early America* (New York, 1977) 198ff.

2. Benjamin Colman, *A Devout and Humble Inquiry* (Boston, 1715), 14; *A*

Blameless and Inoffensive Life (Boston, 1723), 12; see also *A Brief Dissertation* (Boston, 1735), 30–59. Benjamin Wadsworth, *Twelve Single Sermons* (Boston, 1717), 158, 4; sermon preached Jan. 13, 1712, in "Twenty-three Manuscript Sermons, August 19, 1711—April 27, 1712," Harvard University Archives; see also *The Benefits of a Good, and the Mischiefs of an Evil, Conscience* (Boston, 1719), 175. Wadsworth wrote: "He that has truly an humble contrite spirit, will readily make to God such a confession as this, namely, 'Lord, I'm vile and sinful by nature and practice . . .' " (*The Highest Dwelling with the Lowest* [Boston, 1711], 13). Nathaniel Appleton, *A Discourse on the Nature and Excellency of Saving Faith* (Boston, 1742), 34; *The Wisdom of God* (Boston, 1728), 360; *The Clearest and Surest Marks* (Boston, 1743), 197. Foxcroft, *A Discourse on the Great Happiness* (Boston, 1720), 14; *Cleansing Our Way in Youth* (Boston, 1719), 5.

3. Thomas Burnet's *Sacred Theory of the Earth* was listed in the catalogues of Ebenezer Pemberton's library (*A Catalogue of Curious Valuable Books Belonging to Ebenezer Pemberton,* entry 44) and the Harvard library (*Catalogus Librorum Bibliothecae,* entry 7, for the volume published in London in 1697). Robert Middlekauff suggests the influence of Thomas Burnet on the thinking of Cotton Mather (*The Mathers: Three Generations of Puritan Intellectuals 1596–1728* [New York, 1971], 289f.) Colman expressed a particular indebtedness to Burnet in *A Brief Dissertation* (Boston, 1735), 2.

In *Sacred Theory of the Earth* (London, 1697), Burnet argued that the flood came about through the breaking of the smooth crust of the earth and its subsequent caving in on the waters beneath the crust. These waters then overflowed on to the land. The breaking of the crust was part of a process that resulted as well in the formation of mountains. Though Burnet was awestruck by his viewing of the Alps and the Apennines, he had great difficulty reconciling such an emotional experience of nature with an ingrained disposition that favored symmetry and was suspicious of enthusiasm. Burnet described the mountains of the earth variously as "incongruent," "disproportionate," "much disorder'd"; as "rude and irregular"; and as "a confus'd heap of bodies." However, he also insisted on the reasonableness of the divine plan for creation, on the authority of reason, and on the harmony of natural philosophy with revelation. He wrote: "Let every thing be tri'd and examin'd in the first place" in order "to see those pieces of most ancient history, which have been chiefly preserv'd in Scripture, confirm'd anew." In his thinking about nature, Burnet differed in some ways from New Englanders. But his thought can be compared with that of some New Englanders in that he seems to have taken delight in the design, harmony, and vastness of creation, while lamenting perceived irregularity and lack of symmetry, which seemed contrary to the divine order. See Thomas Burnet, *The Sacred Theory of the Earth,* introduction by Basil Willey (London, 1965), 109–29, 16–17; Marjorie Hope Nicolson, *Mountain Gloom and Mountain Glory: The Development of the Aesthetics of the Infinite* (Ithaca, N.Y., 1959), 207f., 220–21.

4. Nicolson, *Mountain Gloom and Mountain Glory.* For discussion of the forest as *vastum* see LeGoff, *L'imaginaire medieval: Essais* (Paris, 1985), 65–69. Henry More, *Democritus Platonissans; or, An Essay upon the Infinity of Worlds,* in *Complete Poems,* stanza 55, 96, quoted in Nicolson, *Mountain Gloom and Mountain Glory,* 134. Compare this with Cotton Mather's vision of life through the microscope, reported in *The Wonderful Works of God* (Boston, 1690), 25–26.

5. The following summary of English theories about absolute time appears in the Harvard commonplace book (1728–35) of John Winthrop:

> From Hopkins's Works. 3d. Edit. Lond. 1710. p. 307. Eternity is a duration which hath neither a beginning, nor end, nor succession of parts; it is but one abiding instant, & hath no part, following one after another. This is hard, if not impossible, to be formed into an idea, yet reason will infallibly demonstrate that being, which hath neither beginning nor end, can have no succession in its duration; for wherever there is succession, there musts needs be a priority, there must needs be beginning.—And if eternity did consist, & were made up of such parts as are equal & commensuarate to our years and days, it must needs follow that these parts themselves must be infinite, for if they were but finite, we shall come to a beginning, which is not granted in eternity. And if they be infinite, then in eternity these must be millions of years as of minutes & consequently, a minute would be equal to a million years; yea, the least part of a minute would be equal to it; which is absurd. It is wholly inconsistent with eternity, & an infinite duration, that there should be anything past, or any thing to come, in it; for what is already past cannot be infinite, because it is already ended; & what is to come cannot be eternal, because there was something going before it; and from hence it likewise appears, that a duration which is eternal, must be without beginning or ending, & without any succession of parts. (John Winthrop, *Commonplace Book 1728–1735* [Harvard University Archives, HUC 8728.394], 56–57)

Ebenezer Parkman occasionally reflected in his diary on time, recording thoughts such as his insight that "revolutions of time" will "be swallowed up in eternity" (Parkman, *Diary,* Jan. 2, 1726, and see also Aug. 31, 1726).

Judge Sewall, like the Mathers, interpreted his life in the world according to a sense of time shaped by anticipation of the end. According to David D. Hall, "Sewall's sense of time was ahistorical. Time was really time*less* in a world where the coincidences mattered, and not the passing moment. Like the artisans who fashioned new England gravestones, he overrode the rhythm of the clock with the time-scheme of the coming kingdom and the resurrection of the saints" (*Worlds of Wonder, Days of Judgment: Popular Religious Belief in Early New England* [New York, 1989], 238). But it should not be supposed that Sewall had no interest in the calculation of time. After hearing Thomas Prince preach about the end of the world, Sewall reflected that "one fly was found in his ointment," and that was an error in computation by Prince of the timetable (*Diary,* 2:974 [Feb. 23, 1721]).

6. Benjamin Colman, *A Humble Discourse of the Incomprehensibility of God* (Boston, 1715), 7, 6, 30. Colman cited George Cheyne in support of the claim about "thousands of rational creatures." *It Is a Fearful Thing* (Boston, 1726), 4–5; *The Glory of God* (Boston, 1743), 16. Colman cited Isaac Watts's *Philosophical Essays* in connection with his comment on the immensity of both God and nature.

The self-conscious use of the term *millions* to express wonder is reflected in a note made by Ebenezer Parkman for a sermon that he preached. Parkman scratched out a short word and replaced it with *millions,* so that the line referred to the "millions of ages" that were to be "spent in the joys of heaven" (Parkman, "Sermon Manuscripts—1724–1762," MHS). Reference to "millions" did not in every case signal a sense of wonder about absolute time, or infinity, however. Colman's proposal that the distance between the sun and the earth was 54 million miles was offered with a mixture of plain wonderment and scientific confidence (*Humble Discourse,* 29). Cotton Mather's calculations (borrowed from other writers) about the speed of light probably were made with the same mixture of affect.

> Mr. Romer, from his accurate observations of the eclipses on the satellits of Jupiter, their immersions and emersions, thinks he has demonstrated, that light requires one second of time to move 9000 miles. He shews, that the rays of light require ten minutes of time to pass from the sun to us. And yet Mr. Hugens has shewn, that a bullet from a canon, without abating its first velocity, would be 25 years passing from us to the sun. So that the motion of light is above a million times swifter than that of a cannonball. (*Christian Philosopher,* 11)

Colman, preaching after the death of fifteen-year-old Elizabeth Wainwright, warned that there were "a million dangers" that a person might encounter in the course of growing into adulthood, which could derail one from progress toward sanctification (*A Devout Contemplation* [Boston, 1714], 9). Colman's description of the joys of heaven, on the other hand, included references to enormity expressed with reference to "millions" (Colman, *The Faithful Servant* [Boston, 1740], 9). That Colman, like Mather, was not disnumerate, capable only of a kind of exaggerated arithmetic, is clear from his reference in the same sermon to the fact that a man had donated 4,807 pounds, New England currency, to pay for the promotion of "the knowledge and the practice of religion" (14). Conversely, one might wonder about the arithmetic of Wadsworth, who estimated the cost of rebuilding the church after a fire to be "several thousands of pounds," when in fact the new church actually cost 680 pounds (Wadsworth, *Five Sermons* [Boston, 1714], 149, ix). When Colman referred to the experience of the pure love of God as "ten thousand pleasures in one," he was not counting but, rather, was indicating inexpressible pleasure (*Government and Improvement of Mirth* [Boston, 1710], 128).

7. Wadsworth, *Exhortations to Early Piety* (Boston, 1702), 13, 47; Sermon preached Aug. 24, 1712, Wadsworth Sermon Notes, Congregational Library. Thomas Foxcroft, *The Voice of the Lord* (Boston, 1727), 4. Foxcroft was troubled in two sermons, preached six years apart, about the relation between life expectancy in the distant past, perhaps *in illo tempore,* and the relatively short lifetimes of his day. According to Foxcroft, persons at one time commonly lived to an age of a "thousand" years, but his own contemporaries now died before a tenth of that length of time had elapsed. Although Foxcroft's primary concern in his reflection on this was to understand why the lifespan of human beings had been shortened, it may have been as well contemplation of the "thousand" that disturbed him and caused him to confess: "And this universal abbreviation of humane life is what no philosophical account can be given of, to any tolerable degree of satisfaction. After all natural inquiries, it must be religiously solv'd. It is an article of divine conduct full of mystery" (*Divine Providence Ador'd* (Boston, 1727), 11; see also Thomas Foxcroft, *Lessons of Caution* (Boston, 1733), 4). Foxcroft's thinking about time, and about numbers, tended to include some element of the mysterious, such as in *A Discourse Preparatory to the Choice of a Minister* (Boston, 1727), in which he connected the casting of lots to the divine will: "In some special cases it shou'd seem proper to refer the matter to a lot, for determination; and if this be done in a regular and solemn manner, the issue may justly be look'd upon as a manifestation of the will and mind of Christ." Foxcroft proposed the following three-part procedure for the choosing of a minister: First, "some certain candidates be singled out and nominated by general consent in a voluntary vote," second, the church was to carefully examine these candidates, and "3. The lot must be employed in a solemn and religious manner" (24, 32–33).

8. Benjamin Colman, *A Discourse Had in the College-Hall* (Boston, 1722), preface.

9. For Perry Miller the centerpiece of Puritan thinking was the covenant, and around it he arranged his history of the ideas of New England's Puritans. Miller viewed the early eighteenth century essentially as the time of decline of the covenant theology, and with it, of Puritanism itself. He accordingly was inclined to cast his history of the period into the categories of "liberal" and "conservative" Puritanism and to employ as a litmus test for liberalism the degree to which a minister strayed in his thinking from covenant theology. Had Miller been concerned with the transformation of Puritanism into new forms of religion, rather than with its demise, and had he not regarded loyalty to covenant theology as the proof above all of party, he might have seen more clearly the similarities and differences in the thinking of Congregational ministers in the early eighteenth century. See *The New England Mind: From Colony to Province* (Boston, 1953), 450, 452, 454–55, 469.

10. Foxcroft Papers, Congregational Library; *The Blessings of a Soul in Health* (Boston, 1742), 9, 7.

11. Miller, *From Colony to Province,* 459. Miller's having overlooked the covenant theology in this treatise is puzzling. Appleton, *The Wisdom of God* (Boston, 1728), 211, 192, 146, 311, 309. In 1741, after hearing George Whitefield preach, Appleton lamented, "It has been a dead & dull time upon us with spiritual accounts of late," a condition evidenced by the fact that there were "but few coming in to own the covenant" (*God, and Not Ministers* [Boston, 1741], 21).

12. Wadsworth, *The Benefits of a Good, and the Mischiefs of an Evil, Conscience* (Boston, 1719), 98ff.; sermon preached Mar. 30, 1712, "Twenty-three Manuscript Sermons, August 19, 1711–April 12, 1712," Harvard University Archives; quoted in Harry S. Stout, *The New England Soul: Preaching of Religious Culture in Colonial New England* (New York, 1986), 155, citing "Sermon on 2 Samuel 11:5" Dec. 4, 1709, in "Sermons, 1709–1719," AAS; see also Wadsworth, Sermon preached Dec. 23, 1711, Wadsworth Sermon Notes, Congregational Library. The following are in the Foxcroft Notebooks, Congregational Library: Wadsworth, Sermon preached Sept. 2, 1722; Pemberton, Sermons preached Sept. 23, 1703, Sept. 2, 1711, Dec. 7, 1711. Colman, *Early Piety Again Inculcated* (Boston, 1720), 5–6; *A Sermon for the Reformation of Manners* (Boston, 1716), 1; *The Doctrine and Law of the Holy Sabbath* (Boston, 1725), 34; *The Hope of the Righteous* (Boston, 1721), 6; see also *The Gospel-Order Revived* (New York, 1700), 12, 118, and *The Lord Shall Rejoice* (Boston, 1741), 12.

13. On the Reformed background of the development of the covenant of grace see R. T. Kendall (*Calvin and English Calvinism to 1649* [Oxford, 1977]), who argues that Beza and Hooker introjected into Calvin's theology an element of voluntarism that transformed the covenant of grace into a covenant of works. Jens Moller ("The Beginnings of Puritan Covenant Theology," *Journal of Ecclesiastical History* 14 [1963]: 46–67), Leonard J. Trinterud ("The Origins of Puritanism," *Church History* 20 [1951]: 37–57), William Clebsch (*England's Earliest Protestants, 1520–1535* [New Haven, 1964]), and Michael McGiffert ("Tyndale's Conception of the Covenant," *Journal of Ecclesiastical History* 32 [1981]: 167–84, and "Grace and Works: The Rise and Division of Covenant Theology in Elizabethan Puritanism," *Harvard Theological Review* 75 [1982]: 463–502) have identified, in various ways and to different degrees, a contractual sense of covenant in William Tyndale (and others). Moller, Trinterud, and Clebsch generally argued that covenant theology among Puritans was a major departure from

Calvin's theology and tended toward legalism. McGiffert, responding to this claim, has argued that Puritan writers such as Bulkeley preserved the sovereignity of grace, but in tension with a developing covenant of works. William K. B. Stoever (*A Faire and Easy Way to Heaven: Covenant Theology and Antinomianism in Early Massachusetts* [Middletown, Conn., 1978]) points out the importance of the difference between "order of nature" and "order of time," among other things, and stresses the fragile dialectecs of covevant theology (125, 178–83). It might be noted that Appleton, explaining that the understanding was enlightened first and that it persuaded the will, wrote: "But now when I speak of this as another step that God takes in our conversion, I don't suppose any distance of time in this work of God upon the soul from the other, but that the will and the understanding are both wrought upon together, the one is before the other in order of nature only, not in time." See also Appleton's discussion of "second causes" in conversion (*Wisdom of God,* 212–13, 227). John Coolidge (*The Pauline Renaissance in England* [Oxford, 1970]) and John von Rohr (*The Covenant of Grace in Puritan Thought* [Atlanta, 1986]) also argue that the covenant was both conditional and absolute, the latter claiming that Puritan theologians for the most part did not depart from Calvinism. A recent work that emphasizes the conditional side of the covenant and its tendency to take "legalistic, combative forms" is Stephen Brachlow, *The Communion of Saints: Radical Puritan and Separatist Ecclesiology 1570–1625* (Oxford, 1988).

14. Philip Greven has argued that the Protestant of "moderate" temperament was inclined to a gradual conversion. Greven writes, "He thought of conversion as a gradual process, which employed reason rather than exploiting the passions." Catholicks were like moderates in that they supposed that conversion was gradual and that reason played an important role in conversion. Catholicks, however, gave more of a place to the affections in the process of conversion, and to the aftermath of conversion, than the moderates profiled by Greven (*Protestant Temperament,* 229).

15. Wadsworth, *A Guide for the Doubting* (Boston, 1711), 95–96; Appleton, *Faithful Ministers of Christ* (Boston, 1713); *The Wisdom of God,* 214, 230; Colman, *A Brief Dissertation* (Boston, 1735), 12. Jerald C. Brauer has written that English Puritans could usually "pinpoint the moment of conversion" ("Conversion: From Puritanism to Revivalism," *Journal of Religion* 58 [1978]: 241). David D. Hall thinks that the laity, in "testifying to a 'work of grace' before a body of church members," remained concerned with locating "the moment of 'election' to salvation" (*Worlds of Wonder: Days of Judgment: Popular Religious Belief in Early New England* [New York, 1989], 123, 143). J. William T. Youngs, Jr., reports that John Hancock (H.C. 1719) could not pinpoint the time of his election (*God's Messengers: Religious Leadership in Colonial New England, 1700–1750* [Baltimore, 1976], 23–24). Norman Pettit notes that for English Puritans, some conversions were gradual and others were immediate (*The Heart Prepared: Grace and Conversion in Puritan Spiritual Life* [New Haven, 1966], 7–9). Pettit also notes that for Solomon Stoddard, conversion "is wrought in the twinkling of an eye" (from *A Guide to Christ* [Boston, 1714], quoted on 205). Mather Byles wrote during the awakening that in conversion, some persons "are beat upon as with a tempest; others are revived as with a gentle breeze" (*Repentance and Faith,* [Boston, 1741], 13). See also Baird Tipson, "The Development of a Puritan Understanding of Conversion" (Ph.D. diss., Yale University, 1972) and Rodger M. Payne, " 'When the Times of Refreshing Shall Come': Interpreting American Protestant Narratives of Conversion 1630–1830" (Ph.D. diss., University of Virginia, 1989). I tend to agree with Tipson that two models of conversion (immediate/gradual), both of which can be found in the writings of William Perkins, served to guide New Englanders in their thinking

about conversion ("The Routinized Piety of Thomas Shepard's Diary," *Early American Literature* 13 [1978]: 70–71).

16. Emphasis on the understanding as the key faculty (vis-á-vis the will) is in Colman, *A Humble Discourse of the Incomprehensibility of God* (Boston, 1715), 1; *God Deals with Us as Rational Creatures* (Boston, 1723), 13; Pemberton, *A Funeral Sermon on . . . Samuel Willard* (Boston, 1707), 48; *A Christian Fixed in His Post* (Boston, 1704), 7; Appleton, *The Wisdom of God,* 211–13; Foxcroft, sermon preached Jan. 7, 1720, Foxcroft Papers, Congregational Library; Wadsworth, "Sermon Preached March 30, 1712," in "Twenty-three manuscript Sermons," Harvard University Archives. Wadsworth attempted to explain the role of the conscience alongside the understanding in conversion. The influence of Cambridge Platonism may well be present in his description of conscience as "a candle of the Lord" (*Benefits of a Good, and the Mischiefs of a Bad, Conscience,* 24–25, 175). Holyoke and Pemberton also referred to conscience in regeneration but gave no theory of its operation (Pemberton, Sermon preached Dec. 2, 1711, Foxcroft Papers, Congregational Library; Holyoke, *The Duty of Ministers* [Boston, 1741], 34).

17. Nathaniel Appleton, *Superior Skill* (Boston, 1737), 6; Foxcroft, Sermon preached Jan. 7, 1720, Foxcroft Papers, Congregational Library; *Ministers, Spiritual Parents* (Boston, 1726), 36.

18. Pettit, *Heart Prepared,* 185–87 (Pettit quotes from Firmin's *The Real Christian* [London, 1670]). On Firmin see the good summary in James Jones, *The Shattered Synthesis: New England Puritanism before the Great Awakening* (New Haven, 1973), 32–53. Cotton Mather, *A Christian at His Calling* (Boston, 1701), 5.

19. Stout, *New England Soul,* 155. Stout does not believe, however, that the second generation preached only sin and damnation. All the "liberal" clergy whom Stout cites in connection with the more benevolent view of God were catholicks: Wadsworth, Colman, Leverett, and William Brattle. (Stout stresses the English influence in connection with the ideas of the "liberal" clergy.) John Tillotson, *Sermons and Discourses,* 2d ed., vol. 3, (London, 1687), 409. I do not think that catholicks went quite so far as Tillotson in their thinking about the capability of the faculties after the Fall. Simon Patrick, *The Parable of the Pilgrim* (London, 1665), 121; Stillingfleet, Sermon on Hebrews 12.3 in *Sermons Preached on Several Occasions* (London, 1673), 100. J. Sears McGee, "Conversion and the Imitation of Christ in Anglican and Puritan Writing," *Journal of British Studies* 15 (1976): 24. McGee writes, "Anglicans could scarcely have advocated such a strategy if they had not been more optimistic about human nature than the Puritans" (26–27). William M. Spellman shows how Tillotson's moralism did not preclude belief in original sin and the need for supernatural grace ("Archbishop John Tillotson and the Meaning of Moralism," *Anglican and Episcopal History* 56 (1987): 404–22). R. Buick Knox thinks otherwise ("Bishops in the Pulpit in the Seventeenth-Century: Continuity and Change" in *Reformation Conformity and Dissent: Essays in Honor of Geoffrey Nuttall,* ed. R. Buick Knox [London, 1977], 101).

20. Stout, *New England Soul,* 155; Foxcroft, *The Day of a Godly Man's Death* (Boston, 1722), 73; Wadsworth, *Twelve Single Sermons* (Boston, 1717), 133; Nathaniel Appleton, *A Discourse on the Nature* (Boston, 1742), 32–33. King locates the sources of Puritan literary references to melancholy in a tradition of writing that emerged in medieval theology and was enlarged in the Renaissance (*The Iron of Melancholy: Structures of Spiritual Conversion in America from the Puritan Conscience to Victorian Neurosis* [Middletown, Conn., 1983], 13–82, 22).

21. Colman, letter to "Rev'd Mr Hooper," Feb. 12, 1740, Colman Papers, MHS.

The letter seems to be Colman's attempt to correct some misconceptions of New England Congregationalism that he detects in the thinking of the West Church pastor William Cooper. The quotation is from Stout, writing about "third generation ministers." (I would, again, claim that catholicks were leaders in this movement.) Stout stresses that these ministers borrowed from English writers certain language about the experience of nature and God (and the workings of the Holy Spirit in the soul) that emphasized "joy" and "delight" (*New England Soul,* 156–57). Appleton, *Wisdom of God,* 215–16. Appleton asked a congregation the following question: "How shall we know that we have true saving faith? Ans: By the Effects" (Sermon preached Dec. 27, 1719, in Ebenezer Parkman, "Notes of Sermons, 1718–1722," MHS).

22. Charles Lloyd Cohen, *God's Caress: The Psychology of Puritan Religious Experience* (New York, 1986), 5, 272–73, 123; Sibbes quoted in McGee, *The Godly Man in Stuart England: Anglicans, Puritans, and the Two Tables, 1620–1670* (New Haven, 1970), 202. J. Sears McGee stresses the importance of the "communal and corporate identity" in Puritan thinking about the way in which "God dispensed sanctifying grace" (202).

23. Patricia Caldwell, *The Puritan Conversion Narrative: The Beginnings of American Expression* (New York, 1983), 127–28, 121, 134. Cohen, surveying the same narratives, admits that there is in them "less affectivity regarding union than might be anticipated given the preachers' excited recreations of it. In particular, not many people openly exalted in profound joy or sublime peace" (*God's Caress,* 212). As I have argued, some seventeenth-century New England ministers conceived of a role for the affections that served to utilize them and to undermine them at the same time (in somewhat the same manner that early New Englanders mentally destroyed the corporeal image as they meditated on it). Caldwell's claim that the conversion narratives evidence a kind of "spiritual paralysis" should be read in the context of her emphasis on the experience of early New Englanders as "an unexpected deadlock between their experiences of the migration and the fulfillment of their religious hopes" (120). The problem that she refers to as the "structural incompleteness" of the conversion narratives seems to me to be itself structurally similar to the problem (as I have described it) of the inability of New Englanders to come to some resolution in their thinking about whether the affections, and the corporeal image, were to be embraced as useful to religion or rejected as corrupting influences.

Stephen Foster has described the "social peace" of the Bay Colony as rooted in an understanding of community as ordered by love between persons. However, according to Foster, the settlers of the Bay Colony "built their exemplary society on a charity so narrowly defined that it restricted the bonds of love to the regenerate," those who were "able to supply clear testimony of a work of saving grace." The first few years of the Bay Colony may have included the establishment of something like the society that John Winthrop had in mind (as described by Foster). However, it seems to me that in view of Caldwell's analysis, and what Tipson has called the "intellectualization" of piety in New England in the seventeenth century, as evidenced in Shepard (which likely carried over into the social world, where it could serve to undermine the intensity of emotion needed to bond persons together), we ought to take Foster's claim in a rather restricted sense. Foster does note that toward the end of the seventeenth century the original social peace had largely deteriorated, and that Cotton Mather "had also dealt the older ideals a fatal blow by substituting a flaccid moralism for the intense Augustinian piety that had originally given Puritanism its energy and strength." In any event, catholicks differed from early settlers such as John Winthrop in that they were more concerned with persons' attending the Lord's Supper (as a converting ordinance) than they were with regulating church admission, and catholicks tended to overlook differences in the "smaller matters" of religion, accepting fellowship even with Anglicans. Moreover, the catholick clergy viewed conversion as a gradual, ongoing process and therefore were much less eager to distinguish the regenerate from the unregenerate for purposes of identifying those eligible to experience the social bonds of love. See *Their Solitary Way: The Puritan Social Ethic in the First Century of Settlement in New England* (New Haven, 1971), 64, and Stephen Foster and Timothy H. Breen, "The Puritans' Greatest Achievement: A Study of Social Cohesion in Seventeenth-Century Massachusetts," *Journal of American History* (June 1973): 5. In the latter work, the authors claim that the social peace in Massachusetts lasted until the 1680s.

24. It is worth noting that these ministers sought escape not only from the flesh but from time itself. Like their ally Samuel Sewall, they "overrode the rhythm of the clock with the time-scheme of the coming kingdom and the resurrection of the saints." For them, "time was really timeless" (David D. Hall, commenting on Sewall's idea of time in *Worlds of Wonder,* 238). A similar analysis of "Puritanism" has been offered by John F. Lynen, who argued argued that the Puritan sense of time was characterized by a "sharp contrast between the present and eternity," which was fostered by the Puritan "doctrine of grace," or predestination. According to Lynen, this doctrine "accustomed the imagination to conceive experience in terms of the purely present in relation to a total history or conspectus of all times." Puritans stressed the transcendence of God but at the same time insisted that God was immediately present to the individual through grace in conversion, and "although the two aspects of deity can still be held together in thought, the mind is forever engaged in a violent shifting of perspective between the present and eternal points of view." Accordingly, the Puritan sense of time, conditioned as it was by the categories of religious belief, was often a sense of timelessness (John F. Lynen, *The Design of the Present* [New Haven, 1969], 35–36); another relevant analysis, focused on Puritan consciousness of history, is in Sacvan Bercovitch, *The Puritan Origins of the American Self* (New Haven, 1975), and see also Rodger Milton Payne, " 'When the times of refreshing shall come': Interpreting American Protestant Varieties of Conversion, 1630–1830," Ph.D. diss., University of Virginia, 1988. Catholick Congregationalists also sometimes expressed themselves in such a way as to make possible the detection in their discourse of a sense of "timelessness" to existence. Catholicks, however, did not focus their thinking on escape from the flesh and the world. The actions of the regenerate in the world were meaningful, both to the individual and to the community. In fact, such activities themselves could serve as a measurement of time in the world, as in Foxcroft's proposal "Our lives are not to be measure'd by the natural length, but by the moral extent, or the wise improvements of our opportunities. The prophet has such an expression as that, *the child shall die an hundred years old*" (*Divine Providence Ador'd* [Boston, 1727], 29). Pemberton likewise wrote: "Here we are taught the true value and rate of life: It is to be rated not by duration, but by action. It must be reckoned not by the months and years, we have existed, but by the good we have done" (*A True Servant of His Generation* [Boston, 1712], 23).

25. David Thomas Konig, *Law and Society in Puritan Massachusetts: Essex County, 1629–1692* (Chapel Hill, 1979), 129, 130, chap. 5. Roger Thompson, *Sex in Middlesex: Popular Mores in a Massachusetts County, 1649–1699* (Amherst, 1986), 170, 186, 193, 196. See also John M. Murrin, "Trial by Jury in Seventeenth-Century New England," in *Saints and Revolutionaries,* ed. David D. Hall, John M. Murrin, and

Thad Tate (New York, 1984), 153–67. Edmund S. Morgan has pointed out that Thomas Hooker condemned the "civil man," who was outwardly law-abiding, peaceable, and upright but was guilty in his heart of sinning against God (*The Puritan Family: Religion and Domestic Relations in Seventeenth-Century New England* [New York, 1946], 1–2). It seems that the "civil man" may have been more visible in the communities of eastern Massachusetts in the late seventeenth-century.

T. H. Breen stressed the emergence of of factionalism and disunion in ecclesiastical and civil politics after 1660. According to Breen, the "loss of 'sweet union' particularly disturbed the members of the rising [second] generation, for they believed, as their fathers had believed, that a covenanted people should be bound together by the force of Christian love. Yet wherever these Puritans looked after 1660, they found neighbor set against neighbor . . . " (*The Character of the Good Ruler: A Study of Puritan Political Ideas in New England, 1630–1730* [New Haven, 1970], 87).

John Putnam Demos has argued that underlying the witchcraft episode at Salem in the 1690s was the "broader issue of 'neighborliness' *versus* 'individualism,' " or a dedication to "harmony, unity, cooperation and brotherhood" as over against persons' "maneuvering vigorously for personal advantage." I accept Demos's claim that neighborliness suffered setbacks in the late seventeenth century, but I locate that against the emergence of public authority as more rational-legal and bureaucratic, in a society becoming more populous and complex, rather than as against the rise of individualism (though I do not deny that there is evidence for certain kinds of individualistic behavior). See *Entertaining Satan: Witchcraft and the Culture of Early New England* (New York, 1982), esp. 298–300.

Taking Ipswich, Massachusetts, in 1670, as her context, Laurel Thatcher Ulrich presents evidence showing that noninstitutionalized forms of authority, as in the role of women as "neighbors" who chastised or supported other "neighbors," helped to "counterbalance" the public authority of men and money. Ulrich does not argue specifically that public and private aspects of New England life became dissociated in Ipswich, or elsewhere, and she does not aim at showing change over time in the roles of women, preferring instead a synchronic approach to her materials. She does, however, reject the opinion that small communities naturally developed strong emotional bonds between members that took the form of " 'a feeling of collective caring' " (*Good Wives: Image and Reality in the Lives of Women in Northern New England 1650–1750* [Oxford, 1980], 239, and chap. 3). Ulrich's statement is aimed against the work of David H. Flaherty (*Privacy in Colonial New England* [Charlottesville, Va., 1972]), which, she claims (and I tend to agree), "romanticizes" the concept of neighborliness (see Flaherty, *Privacy in Colonial New England,* 110–111). Flaherty proposes that New Englanders generally kept a "holy watchfulness" over each other (151).

26. Agnieszka Salska, "Puritan Poetry: Its Public and Private Strain," *Early American Literature* 19 (1984): 108, 117. Salska writes, "The fact that the best colonial lyrics remained unpublished in their authors' lifetimes cannot be treated as merely accidental" (119). David Leverenz, *The Language of Puritan Feeling: An Exploration in Literature, Psychology, and Social History* (New Brunswick, N.J., 1980), 196–99, 164.

27. Pettit, *Heart Prepared,* 206, 205; Middlekauff, *Mathers,* 319. Pettit interpreted the founding of the Brattle Street Church—and, in particular, the abandoning of the requirement of a relation—as a sign of growing indifference in the eighteenth century to the "inner life" of religion. Catholicks were not at all indifferent to the "inner life";

they expressed their sense of its importance not through the requirement of a relation but through an emphasis on personal piety informing collective life.

28. Christine Leigh Heyrman has argued that the development of the economic resources of Marblehead did not undermine community. In fact, "communal institutions, relationships, and attitudes actually appeared for the first time as the town developed an independent, direct trade during the 1730's" (*Commerce and Culture: The Maritime Communities of Colonial Massachusetts 1690–1750* [New York, 1984], 18). Although it is tempting to seek parallels to this history in Boston, earlier in the century, in the emergence of the catholick emphasis on community, I do not think that a comparison is justified, at least not on the terms set by Heyrman in her analysis of Marblehead. One important reason for this is that the "localism" (as a form of community ideology) that Heyrman identifies as characteristic of Marblehead (and Gloucester) does not fit well with the catholick emphasis on openness to religious differences (especially Anglicans and Anglicanism). In fact, it may have been Edward Holyoke's discomfort with localism in Marblehead that led him to leave the Second Church there for the presidency of Harvard in 1737. Holyoke had been installed as the first pastor of the Second Church in 1716, through the influence of the Brattles, who distinguished Holyoke quite clearly from John Barnard, when both men were in the running for a position at First Church that same year. Second Church was founded by former members of First Church, which hired Barnard. See Stephen P. Hathaway, Jr., "The Second Congregational Church in Marblehead," *Essex Institute Historical Collections* 22 (1885): 81–102; Thomas C. Barrow, "Church Politics in Marblehead," *Essex Institute Historical Collections* 98 (1962): 121–27; John Barnard, "Autobiography of Reverend John Barnard," *Collections of the Massachusetts Historical Society,* 3 ser., vol. 5 (1856), 177–243; Heyrman, *Maritime Communities,* 273–303.

29. Thomas Foxcroft, *The Character of Anna* (Boston, 1723), 35, 23, 48, 41. Foxcroft preached that "the practice of true religion" consisted in "duty to God and neighbor" (Sermon preached Nov. 11, 1711, in Leverett Papers, MHS).

30. Thomas Foxcroft, *Cleansing Our Way in Youth* (Boston, 1719), 59; *A Brief Display* (Boston, 1727), 25; *A Discourse Concerning Kindness* (Boston, 1722), 7; *The Blessings of a Soul in Health* (Boston, 1742), 5–6.

31. Benjamin Wadsworth, *A Guide for the Doubting,* 26; *Christian Advice to the Sick and Well* (Boston, 1714), 2, 33; *The Well-Ordered Family* (Boston, 1712), 3; *An Essay on the Decalogue* (Boston, 1719), 63–65. Preaching at the dedication of a new church, Wadsworth maintained that the churches were distinct from each other but that Christians were joined in the "mystical body of Christ" (*The Lord Jesus Walking in the Midst of the Churches* [Boston, 1721], 25). It is worth noting that Wadsworth proposed a role for "conscience" in the process of regeneration. Drawing explicitly on Fenner and borrowing an idea from Cambridge Platonism, Wadsworth called conscience "a noble faculty of the soul, it should be a candle of the Lord." He defined it as that "faculty of the soul, by which a person considers what God's law requires and forbids: and by which he compares his own carriage with God's law, and approves or condemns the same, according as 'tis found agreeable to God's law, or disagreeable" (*Benefits of a Good, and the Mischiefs of a Bad, Conscience,* 175, 12). The reference to "candle of the Lord" suggests that Wadsworth was thinking about the response of the "whole man" to God, possibly in the same way that Jonathan Edwards understood conscience (See Norman Fiering, *Jonathan Edwards's Moral Thought and Its British Context* (Cha-

pel Hill, N. Car., 1981), 73, 231n; *Moral Philosophy at Seventeenth-Century Harvard: A Discipline in Transition* [Chapel Hill, 1987], 58).

32. Benjamin Wadsworth, Sermon preached Aug. 11, 1723, Foxcroft Notebooks, Congregational Library; *The Churches Shall Know* (Boston, 1717), 9, 22–23; *An Essay to Do Good* (Boston, 1710), 27, 41; Wadsworth argued that the first nine commandements searched the heart and soul, as well as "outward behavior." The tenth commandment referred "directly to inward motions of the soul, whether ever they appear in the outward act or behaviour or not" (*An Essay on the Decalogue* [Boston, 1719], 122–23). Wadsworth argued that human beings, as rational creatures, were "actively" to "shew forth God's glory" (*Early Seeking of God* [Boston, 1715], 14).

33. Benjamin Colman, *A Sermon at the Lecture in Boston, after the Funerals of . . . William Brattle . . . and . . . Ebenezer Pemberton* (Boston, 1717), 17; *The Glory of God* (Boston, 1743), 4; *The Unspeakable Gift of God* (Boston, 1739), 7–8; *David's Dying Charge* (Boston, 1723), 41; *The Lord Shall Rejoice* (Boston, 1741), 3, 12; *Unspeakable Gift of God,* 15.

34. Nathaniel Appleton, *The Great Blessing* (Boston, 1742), 6–8.

35. Ebenezer Pemberton, *A Sermon Preached in the Audience* (Boston, 1706), 25; Nathaniel Appleton, *The Origin of War Examin'd* (Boston, 1733), 8; Benjamin Wadsworth, *Christian Advice to the Sick and Well* (Boston, 1714), 44; Benjamin Colman, *The Government and Improvement of Mirth* (Boston, 1710), 22ff., 41ff., 82ff; *A Holy and Useful Life* (Boston, 1715), 10–16; Benjamin Wadsworth, *An Help to Get Knowledge* (Boston, 1714), 22.

36. See Wadsworth's collection of sermons preached after the destruction of the meetinghouse by fire in 1711, some during a measels epidemic (*Christian Advice to the Sick and Well*). Wadsworth's and Pemberton's sermons in the weeks after the burning of the meetinghouse emphasize the dangers of becoming inordinately attached to the things of the world. In a sadly prophetic moment, Wadsworth preached on Sept. 30, 1711, that persons should be ready to part with earthly enjoyments. The meetinghouse burned two days later ("Twenty-three Manuscript Sermons," Harvard University Archives; "Wadsworth Sermon Notes," Congregational Library; "Foxcroft Notebooks," Congregational Library). Foxcroft condemned lusts in a sermon preached before the General Court after the earthquake of 1727 (*Voice of the Lord* [Boston, 1727]). Some sermons in which Colman mentioned lusts are *The Withered Hand* (Boston, 1740), *The Peaceful End* (Boston, 1736), and *Practical Discourses on the Parable of the Ten Virgins* (Boston, 1747, op. 1707). The years 1716–17 saw an unusually large number of sermons addressed to the matter of sexual sins. Colman's *The Warnings of God to Young People* (Boston, 1716), Foxcroft's *Cleansing Our Way in Youth* (Boston, 1719, but preached in 1717), and Wadsworth's *Unchaste Practices Procure Divine Judgements* (Boston, 1716) all included strongly worded cautions against lusts. The reason for the appearance of these sermons together stems from the fact that a society of young men that was formed about this time had invited the ministers to instruct them. The message of the sermons, I assume, was shaped with an eye to the occasion. Hall, *Worlds of Wonder,* 137; Joshua Gee, *The Strait Gate* (Boston, 1729), 67–69, 88–91.

37. Rudolph Otto, *The Idea of the Holy: An Inquiry into the Non-Rational Factor in the Idea of the Divine and Its Relation to the Rational,* trans. John W. Harvey (New York, 1958), 12–15, 20–22, 31. Otto proposes love, pity, comfort, and so on, as "the ideas and concepts which are parallels or 'schemata' on the rational side of this non-rational element of 'fascination' " (31). The same should be understood with regard to fear and self-depreciation in their connection to the *mysterium tremendum.* According

to Otto, the *tremendum* and the *fascinans* "combine in a strange harmony of contrasts, and the resultant dual character of the numinous consciousness, to which the entire religious development bears witness . . . is at once the strangest and most noteworthy phenomenon in the whole history of religion" (31). I have suggested that some of the New England ministry emphasized fear and self-depreciation, to the detriment of love and comfort. For these ministers, I do not think—in spite of what might be suggested in Otto's statement—that there was, really, a "harmony" of contrasts, but, rather, an uneven combination of elements. There was, however, more of a true harmony in catholick theology.

38. In this discussion about the potential of the "sacred" to cause disorder (social and "cosmic") and the roles of ritual as both precaution and stimulus, I have drawn on Emile Durkheim, *Elementary Forms of the Religious Life,* trans. Joseph Ward Swain (1915; 2nd ed., 1976); A. Van Gennep, *The Rites of Passage* (London, 1960); Victor Turner, *The Ritual Process: Structure and Anti-Structure* (Ithaca, New York, 1969). The test of a public relation (for church admission) might have contributed substantially to an intellectualizing of piety among persons of whom it was required, particularly in view of the fact that it was a "test" of some measure of conformity of a person's experience to a fairly specific set of guidelines (although the expectation of conformity varied from church to church and probably decreased as the seventeenth century wore on). If this is true, then catholick deemphasis or abandonment of the public relation ought to be seen as a sign of their moving away from aspects of church life that served to intellectualize piety. (As I have noted I do not accept John King's claim that the relation was not really a test for admission, and that it in fact served to draw the church members more closely together [*Iron of Melancholy:* 44–45]).

It is worth noting that the theory of Mary Douglas regarding the elaboration of symbols within a given social context is relevant to a consideration of changes that took place in Congregationalism in the late seventeenth and early eighteenth centuries. The process of social and intellectual change in New England during that time was highly complex, and full of exceptions and irregularities, and a consideration of that process according to categories proposed by Douglas is no substitute for a "historical" explanation. Nevertheless, Douglas's notion of "group" and "grid" is useful here as a way of arranging the data in ways that allow for a new angle of analysis and provoke fresh questions. Specifically, Douglas's claim that witchcraft fears are likely to be found in "high group/low grid" contexts bears obvious relevance to the Salem episode. (John Demos, among others, has drawn on Douglas's theories about witchcraft in seeking to determine what happened in Salem [*Entertaining Satan: Witchcraft and the Culture of Early New England* (New York, 1972), 278–79].) More relevant to the emergence of catholick Congregationalism, however, is Douglas's theory that a more highly elaborated symbolic system (in New England, probably "high group/high grid") is associated with a high value placed on sacramental religion and ritualism in general. See *Natural Symbols: Explorations in Cosmology* (New York, 1973), esp. chaps. 7, 5, 3.

39. Hall, *Worlds of Wonder,* 196; Joseph S. Clark, D.D., *A Historical Sketch of the Congregational Churches in Massachusetts from 1620–1858* (Boston, 1858), 140ff.; Youngs, *God's Messengers,* 81; John M. Murrin, "Anglicizing an American Colony: The Transformation of Provincial Massachusetts" (Ph.D. diss., Yale University, 1966), 28–45; David D. Hall, *The Faithful Shepherd: A History of the New England Ministry in the Seventeenth-Century* (New York, 1974), 272–73.

40. E. Brooks Holifield, *The Covenant Sealed: The Development of Puritan Sacramental Theology in Old and New England* (New Haven, 1974), 197–224. Holifield

notes sacramental meditations by Cotton Mather, Willard, Stoddard, Colman, and Wadsworth. He stresses, however, "The sacramental meditations differed in tone and emphasis," arguing, "Cotton Mather's were intensely subjective and preoccupied with analyzing the dispositions of the soul," and Willard's were focused essentially on the review of doctrine (202). The meditations by Wadsworth and Colman (including those cited later) were hardly subjective at all and were not focused on doctrine. Instead Wadsworth and Colman, and Appleton as well, tended to view the Lord's Supper as a converting ordinance, in a manner roughly similar to Stoddard, and to stress, at the same time, its character as a "publick" activity. Pemberton, *Funeral Sermon on Samuel Willard,* 13; Benjamin Colman, *Parents and Grown Children* (Boston, 1727), 6, passim; *The Credibility* (Boston, 1729), 31. In *A Brief Inquiry* (Boston, 1716), Colman argued that terms that limit the participation of persons in the Lord's Supper, and that are not to be found in the New Testament, ought not to be continued by the church (21). Appleton, sermon preached Oct. 11, 1719, in Ebenezer Parkman, "Notes of Sermons, 1718–1722," MHS; *The Wisdom of God,* (Boston, 1728), 297–312; Wadsworth, *A Dialogue between a Minister and His Neighbour about the Lord's Supper* (Boston, 1724), 68, passim. Arthur D. Kaledin thinks that the Brattle Street Church itself "became an instrument of conversion rather than simply a home for the converted" ("The Mind of John Leverett" [Ph.D. diss., Harvard University 1965], 241). I have been unable to locate a copy of Colman's sacramental meditations entitled *Some of the Glories of Our Lord* (London, 1728).

41. Wadsworth, *Dialogue between a Minister and His Neighbour,* 83, 99, 14, 74–75. Part of Wadsworth's sermon was focused on the problem of the excessive scrupulosity of persons in examining themselves for participation in the Lord's Supper. Here, and elsewhere, Wadsworth warned against such excess: "As for that awe and dread that keeps you from this ordinance, it's plain that 'tis not from God," but it may be from "the devil" (69, and see also Wadsworth's warning against "overwhelming melancholly" in *Twelve Single Sermons* [Boston, 1717], 133). David D. Hall has recently given evidence that the custom of a person's avoiding the Lord's Supper, if he or she was quarreling with someone who also would be present at the rite, was a part of New England religious culture before the eighteenth century. He notes, "Enemies and anger—these two did not mix with the ritual of communion" (*Worlds of Wonder,* 160). My point here is that Wadsworth's publicly proposing "social peace" as a virtual requirement for communion, in the midst of a sacramental "renaissance," reflected the emergence of a "catholick" mentality in New England.

42. Benjamin Wadsworth, *The Faithful Reprover* (Boston, 1711), 39, 55, 57ff.; Thomas Foxcroft, *A Practical Discourse Relating to the Gospel Ministry* (Boston, 1718), 15–16. Foxcroft believed that failure to point out to neighbors their errors would also bear bad fruit for a person in the afterlife. Foxcroft explained this using an unusual turn of phrase: "The transmigration of sin from perishing souls unto unfaithful watchment is no Platonic dream, or airy notion, but a doctrine according to godliness taught in the school of Christ."

43. Benjamin Wadsworth, *Surviving Servants of God* (Boston, 1724), 21; *Assembling at the House of God* (Boston, 1711), 2, 7; Appleton, *Wisdom of God,* 302, 300; Benjamin Colman, *An Argument* (Boston, 1747), 3. For Colman, Christians "loved to worship" (*The Death of God's Saints Precious* [Boston, 1723], 22).

44. Ebenezer Turell, *The Life and Character of the Reverend Benjamin Colman,* (Boston, 1749), 217; Colman, *Argument* 42, 2; *Jesus Weeping* (Boston, 1744), 44; *Faith Victorious* (Boston, 1702), A2 (preface), 33; *David's Dying Charge,* 9; Wadsworth,

Well-Ordered Family, 4; *Dialogue between a Minister and His Neighbor,* 22; *Essay on the Decalogue,* 54; Foxcroft, *A Serious Address to Those Who Unnecessarily Frequent the Tavern* (Boston, 1726), 9.

45. Colman, *Argument,* 3, 2, 4, 5; Appleton, *Wisdom of God,* 289; Foxcroft, *Ministers, Spiritual Parents,* 6; *Voice of the Lord,* 41, 38; Charles Hambricke-Stowe, *The Practice of Piety: Puritan Devotional Disciplines in Seventeenth-Century New England* (Chapel Hill, 1982), 147–75.

46. Benjamin Wadsworth, *Churches Shall Know* (Boston, 1717), 37; *Men Self-Condemned* (Boston, 1706), 30; Nathaniel Appleton, *Righteousness and Uprightness* (Boston, 1738), 26–27; Appleton, in Solomon Prentice *Notes on Sermons* (1724–26), 77, Harvard University Archives; *Wisdom of God,* 81; Ebenezer Pemberton, *A Sermon Preached in the Audience* (Boston, 1706), 14, 12–13.

47. Appleton, *Wisdom of God,* 230. The South Shore Arminians for the most part did not conceive of the community of the elect in these terms, preferring instead a separation of reason from the affections, and a public life that was legal and relatively unemotional. See Lemuel Briant, *The Absurdity and Blasphemy of Depreciating Moral Virtue* (Boston, 1749); Ebenezer Gay, *Natural Religion as Distinguished from Revealed* (Boston, 1759); Wilson, *The Benevolent Deity,* 82–83, 85, 134, 158–59, 173–81. Foxcroft was by no means an Arminian, but he seems to have found common ground of some sort with the Arminians Robert Breck and Samuel Osborn (Clifford K. Shipton, *Biographical Sketches of Those Who Attended Harvard College,* vol. 6 [Boston, 1873–1975], 51; Robert J. Wilson III, *The Benevolent Deity: Ebenezer Gay and the Rise of Rational Religion in New England, 1696–1787* [Philadelphia, 1984], 75).

David D. Hall ("On Common Ground: The Coherence of American Puritan Studies," *WMQ* [1987]) has observed that American Puritan studies since 1970 have begun to identify "affective, aesthetic, and ritual dimensions of Puritanism" (222). Although I do not disagree with this statement, I would add that this scholarship has been carried on largely against an earlier history that stressed "morality," understood as rational-legal and emotionally impoverished, as characteristic of Puritan religion. It seems to me that, in spite of the work of Robert Middlekauff and Norman Fiering, American Puritan studies are still largely inclined to an approach that accepts a juxtaposition of intellect to piety, or morality to affection. Although in many cases such an approach uncovers aspects of the history, it sometimes misses opportunites to identify ways in which some New Englanders—in my case, these catholick clergy—attempted to describe the integration of piety and intellect, morality and affection, public and private aspects of religion. In some ways, scholars in the field are still attempting to work out the details of the dichotomy suggested by Joseph Haroutunian's book, published over fifty years ago, entitled *Piety versus Moralism* (New York, 1932).

Chapter 5

1. Benjamin Colman, *The Religious Regards We Owe Our Country* Boston, 1718), 23; *The Hainous Nature of the Sin of Murder* (Boston, 1713), 10; Letter to "Rev'd Mr. Hooper," Feb. 12, 1740, in Colman Papers, Massachusetts Historical Society; Benjamin Wadsworth, *The Benefits of a Good, and the Mischiefs of an Evil, Conscience* (Boston, 1719), 24; Sermon preached Oct. 7, 1722, in Foxcroft Notebooks, Congregational Library; Thomas Foxcroft, *The Character of Anna* (Boston, 1723), 40.

2. Stephen Foster, *Their Solitary Way: The Puritan Social Ethic in the First Century of Settlement in New England* (New Haven, 1971), 42–43, including the quotations from Winthrop and Hooker; John Wilkins, *Of the Principles and Duties of Natural Religion* (London, 1675), 12; Simon Patrick, *The Parable of the Pilgrim* (London, 1665), 175; John Tillotson, *Sermons Preached on Several Occasions* (London, 1671), 127. Tillotson explained in clear terms that religion was entirely reconcilable to "the happiness of mankind" and "the greatest friend to our temporal interests; and that it doth not only tend to make every man happy, consider'd singly and in a private capacity, but is excellently fitted for the benefit of human society" (127–28).

3. Benjamin Wadsworth, Sermon preached Sept. 13, 1696, in "Nineteen Sermons," Harvard University Archives; Richard L. Bushman, *From Puritan to Yankee: Character and the Social Order in Connecticut, 1690–1765* (New York, 1970, op. 1967), 279. Catholicks gave no detailed abstract explanation of the nature(s) of self-love (but their thinking about it can be followed in their discussions of their self-love in practical contexts [e.g., commerce, government]). Theirs does not seem to have differed substantially, however, from the treatment given self-love by Solomon Stoddard (*Three Sermons Lately Preach'd at Boston* [Boston, 1717]), in that they recognized various forms of self-love (35). A discussion of the "pursuit of happiness" in the colonies in connection with individualism and the profit motive, with the caution that this should not be taken as prima facie evidence for the secularization of American culture, is in Jack P. Greene, *Pursuits of Happiness: The Social Development of Early Modern British Colonies and the Formation of American Culture* (Chapel Hill, 1988), 196–206. The pursuit of happiness accompanied by the constriction of emotion is discussed at length in Jan Lewis, *The Pursuit of Happiness: Family and Values in Jefferson's Virginia* (New York, 1983). A summary of some ideas about self-love in the seventeenth century (e.g., Pascal, La Rochefoucauld, Jansen) that suggests some of the slipperiness of the term is in Anthony Levi, *French Moralists: The Theory of the Passions, 1585–1649* (Oxford, 1964), 225–33. Norman Fiering gives an excellent summary of the various (and at times near-contradictory) meanings of self-love in the early and late writings of Edwards in *Jonathan Edwards's Moral Thought* (Chapel Hill, 1981), 150–99.

4. John Passmore, *The Perfectibility of Man* (New York, 1970), 120; Cotton Mather, *Piety and Equity, United* (Boston, 1717), 18, 34; Nicholas Noyes, *New-Englands Duty and Interest* (Boston, 1698), 56; Joshua Gee, *The Strait Gate* (Boston, 1729), 57, 11.

5. Catholick clergy do not seem to have been particularly worried about the influence of the unregenerate in society, even though there were a great many unchurched persons. It may have been the first flush of optimism of an Enlightenment sort that was responsible for this apparent diminished concern for how the unregenerate were to fit into a society founded on the brotherly love of the regenerate. Catholicks, removing the barriers to communion and proclaiming that the "smaller matters" of religion were unimportant as far as Christian union was concerned, may have simply wished that the unchurched would eventually be brought into the fold. They do not seem to have given much consideration to the possibility that some persons were simply predestined to hell. However, they did not go as far as Charles Chauncy, Foxcroft's junior colleague at First Church, in proposing universal salvation (*The Mystery Hid from Ages and Generations* [Boston, 1784]).

6. T. H. Breen, *The Character of the Good Ruler: A Study of Puritan Political Ideas in New England, 1630–1730* (New Haven, 1970); J. E. Crowley, *This Sheba, Self:*

The Conceptualization of Economic Life in Eighteenth-Century America (Baltimore, 1974).

7. Charles Lloyd Cohen, *God's Caress: The Psychology of Puritan Religious Experience* (New York, 1986), 129 (including the quotation of Sibbes). Cohen also quotes Shepard on the necessity for investment of love in action. Benjamin Wadsworth, *Surviving Servants of God* (Boston, 1724), 5; Thomas Foxcroft, *Cleansing Our Way in Youth* (Boston, 1719), 117, 114; Benjamin Colman, *A Sermon at the Lecture in Boston, after the Funerals of . . . William Brattle . . . and . . . Ebenezer Pemberton* (subtitled "Industry and Diligence in the Work of Religion") (Boston, 1717), 12, 17; Ebenezer Pemberton, *A Christian Fixed in His Post* (Boston, 1704), 5–6; *A True Servant of His Generation* (Boston, 1712), 18. Anglicans as well as Puritans in England believed that a calling was indispensable to the Christian life. According to J. Sears McGee, "full holiness," for Anglicans, required that a person be "at peace with others" and actively engaged in a calling (*The Godly Man in Stuart England: Anglicans, Puritans, and the Two Tables, 1620–1670* (New Haven, 1970), 164–65. John Tillotson wrote that the consideration of heaven ought to "make us very active and industrious, to be as good, and to do as much as we can in this life" (*Sermons Preached on Several Occasions* [London, 1671], 294).

8. Pemberton, *Christian Fixed in His Post,* 20; Cohen, *God's Caress,* 130; Foster, *Their Solitary Way,* 105.

9. Benjamin Wadsworth, *Exhortations to Early Piety* (Boston, 1702), 54; *Men Self-Condemned* (Boston, 1706), 85; Benjamin Colman, *A Holy and Useful Life* (Boston, 1715), 5; Thomas Foxcroft, *The Voice of the Lord* (Boston, 1727), 41.

Foxcroft's reference to the earthquake's "awakening" persons from idleness suggests other references to inappropriate sleep as indicative of the failure of persons to remain actively engaged in their religious duties of work and worship. Unlawful sleeping was viewed in much the same way as was idleness. Wadsworth seems to have encountered persons who were "sleeping and drouzing" in church. Other persons did not even bother to appear in church during time set aside for public worship: "Possibly they're so tire and wearied with their past frolicks, that they spend it chiefly drouzing and sleeping." Drowsiness and idleness were similar in that they both constituted a disregard for the active nature of the soul, and regenerate life, and so, Wadsworth said, God "sometimes chastens them, to awaken them out of their dull, drouzy, secure frames." Too much sleeping, or sleeping at the wrong time, left open the door for danger. Wadsworth, addressing a group of "Christian souldiers going to war," observed, "To sleep on the watch has been counted a capital crime, and (I believe in many cases) it ought to be look'd upon as such." Appleton, applying to sleep the popular warning against idleness, suggested, "The devil takes the Oportunity [*sic*] of men's being asleep" to influence them toward evil. Sleep, like idleness, was characterized by a disjunction of internal and external life. Charles Morton suggested such a view in his definition: "Sleep [is] a state or mode of existing, wherein the exteriour senses, & (that which is called) common sense are obstructed on their operations." And not only did this condition result in the obvious inability of the sleeping person to act, to do good, but it could cause a commotion in the interior life of the individual. In a telling comment on dreams, Morton explained that they "are therefore very confused & independent, much like the . . . impertinent thoughts of idle and unemployed persons." See Benjamin Wadsworth, *An Essay on the Decalogue* (Boston, 1719), 57; *Faithful Warnings* (Boston, 1722), 9; *Assembling at the House of God* (Boston, 1711),

17; *Considerations to Prevent Murmuring* (Boston, 1706), 15; Appleton in Solomon Prentice, *Notes on Sermons,* Harvard University Archives.

The drinking of alcoholic beverages also was of potential danger to those who were obliged to remain diligent in their activity in the world. In excess, it severely diminished physical capability and caused a dreamlike confusion, in which "the whole faculties of the soul are . . . disordered" and "memory drowned." This is not to say that all drinking was dangerous. Wadsworth, Foxcroft, and Colman stated publicly that moderate consumption of alcoholic beverages was no sin. The frequenting of taverns was a legitimate "diversion" (along with activities such as "running, racing, wrestling, leaping, fencing and sundry other exercises") that could be "undoubtedly innocent, yea profitable & of use, to fit us for service, by enlivening & fortifying our frail nature, invigorating the animal spirits, and brightning the mind, when tired with a close application of business." Drinking was acceptable "at such times and occasions, when there is proper occasion" for it. See Benjamin Wadsworth, *Essay on the Decalogue,* 84; *An Essay to Do Good* (Boston, 1710), 3; Thomas Foxcroft, *A Serious Address to Those Who Unnecessarily Frequent the Tavern* (Boston, 1726), 10; Benjamin Colman, *The Government and Improvement of Mirth* (Boston, 1710), 30.

10. Thomas Foxcroft, *A Brief Display* (Boston, 1727), 24; Pemberton, *The Souldier Defended* (Boston, 1701), 24.

11. Nathaniel Appleton, *The Great Blessing* (Boston, 1742), 20; Foxcroft, *Brief Display,* 25–26; sermon preached Aug. 4, 1720, Foxcroft Notebooks, Congegational Library; Ebenezer Pemberton, *A True Servant of His Generation* (Boston, 1712), 30, 13; *A Sermon Preached in the Audience* (Boston, 1706), 27.

12. Wadsworth, *The Saint's Prayer* (Boston, 1715), 23; Foxcroft, *Serious Address,* 29; Pemberton, *True Servant of His Generation,* 14; Sermon preached July 16, 1708, in Pemberton, *Sermons June 13, 1708–April 3, 1709,* MHS. Wadsworth expressed concern about persons' pursuing "unlawful callings and imployments": "stageplays, shows," and other activities. And he pointed out that certain employments might place a person in contact with deceivers: "It may be our particular calling . . . is such, that it's scarcely (if at all) possible" to avoid bad influences (*Faithful Warnings* [Boston, 1722], 6). William Brattle seems also to have accepted that some professions endangered Christian holiness, but he cautioned against too quick a criticism of such professions: "We may infer that persons are sometimes rash & censorious in judging their neighbours for taking up a profession that is of an ensnaring nature" (Solomon Prentice, *Notes on Sermons,* Harvard University Archives).

13. Crowley, *This Sheba, Self,* 124, 65. It seems that Crowley cites Colman, Wadsworth, and Pemberton generally as examples of a kind of thinking that evidences movement away from belief in a religious basis for social order (cf. 65, 82). It is not always clear from his analysis, however, how we are to view them. He seems to cast them as representative of a kind of thinking that was opposed to the mentality of the revival (and the emphasis on brotherly love), but Colman supported the revival (Pemberton and Wadsworth being deceased). My understanding of his use of their writings in support of his argument also has been complicated by problems arising from the sometimes imprecise chronology of his history. He identifies the 1730s as a turning point in American thinking about economic life (56, 76, 80) but often gives as examples of such change works published much earlier, or later. All of this is to say that his interpretation of catholick writers does not fit well with an otherwise useful study.

14. Colman, *Religious Regards We Owe Our Country,* 15, 22, 23, 24, 30. Colman stressed that each person was to be "the other's keeper" (15).

15. Foxcroft, *Cleansing Our Way in Youth,* 104, 102, 106–8.

16. Wadsworth, Sermon preached Oct. 5, 1707, Wadsworth Sermon Notes, Congregational Library; *Faithful Warnings,* 19; Foxcroft, sermon preached July 31, 1737, Foxcroft Notebooks, Congregational Library; *Cleansing Our Way in Youth,* 75. Foxcroft argued that even persons who were already wealthy could benefit from religion, in a temporal way, because religion "will still serve your temporal interest, as it teaches you how to abound, directs and influences the enjoyment and improvement of your estate, so as tends to secure and increase it" (75).

17. Appleton, *Great Blessing,* 21; *Wisdom of God,* 33; Holyoke, *The Duty of Ministers* (Boston, 1741), 24; Benjamin Colman, *The Doctrine and the Law of the Holy Sabbath* (Boston, 1725), iii; *Righteousness and Compassion* (Boston, 1736), 29, 24, 23; Wadsworth, *Fraud and Injustice Detected* (Boston, 1712), 16; Silverman, *The Life and Times of Cotton Mather* (New York, 1984), 366.

18. Colman, *Brief Inquiry,* 20. Ward quoted in *Boston: A Chronological & Documentary History, 1602–1970,* ed. George J. Lankevitch (Dobbs Ferry, N.Y., 1974), 82. One wonders how to interpret the note, taken from the geographical catechism in the tutor Henry Flynt's class at Harvard, about religion in Holland: "What is the religion of this country? A. No country in Europe has more religion (all being tolerated for the sake of trade)" (*A Catechism Geographicall Historicall and Chronologicall,* Harvard University Archives).

19. Breen, *Character of the Good Ruler,* 217, 216, 213, 212. I have assumed that Breen's discussion of Colman's justification of Governor Dudley's behavior, in a funeral sermon, is to be taken as a sign of Colman's sympathy with the court position (236). Breen suggests that the court faction lacked confidence in the capability of civil magistrates to wield power wisely (217). In the context of Breen's analysis, I see nothing particularly distinctive in this. Breen's "country" theorists, who shared "Cato's" suspicion of power, seem to have felt the same way (242, 263ff.). Breen also suggests that the court faction distinguished persons into different "orders" in society, and that such a distinguishing differed from the separation of orders that Governor John Winthrop had defended in the seventeenth century. Catholicks most certainly believed that God had separated persons into various orders, or "spheres," in life, some high and some low. But Breen's claim for a difference between catholicks and Winthrop on this account is lacking in evidence and seems to be based largely on the notion—assumed rather than proved—that "the court was the product of a secular environment" (212, and see also 217). Catholicks certainly differed in some ways from their seventeenth-century forebears, but they nevertheless continued to view government through the lens of religion.

20. Benjamin Wadsworth, *Rulers Feeding and Guiding Their People* (Boston, 1716), 1, 60, 6, 5, 54, 49–50. Wadsworth did credit the college but in connection with its offering an education for those "who desire that they may know and do God's will" (17).

21. Ebenezer Pemberton, *The Divine Original and Dignity of Government* (Boston, 1710), 18, 14, 11, 3, 21–23, 78, 27, 1–2. Breen writes, "This sermon is one of the clearest statements of the court persuasion to come out of this period." Breen's analysis, however, is based on an unwarranted dismissal of the religious character of the sermon, of "Pemberton's spiritual language" (212). I see no reason not to take seriously Pemberton's emphasis on the spiritual aspect of government.

22. *Appleton's Cyclopedia of American Biography,* vol., 6 (New York, 1889), 149; Foxcroft, *Brief Display,* 6, 2, 4, 9, 20, 25, 26, 15–18.

23. Colman, *Religious Regards We Owe Our Country,* 37, 3, 5–6, 15, 30, 22–25. Breen thinks that a particular "life-style" based on the adoption of English dress and manners was characteristic of persons of the court persuasion (208).

24. Appleton, *Great Blessing,* 8, 18, 21.

25. Peter Brown, "The Saint as Exemplar in Late Antiquity," *Representations* 1 (1983): 9–10; Sacvan Bercovitch, *The Puritan Origins of the American Self* (New Haven, 1977), 1–34; J. Sears McGee, "Conversion and the Imitation of Christ in Anglican and Puritan Writing," *Journal of British Studies* 15 (1976): 27–28; Middlekauff, "Piety and Intellect in Puritanism" *WMQ* 22 (1965): 462–64; *The Mathers: Three Generations of Puritan Intellectuals 1596–1728* (New York, 1971), 255.

26. Catholicks most often spoke of the imitation of Christ in regular sermons, but see the published lecture sermon by Wadsworth, *The Imitation of Christ* (Boston, 1722). Other sermons are Appleton, sermon preached Sept. 7, 1718, in Parkman, *Notes of Sermons,* MHS; Sermon preached Feb. 27, 1726, in Prentice, *Notes on Sermons,* HUA; Foxcroft, Sermon preached May 19, 1717, in Samuel Moody, *Commonplace Book 1746,* HUA; Pemberton, Sermon preached July 18, 1708, in *Sermons June 13, 1708–April 3, 1709,* MHS; Benjamin Colman, *Jesus Weeping,* (Boston, 1744). On Christ as human and divine (and as a mediator) see, for example, Colman, *The Great Duty* (Boston, 1737), 16; *A Dissertation of the Image of God* (Boston, 1736), 43; *The Rending of the Vail of the Temple* (Boston, 1717), 11; Pemberton, *Funeral Sermon on . . . Samuel Willard;* Benjamin Wadsworth, Twelve Single Sermons (Boston, 1717), 112, 196–97, 170; *The Imitation of Christ;* Nathaniel Appleton, *The Wisdom of God* (Boston, 1728), 19–20, 22, 31. Foxcroft's notes (Congregational Library) show the direct influence of Tillotson's thinking about the imitation of Christ. See also Tillotson, *Sixteen Sermons,* 2d ed., vol. 2 (London, 1700), sermon 8, esp. 222–48; Stillingfleet, "Sermon VI," in *Sermons Preached on Several Occasions* (London, 1673), 97–119; Simon Patrick, *the Parable of the Pilgrim,* (London, 1665), 107–36. Patrick, who, as noted, seems to have had one foot in latitudinarianism and the other in Puritanism, called attention to Jesus as an example of "private piety," as well as of public charity. McGee ("Conversion and the Imitation of Christ") stresses that Puritans and Anglicans viewed the imitation of Christ differently, the former remaining very uncertain about their capability to imitate Christ truly, the latter believing it to be relatively "easy" (31).

H. R. McAdoo (*The Spirit of Anglicanism: A Survey of Anglican Theological Method in the Seventeenth-Century* [London, 1965], 172), following Norman Sykes ("The Sermons of Archbishop Tillotson," *Theology* 58 [1955], 297), claims that Tillotson abandoned the use of *exempla.* Foxcroft's citation of Tillotson on the imitation of Christ suggests otherwise. Barbara Shapiro argues that latitudinarians emphasized God, not Christ, in their theology and urged their audiences to employ reason in a project of developing a rational morality aimed at charity and moderation (*Probability and Certainty in Seventeenth-Century England* [Princeton, 1983], 88–89, 104–6). I agree, for the most part, with her judgment. However, I would add that the figure of Jesus is of course still present in their thinking, even if imitation of his example was largely a matter of corporal works of charity, rather than a more specifically spiritual emulation. McGee (*Godly Man in Stuart England,* 208–34, 171–73) thinks that "love to brethren" was understood by Anglicans (1620–70) as concern for the material comfort of others, as a "bland charity," rather than as an emotional bond founded on a sense of spiritual union. This was probably true as well of latitudinarians later in the seventeenth century. Foxcroft, in drawing from Tillotson some ideas on the imitation of Christ, did not give up any emphasis on the spiritual aspects of brotherly love.

Foxcroft's reading of Tillotson may have been balanced by study of the Cambridge Platonists, who viewed the imitation of Christ more as a matter of the cultivation of spirituality (see Gordon Rupp, "A Devotion of Rapture in English Puritanism," in *Reformation Conformity and Dissent: Essays in Honour of Geoffrey Nutall,* ed. R. Buick Knox [London, 1977], 126).

27. According to Foxcroft, ministers "must follow the example of CHRIST," and in so doing set an example for others. Appleton insisted, "Ministers must water their word by their own example," because "the example of ministers will add a great deal, of light and weight" to the arguments made from the pulpit. Ministers were to undertake "to explain the mysteries of the Gospel," but it was most important that they be "very exemplary in their lives and conversations. This is the main point, without which, all the rest will signifie little." Pemberton, in his sermon for Samuel Willard, proposed that ministers should "nourish their people" with their "private and secret addresses to God," as well as through sermons that would inspire the "true spirit of devotion," but "in fine, they are to feed them by their good example. . . ." And Foxcroft, preaching at his own ordination, stressed the importance of example as well, arguing that ministers must "transcribe their public sermons into their private visible actions and behaviour," and by this he meant that piety should be visible in public action. See Thomas Foxcroft, *A Practical Discourse Relating to the Gospel Ministry* (Boston, 1718), 25, 20; Nathaniel Appleton, *God and Not Ministers,* 19; Appleton, *Faithful Ministers of Christ* (Boston, 1743), 28; *Superior Skill* (Boston, 1737), 24, 30; Ebenezer Pemberton, *Funeral Sermon on . . . Samuel Willard* (Boston, 1707), 14–15; Colman, *Sermon at the Lecture in Boston, after the Funerals of . . . William Brattle . . . and . . . Ebenezer Pemberton,* 44; *A Sermon Preached at the Ordination of . . . William Cooper* (Boston, 1716), 6; Benjamin Wadsworth, *Ministers Caring for Souls* (Boston, 1715), 20.

28. Benjamin Colman, *Faith Victorious* (Boston, 1702), 1; Thomas Foxcroft, *Practical Discourse Relating to the Gospel Ministry,* 19; *The Character of Anna* (Boston, 1723), 49–50; Appleton, Sermon preached Mar. 16, 1720, in Ebenezer Parkman, *Notes of Sermons,* MHS; *The Diary of Ebenezer Parkman 1703–1782,* Jan. 24, 1727.

29. Robert Henson, "Form and Content in the Puritan Funeral Elegy," *American Literature* 32 (1960–61): 21. David E. Stannard (*The Puritan Way of Death: A Study of Religion, Culture, and Social Change* [New York, 1977], 149, 147–63) argues that New Englanders by the early eighteenth century had largely abandoned belief in the spiritual mission of the community and had begun to emphasize the individual. Rather than consoling the community for its loss and reiterating the importance of its survival, ministers preached instead, in increasingly sentimental tones, about "the individual who had been so fortunate as to die" and who now experienced the joys of heaven (155). Emory Elliot ("The Development of the Puritan Funeral Sermon and Elegy: 1660–1750," *Early American Literature* 15 [1980]: 151–64) also detects a shift to a concern for the individual in sermons preached after 1700. As I suggest later, the emphases placed on a shift to "individualism" (in funeral sermons) by Stannard and Elliott is not well supported by the literature that they cite. Moreover, I reject Elliott's claim that "emotional" language in catholick funeral sermons is the product of a perceived conflict between the necessity to defend doctrine and the obligation to praise persons who were not members of the church. Catholicks preached funeral sermons well aware that the occasion afforded them an opportunity to instruct their audience by calling attention to the example of the deceased. Moreover, like Parkman, they knew that example struck hardest when it stirred the affections, and they consciously endeavored to use language for that purpose.

30. I include here Foxcroft as well as the other four ministers cited by Elliot.

31. Catholicks paid considerable attention to the examples that had been set by the deceased. Elliott's work does not address this.

32. Henson, "Form and Content in the Puritan Funeral Elegy," 21, 16; Wadsworth, *Ministers Naturally Caring for Souls,* 15–16, 9; *Man's Present State* (Boston, 1715), 16–17. Bridge served as an assistant at First Church for ten years leading up to his death.

33. Benjamin Colman, *A Blameless and Inoffensive Life* (Boston, 1723), 3, 12.

34. Benjamin Colman, *A Blameless and Inoffensive Life* (Boston, 1723), (title page), 2, 3, 12, 5, 18–19.

35. Benjamin Colman, *The Hope of the Righteous* (Boston, 1721), preface, 4, 6, 8.

36. Benjamin Colman, *The Faithful Servant* (Boston, 1740), 3, 4, preface.

37. Pemberton, *True Servant of His Generation,* 12, 1, 2, 3, 4, 23, 29, 27, 31. Elliott ("Development of the Puritan Funeral Sermon") thinks that Pemberton was "urging others to follow Wally's example not so much in his spiritual life but in his intellectual life" and suggests that Pemberton used the occasion to promote "literature and learning" as opposed to "true religion" ("Development of the Puritan Funeral Sermon," 160). Although it may be true that there was more emphasis on "learning" in this funeral than in most, Pemberton in no way sacrificed piety to intellectual accomplishment.

38. Nathaniel Appleton, *Righteousness and Uprightness* (Boston, 1738), iii, 6–7, 7–10, 16, 26.

39. Ibid., 30, 29, 16. Since Appleton based his explanation of righteousness on an entirely conventional notion of its connection to conversion, I see no reason to suppose, as does Elliott, that Appleton invested the term *righteous* with a "new meaning," in order to be able to speak of Foxcroft's righteousness (Elliott, ["Development of the Puritan Funeral Sermon"] 158). Appleton's sermon was catholick in its point of view not only because of its connection of piety to activity but because he accepted Foxcroft's piety as genuine, in spite of the fact that Foxcroft was Anglican. Moreover, I do not think that the sermon was made difficult for Appleton by the fact that it was for a man who was not a member of the congregation. Colonel Foxcroft, as father to Appleton's friend Thomas Foxcroft, was hardly a stranger to Appleton.

40. Nathaniel Appleton, *A Great Man Fallen in Israel* (Boston, 1724), 6, 12, 15, 24–26, 27, 30–31. Wadsworth, in his sermon for Leverett, reminded his audience, "Practice is the end of knowledge." Claiming that he could not know the content of Leverett's faith, Wadsworth nevertheless declared, "Yet I think I might truly say, he was a great man." Praising Leverett and explaining why his "good example . . . should be imitated," Wadsworth emphasized that Leverett was "a great, worthy, useful person," who had been furnished by God with many "very great and useful endowments" and whose "usefull instructions and directions" should be followed. Such usefulness, in fact, lay chiefly in his service to society. He held "sundry different stations and offices, and he was very useful and serviceable therein. . . . He was eminently serviceable to the college for many years as a tutor" and as president. As was the practice, Wadsworth brought his sermon to a conclusion with a reference to virtue and public order, exhorting the assembly: "By your examples, counsels, prayers, government, endeavour to maintain good order in the society; to encourage all that's holy, just, good, vertuous, praiseworthy." But he warned that such effort for the public good should be balanced with "secret prayer morning and evening" (*Surviving Servants of God,* 5, 10, 20, 9, 21). Colman used the occasion of Leverett's death as an opportunity to urge the mourners

themselves to be "exemplary" after the manner of the deceased, particularly in their "humiliations, and godly sorrowing unto repentance." Colman instructed his listeners to make "supplications and cries to heaven" that they might receive "the spirit of light and grace upon themselves." Such striving after personal spiritual growth was to be balanced, however, with activities undertaken for the good of the whole: "And finally, exemplary each one . . . in a proper activity and present diligence, in what is respectfully incumbent on us for the good of the bereaved society" (*The Master Taken Up* [Boston, 1724], 11).

41. If catholicks were inclined to view public life largely in connection with social institutions such as those mentioned here, then it is possible that they understood "love to neighbor" in a more routinized," or, even, "intellectualized" way than I have here suggested. But the evidence of funeral sermons is rather limited and cannot be relied on in the absence of other research, which is beyond the scope of this inquiry. Moreover, the topics and arguments of many catholick sermons suggest that public life was often seen as simply neighbors talking over the fence. According to Lonna M. Malmsheimer, one-fourth of the funeral sermons preached in New England between 1672 and 1792 were for women ("New England Funeral Sermons and Changing Attitudes towards Women, 1672–1792" [Ph.D. diss., University of Minnesota, 1973], 32). Malmsheimer is most concerned with the middle and late eighteenth century.

42. Nathaniel Appleton, *The Christian Glorying* (Boston, 1736); Benjamin Colman, *The Death of God's Saints Precious* (Boston, 1723), 14–14, 23–24; Benjamin Wadsworth, *Early Seeking of God* (Boston, 1715). The fact that Wadsworth was willing to preach a funeral sermon for a young woman who apparently had never been admitted to communion suggests that he perceived a distinct difference between women's lives and men's. More surprising, however, is a lack of emphasis in these sermons on women as "tender-hearted" creatures. Given the nature of the female role (among others) of "tender mother," one expects more attention to this aspect of the character of the deceased. It is, of course, possible that none of these three women were in fact mothers. On "mother" as a role in New England at this time see Laurel Thatcher Ulrich, *Good Wives: Image and Reality in the Lives of Women in Northern New England, 1650–1750* (New York, 1982), 146–63, 238–39.

Conclusion

1. Hornberger, "Benjamin Colman and the Enlightenment," 240.

2. As I have noted (chap. 4, n. 47), much scholarship still seems to follow the paradigm of analysis suggested by Joseph Haroutunian's *Piety versus Moralism* (New York, 1932). A recent work in this vein is Edwin S. Gaustad, *Faith of Our Fathers: Religion and the New Nation* (San Francisco, 1987), 77, 96.

3. Peter Gay, *The Enlightenment: The Science of Freedom* (New York, 1969), 301–6, 187–207. Gay writes: "Long before Romanticism, and without the aid of Romantics, the age of the Enlightenment discovered and managed to gratify a taste for pathos, for graveyards, for moonlight, for the dark and the infinite" (306). Henry May, on the other hand, has argued that there was a "tidal variation between ages of . . . reason and (loosely speaking) romanticism" (*The Enlightenment in America* [New York, 1976], 42–43). May's juxtaposition of "rationality" and "religious emotion" is referred to in the preface to this book. Jay Fliegelman's excellent study, which he

describes as a chapter in the "history of American affections," includes evidence drawn from a wide range of sources, in support of the thesis that an affectional model of authority replaced a patriarchal model in the second half of the eighteenth century (*Prodigals and Pilgrims: The American Revolution against Patriarchal Authority 1750–1800* [New York, 1982]).

4. R. S. Crane, "Suggestions toward a Genealogy of the 'Man of Feeling,' " in *The Idea of the Humanities* (Chicago, 1967), 188–213. Crane suggested that the notion of man as a social creature inclined to love was found in some latitudinarian writers.

5. Robert J. Wilson III, *The Benevolent Deity: Ebenezer Gay and the Rise of Rational Religion in New England, 1696–1787* (Philadelphia, 1984); John Barnard, "Autobiography of John Barnard," *Collections of the Massachusetts Historical Society,* 3 ser., vol. 5 (1856), 177–243.

6. Norman Fiering, *Moral Philosophy at Seventeenth-Century Harvard: A Discipline in Transition* (Chapel Hill, 1981), 138. Fiering notes that Edwards grew up in a household that was well stocked with theological writings, but especially with works by Benjamin Colman (Norman Fiering, *Jonathan Edwards's Moral Thought and Its British Context* [Chapel Hill, 1981], 25).

7. Nathaniel Appleton, *The Wisdom of God* (Boston, 1728), 282–83.

8. Bruce Tucker, "The Reinvention of New England, 1691–1770," *New England Quarterly* 59 (1986), 315–40; Bruce Tucker, "The Reinterpretation of Puritan History in Provincial New England," *New England Quarterly* 54 (1981), 481–84.

9. I have described that dialectical theology in *The Hidden Balance: Religion and the Social Theories of Charles Chauncy and Jonathan Mayhew* (New York, 1987).

10. Patricia V. Bonomi, *Under the Cope of Heaven: Religion, Society and Politics in Colonial America* (New York, 1986), 221.

Index